UNABOMBER

UNABOMBER
How the FBI Broke Its Own Rules to Capture the Terrorist Ted Kaczynski

JIM FREEMAN
Special Agent in Charge
TERRY D. TURCHIE
Assistant Special Agent in Charge, UNABOM Task Force
DONALD MAX NOEL
Supervisory Special Agent, UNABOM Task Force

History Publishing Company
Palisades, New York

Copyright©2014 by Jim Freeman, Donald Max Noel & Terry D. Turchie
Freeman, Jim
Noel, Donald Max
Turchie, Terry D.

LCCN: 2014930212
ISBN: 9781940773063 (HC)
ISBN: 9781940773049 (eBook)
SAN: 850-5942

Freeman, Jim R.

Unabomber : how the FBI broke its own rules to capture the terrorist Ted Kaczynski / Jim Freeman, Terry D. Turchie, Donald Max Noel. -- Palisades, NY : History Pub. Co., c2014.

p. ; cm.

ISBN: 978-1-940773-06-3 ; 978-1-940773-04-9 (ebook)
Includes bibliographical references and index.
Summary: As told by the three FBI agents who led the chase, this is the story of how the FBI broke its own rules, blasting away the layers of bureaucratic constraints that had plagued earlier efforts, to catch the notorious Unabomber and end his 16-year trail of terrorism.--Publisher.

1. Kaczynski, Theodore John, 1942- 2. Bombing investigation--United States--Case studies. 3. Serial murder investigation--United States--Case studies. 4. United States. Federal Bureau of Investigation--Rules and practice. 5. Bombings--United States--Case studies. 6. Bombers (Terrorists)--United States--Case studies. 7. Serial murderers--United States--Case studies. 8. Terrorists--United States--Case studies. I. Turchie, Terry D. II. Noel, Donald Max. III. Title.

HV6248.K235 F73 2014   2014930212
364.15/230973--dc23   1404

Published in the United States of America by
History Publishing Company, LLC
Palisades, New York

Printed in the United States on acid-free paper.
First Edition

This book is dedicated to the victims and families of the victims of the Unabomber's crimes; the hundreds of Federal, state and local law enforcement officers and agencies who worked tirelessly on this investigation for over 18 years; and to the American public, represented in this story by the *Washington Post*, the *New York Times*, and David Kaczynski, who have proven thousands of times the importance of the relationship between law enforcement and the public in solving crimes and preventing a wide range of criminal and terrorist activity.

Table of Contents

INTRODUCTION

THE UNABOMBER—JUST MENTION OF THE NAME CONJURES UP AN iconic image of a mysterious figure enshrouded in a gray hooded sweatshirt and wearing darkened aviator sunglasses. For almost eighteen years, beginning in May of 1978 until his identification and arrest on April 3, 1996, the Unabomber's terrorist bombing crusade reached inside the homes, universities and places of business of his innocent victims, viciously murdering three of them and injuring twenty-three others. In November, 1979, the Unabomber's third bomb would have downed an airliner flying from Chicago to Washington, D.C. if the pilots hadn't skillfully implemented an emergency landing of the aircraft as its cabin filled with smoke.

Throughout almost two decades of his terrorist campaign, Federal and local law enforcement officers had settled into a hot and cold pattern of isolated and independent investigations of his crimes. First in Chicago and then following the trail of crime scenes to Salt Lake City, Sacramento, San Francisco, New Haven and Newark, dozens of agents from the FBI, Bureau of Alcohol, Tobacco and Firearms (ATF), and the United States Postal Inspection Service were joined by a myriad of police officers and deputies who rushed to crime scenes in search of quick solutions. When the identification of the bomber eluded them, investigators were left with the mundane and tedious chore of collecting evidence that had often been obliterated by the explosions. The process was complicated by multiple and overlapping layers of bureaucracy, institutional pride, professional jealousies, and individual egos.

When resolution was nowhere to be found and public attention calmed down, resources were routinely drained from the investigation until the next bombing. Then the sequence repeated itself all over again. As the trail of the Unabomber grew colder over the years, the morale of local officers and Federal agents suffered under a barrage of media criticism as to why the case hadn't been solved. The Unabomber must have loved the spectacle of the inept "Wiley Coyote" like federal agents chasing the elusive roadrunner and repeatedly crashing against one obstacle after another he had put in their path.

None of the usual "tried and true" law enforcement tactics seemed to work in the battle against time to identify the Unabomber. Except for a 1987 Salt Lake City bombing, there weren't any witnesses to the bomber's activities. Forensics and exhaustive lab exams didn't work. Following leads generated at each crime scene didn't work. Appealing to the public for help didn't work. Time after time, the high profile bomber in the gray hooded sweatshirt appeared unseen out of nowhere, and then vanished into nothing.

There was a reason why all the roads the investigators took over the years to identify and find the Unabomber failed to lead them to his doorstep. He wasn't their normal prey. Every thought the bomber had and everything he did was designed to throw his pursuers off his trail, to put them on the wrong roads, and to sabotage their methodical collection of evidence at crime scenes. His victims were randomly selected. There weren't any connections among them. None of them had any connections to him. His bombs were built to maim and kill. They were also built to deceive and confuse.

To the investigators who searched for him, the Unabomber's motives and tactics remained a mystery until his own words were eventually revealed to explain the keys to his success:

"A while back I obtained 2 human hairs from the bathroom in the Missoula bus depot. I broke one of these hairs into two pieces, and I placed one piece between the layers of the electrical tape I used to wrap the wire joints inside the package...The reason for this is to deceive the policemen, who will think that the hair belongs to whoever made the device."

But no matter how hard he tried the bomber couldn't completely purge his words, his patterns, and his own personality traits, that were so deeply embedded in the totality of the crimes he committed. In fact, the physical and psychological puzzle pieces that would define and unlock the identity of the Unabomber were left hidden along the road of terror he traveled for eighteen years.

When a new team of investigators devised a different strategy to crack the genetic code that protected the Unabomber's anonymity, the first task was to begin blasting away the layers of bureaucratic constraints that had plagued the earlier efforts to retrace the trail of crimes. Ultimately, the puzzle pieces that he left behind were found and the puzzle collapsed around the Unabomber like a deck of cards.

Buckley Crist, Jr. was a materials engineering professor at Northwestern University's Technological Institute in Evanston, Illinois in May of 1978. He was also listed as the return addressee on the first mail bomb associated with the Unabomber. Ten dollars in un-canceled stamps were affixed to the parcel, which was found by a passerby in a University of Illinois, Chicago Circle Campus parking lot, adjacent to the Science and Technology building. The parcel was returned to Crist, who called campus security at Northwestern University. With Crist present, police officer Terry Marker was injured as the package detonated while he tried to open it. Crist claimed to have no idea who would have used his name to send the package to its intended recipient - Professor E.J. Smith at Rensselear Polytechnic Institute in Troy, New York. The device would contain the clues to where the bomber might have been born.

A year later, in May of 1979, graduate research student John Harris of Northwestern University in Evanston attempted to open a cigar box wrapped in pink polka dot paper that had been left behind in a room used by graduate students on the second floor of the Technological Institute. As the package exploded, Harris suffered burns and cuts on his face and arms. The force of the blast blew the glasses off his face and singed his eyebrows. While the first bomb was targeted at a named individual, this device was placed where any unsuspecting student or faculty member would be harmed. A portrait of the Unabomber's operational comfort zone within university environments was emerging.

American Airlines Flight # 444 left Chicago for Washington, D.C.'s National Airport on November 15, 1979. When the plane reached an altitude of about 34,500 feet, the cabin filled with smoke. After an emergency landing at Washington Dulles International Airport, investigators found a partially detonated bomb containing a barometer switch in the airplane's baggage compartment. The switch was altered to function as an altimeter, causing the bomb to explode when the plane reached a certain altitude. Eighteen passengers suffered smoke inhalation, but a disaster was narrowly averted by a failure in the bomb's construction. Explosives experts from the FBI Laboratory examined the bomb's components and were able to connect this and the first two bombs as having been made by the same bomber. The FBI dubbed the case "UNABOM" because the early targets were universities and airlines. His targeting of a passenger aircraft added yet another facet to his mosaic.

Percy Wood was the President of United Airlines in June of 1980 when he received a letter at his home in Lake Forest, Illinois. The letter was from an individual unknown to him, "Enoch Fischer." Fischer's letter told Wood to expect a book in the mail that all business executives should read. On June 10, in the safety of his own home, Wood opened a parcel delivered by the U.S. mail service to find a book titled, "Ice Brothers," by author Sloan Wilson. As he opened the book, a massive blast injured his hands and face. The use of a letter to set expectations for a package delivery was a new touch and it also introduced the bomber's love for pseudonyms.

In October of 1981, a bomb wrapped in brown wrapping paper and secured with string, was found in the third floor hallway of the Bennion Hall Business Building at the University of Utah in Salt Lake City. The bomb was discovered and subsequently detonated to render it safe in a women's restroom in proximity to where it was found. This bomb and the one that followed solidly connected the Unabomber to a different geographical location, but continued to illustrate his comfort zone within university environments.

Patrick Fischer was the head of the Computer Science Department at Vanderbilt University in Nashville, Tennessee. On May 5, 1982, Fischer's secretary, Janet Smith opened a package addressed to him and noticed that it had been forwarded from his previous place of employment, Pennsylvania State University. The package had been mailed from Provo, Utah and had a return address of a professor at Brigham Young University. A pipe bomb inside a wooden box exploded, causing injuries to Smith's chest, arms and hands.

Two months later in July of 1982, Diogenes Angelakos walked into a small coffee room adjacent to his fourth floor office in Cory Hall at the University of California in Berkeley. He reached to pick up a package that had been left on the floor. An electrical engineering professor of long standing at U.C. Berkeley, Angelakos suffered serious injuries to his right hand as the package exploded in front of him. The Unabomber would strike Cory Hall again in 1985. What was the connection that drew him back?

After two bombings attributed to the Unabomber in three months, he dropped from sight in July of 1982 and wasn't heard from again until 1985. When he re-emerged, 1985 became the year of the Unabomber. His bombs found their targets four times in eight months. First, a mail bomb addressed to the Boeing Fabrication Division at Auburn, Washington, was removed from the plant as being "suspicious" and rendered safe in a nearby sludge pond. Most of the forensic evidence connected to the device was lost in its detonation.

Just a few days later, the Unabomber backtracked on his trail, returning to the scene of his last crime in 1982, Cory Hall at the University of California in Berkeley. U.S. Air Force Academy graduate and pilot John Hauser was an engineering student who wanted to be an astronaut. In a first floor computer room utilized by graduate students at Cory Hall, Hauser noticed a three ring binder attached to a box by a rubber band left unattended on a table. As he examined the binder in an attempt to determine the owner, a thunderous blast ripped his Air Force Academy class ring off his hand, hurling it across the room, and leaving its imprint etched into the wall. Mr. Hauser lost four fingers from his right hand, suffered severe nerve damage to his forearm, and lost partial vision in his left eye. His dream to be an astronaut was ended by the Unabomber's work.

Nicklaus Suino was a research assistant for University of Michigan psychology professor James McConnell, who had developed a reputation for his work in psychology and invertebrate behavior. In November of 1985, McConnell had caught the attention of the Unabomber. As Suino opened a manuscript received in the mail, he found an attached letter from the sender who requested Professor McConnell to read his graduate thesis on the "history of science"; when it suddenly exploded with lead fishing sinkers packed into the bomb as shrapnel causing wounds and burns to Suino's chest and arms. McConnell, standing eight feet from the blast, experienced hearing loss as a result of the attack. What kind of discipline was the "history of science?" None of the investigators on the UNABOM Task Force had ever heard of it.

The fourth UNABOM device of 1985 was the deadliest. Hugh Scrutton was only 38 years old when he walked outside behind RenTech Computer Rentals, the business he built in Sacramento, California. Seeing two by fours with protruding nails lying in the parking lot near his car, he bent over and reached down to remove them. A bomb concealed within the wooden frame showed little mercy as Scrutton made contact, sending shrapnel over one hundred feet into the air, with some of it hitting him in the heart. Mr. Scrutton died almost instantly from the horrendous blast. It was December 11, 1985.

The world wouldn't hear from the Unabomber again for fourteen months. The bomb that killed Mr. Scrutton had the same deadly design as the bomb that was to follow it in 1987.

Seven years of unsolved bombings and the murder of Mr. Scrutton catapulted the case to the top tier of the FBI's investigative priorities. The investigation was designated as Major Case #75 and assigned the acronym UNABOM since the early targets were universities (UN) and airline (A) bombings (BOM). Previously referred to by investigators as the "junkyard bomber," because his bombs were made from construction debris and items commonly found in junkyards, the subject became known as the Unabomber from this point on.

On February 20, 1987, the mysterious bomber walked casually toward the rear of CAAMS Computer store in Salt Lake City, gingerly placing his bomb next to a car in the parking lot. Hearing voices inside the store, he looked up at a back window to see an employee watching him intently. She turned to get the attention of other employees, screaming about the suspicious figure in their midst. Gary Wright, the son of the owner of CAAMS, drove into the parking lot shortly after the shadowy figure disappeared into the neighborhood.

Sensing the "road hazard" lying on the ground was potentially dangerous for people and cars, Wright knelt down to remove it. As he touched it, the lethal bomb exploded with the same force that killed Mr. Scrutton in 1985. Wright was fortunate that his positioning at the time of the blast saved his life. The Unabomber was not so lucky. The witness image of him wearing a gray hooded sweatshirt and shaded aviator sunglasses captured the public's interest, forever landing him a prominent position in the annals of the world's wanted criminals.

The Unabomber vanished from sight for another seven years. Only a single full time FBI agent in San Francisco, John Conway, remained assigned to the case amid increasing assumptions and wishful thinking that after seven years the bomber had likely died, perhaps a victim of his own bomb-making. But, John didn't like loose ends and wanted closure. So, he worked with the time and resources he had.

Early in the summer of 1993, the Unabomber returned with a vengeance. He mailed two bombs from Sacramento, California. One of them found its target on June 22, as it was opened in the kitchen at the home of Dr. Charles Epstein, head of the Genetics Department at the University of California Medical School in San Francisco. The other bomb was delivered three thousand miles away to Dr. David Gelernter, a professor of computer science at Yale University. He opened the package in his Yale office only two days later, on June 24th. Both men sustained massive injuries from the Unabomber's newer, smaller and more potentially lethal bombs.

The Unabomber wasn't finished with reintroducing himself to America after his hiatus of seven years. A few days after the coast to coast blasts, Warren Hogue, Assistant Managing Editor for the *New York Times* received a letter from "an anarchist group, F.C.," which was an acronym affixed inside several of the bombs and was known by FBI Laboratory examiners as the bomber's calling card. The letter contained a nine digit number written to resemble a Social Security Account number, and the bomber told the Times that they should use this number to verify future correspondence from him that would also contain the secret number. Or, if the *New York Times* doubted this letter, they could go to the FBI who the Unabomber claimed would vouch for his veracity.

The *New York Times* handed the letter over to the FBI. A major discovery was made. Indented writing appeared under ultraviolet examination of the letter - "CALL NATHAN R. WED 7 PM."

The questions surrounding the document flowed endlessly. Could the bomber have carelessly applied the notation by over-writing the blank sheet of paper that he later used in the letter to the *New York Times* editor? Did the Unabomber have a friend, rel-ative, or associate whom he casually referred to as Nathan R? Could the indented writings have been inadvertently applied by the newspaper editor himself, or someone in the mailroom?

Whether it was the resurgence of bombings or the audacity of the Unabomber's letter to an editor of the *New York Times*, the UNABOM case once again was thrust into the limelight. Attorney General Janet Reno, with the concurrence of the Secretary of the Treasury (ATF) and the Post Master General (PIS) ordered the creation of the UNABOM Task Force (UTF) under the direction of the FBI. Reno decreed that all three

Federal Agencies, each of which had investigative responsibilities for some of these bombings, contribute equal amounts of investigators, administrators and resources to the UTF. They would work together under the direction of the Task Force Leader-FBI Chief Inspector George Clow. Clow was appointed to this position by new FBI Director Louie Freeh. Clow decided to headquarter the UTF within the San Francisco office of the FBI. A short time later, nine upper level FBI officials were dispatched from FBI Headquarters in Washington, D.C. to San Francisco to develop a coordinated response to identifying and arresting the Unabomber along with this so-called anarchist group – F.C. The Bureau of Alcohol, Tobacco and Firearms (ATF) contributed some of its management officials and investigators to the case, while the U.S. Postal Inspection Service joined in with one supervisor and several of its investigators. Additionally an arm of the UTF was established within the Sacramento office of the FBI. Finding "Nathan R" became almost as important as finding the Unabomber. The "Nathan R Project" became a lynchpin of a multi-pronged strategy developed by the newly created UNABOM Task Force (UTF). The UTF coordinated and directed the subsequent UNABOM investigation all over the nation.

Seven months later the trail was once again growing cold. The FBI officials managing the investigation in San Francisco were continuing to progress in their individual career paths, with some receiving promotions and wanting to get on to their new assignments. They could leave UNABOM, but the San Francisco FBI and Major Case 75 had nowhere to go. And, the UNABOM case remained unsolved.

As the Special Agent in Charge of the San Francisco FBI Field Division, I was responsible for several hundred agents and support personnel, covering the populous coastal communities from Monterey, through the San Francisco Bay Area, and up to the Oregon border. Now, I had to make a decision. Would FBI

Headquarters simply replace the outgoing Bureau managers with another round of transfers to San Francisco? Or, was it time for different thinking if we were ever to solve UNABOM. I knew what I had to do. I picked up the phone and called FBI Director Louis Freeh in Washington, D.C.

PROLOGUE

A DERANGED AND BRILLIANT HERMIT, HE BECAME MORE AND MORE deadly as he experimented with and tested his bombs near his mountain cabin in Montana. In 1978, they were little more than large firecrackers, but through years of library research and practice in the mountains near his rural cabin, he got his first kill in 1985 by placing a package bomb behind a retail computer store in Sacramento. Upon moving the device, the owner of the store had his chest torn apart by shrapnel from the exploding bomb. A similarly targeted bomb was placed some fourteen months later in Salt Lake City. But this time there was a lapse in the bomber's security protocol. An office worker watched him place the package in a parking lot and gave his description to a police artist after a tremendous explosion savagely injured another victim. The publicity that followed was exhilarating for him, but the fear of discovery overshadowed it all and he withdrew inwardly, frustrated by his inability to kill.

Six years of quiet followed while he worked to perfect his killing machines. Through study of previous equipment malfunctions and intense library research, he worked to achieve a critical reduction in the size of the bombs and to improve their durability, insuring reliable delivery via the mails while increasing their destructive power.

No small task for a bomb maker that eschewed manufactured construction materials; instead, preferring hand crafted wooden and metal components. His laboratory was within the rugged Montana terrain, near the small town of Lincoln, Montana, in an area dimpled by abandoned mineshafts and scarred with ravines and rock outcroppings that gave the privacy and shelter needed for his test detonations. Notebooks were filled with mathematical equations computing the optimum wire composition and recording his test results of the precise wire diameter and length required to bring the exact electrical charge to detonate the various chemical mixtures and explosive accelerants.

Research, experimentation, and repeated trial and error, brought a little progress each time. Time was not an enemy in these mountains, a seemingly endless supply of it was wrapped daily in the summer sunlight or sheathed in the snow and cold winter wind. This mountain recluse—turned urban vigilante— had long ago come to terms with time and boredom. Under winter's icy mantle, he appeared modeled after Abe's own stereotype, in a town carrying that namesake. Day by day, he studied library books and other publications in front of a pot-bellied iron stove and read by the light of the cabin's only small window. The theoretical calculations that darted within his head were composed and recorded in the notebooks toward that day when there was a break in the weather and they could be put to the test.

The bombs were his voice. At first he was content for the explosive devices to speak for him. Soon, however, he began to tag them with the mysterious "F.C." inscribed on small metal tags or end caps designed to withstand the explosion. The FBI accepted it for what it was—a subtle message to taunt and confound the investigators. Eventually, he would find the power to speak for himself.

He read and he wrote, endlessly. In letters to his brother as well as abstract treatises, he sought to match his deadly tactical message with a strategic manifesto for the entire world to know and learn and follow. The words that came forth were pulled from the notes and ideas inscribed in his journals and letters to his brother that were broad statements on the ills of modern industrialized society.

The Unabomber changed the rules of the game when he sent a letter to the *New York Times* in June of 1993:

"We are an anarchist group calling ourselves FC. Notice that the postmark on the envelope precedes a newsworthy event that will happen about the time you receive this letter, if nothing goes wrong. This will prove we knew about the event in advance, so our claim of responsibility is truthful. Ask the FBI about FC. They have heard of us. Right now we only want to establish our identity and provide an identifying number...Keep this number secret so that no one else can pretend to speak in our name."

He couldn't have realized his pursuers were ready and willing to break their own rules this time around to find the leads hidden within his own writings that would land them on the trail to his mysterious identity. He didn't know it then, but he was no longer in control of his own game.

CHAPTER ONE

CHANGING THE FBI CULTURE TO TRACK A SERIAL BOMBER

(The traditional field office approach to FBI investigations dating back to the days of J. Edgar Hoover hindered fast moving, multi-jurisdictional investigations. I had to change the culture, structure, and strategy so that we would have a fighting chance to succeed at solving UNABOM).

AS MY FLIGHT TO WASHINGTON, D.C. CLIMBED OUT OF THE FOG blanket around San Francisco, I settled back in my seat with a feeling of weariness and some concern about my upcoming meeting with FBI Director Louis Freeh.

"I may have really stepped in it this time," recurring doubt played in my head as I recalled my phone call to Louie.

With unbounded optimism, I had expressed confidence in my ability to manage and even solve this sixteen-year old monstrosity of a case. The realization flooded my thinking. This was the UNABOM investigation and I had just volunteered for a career-bending and potentially career-breaking case. Not completely out of character, I conceded to myself, but did this really compare with my previous experiences? In Miami, I had contended with spies, drug traffickers, and cold-blooded killers. More recently I had guided the San Francisco FBI team that tracked down and arrested Richard Allen Davis for the kidnapping and murder of Polly

25

Klaas. But no high-profile FBI case that I could recall had lingered and festered on the vine like UNABOM.

Sometimes dozing and then awakening from my surreal dream, my memories turned to the succession of bombings and briefings I had received from agents currently assigned to the investigation. I mentally prepared for my meeting with Louie by asking my own questions and then trying to answer them. What did I know about the case? For that matter, what did anyone really know about the Unabomber?

When the six- hour plane ride was over, I ended up with far more questions than answers. During the cab ride from Dulles Airport to downtown Washington, I jotted notes into my business plan for the discussions with Louie. I decided to focus my requests on an issue that I considered necessary for success. First, the 1993 creation of the UNABOM Task Force (UTF) gave FBI Inspector George Clow centralized management authority over the efforts of local, State, and Federal investigators around the country. Other FBI field divisions were also required to take their guidance from the San Francisco based UTF, which was designated by the Department of Justice as responsible for the administration and management of the overall UNABOM investigation. This included agents and investigators from across the FBI, the United States Postal Inspection Service (USPS), and the Bureau of Alcohol, Tobacco and Firearms (ATF). While the San Francisco FBI contributed the majority of agent and support employee staffing to the UTF, significant manpower was also assigned to the case in the FBI's Chicago, Salt Lake City and Sacramento Field Offices because of UNABOM crimes committed in those territories.

In actual practice, there were too many investigators still doing their own thing. Their investigative priorities had eroded into parochial and misguided efforts lacking focus and leadership. These individuals and small teams had operated as isolated silos of investigation at or near the various crime scenes for sixteen years with little actual coordination or central direction. At every move they seemed to fight change. I was against accepting the assignment without a firm reaffirmation of unparalleled support and delegation of authority from the Director—both inside and outside the FBI.

Upon my arrival at FBI Headquarters long-time friends and associates greeted me on my way to the Director's office. Other Bureau officials invited to the meeting met me in the Director's reception room, outside of an executive hallway that ran between the offices of the Director, Deputy Director and a handful of other FBI executives who managed the Bureau from FBIHQ. After the Director greeted us and everyone exchanged cordial and brief formalities, we were escorted to a small group setting in the Director's conference room. He quickly got down to business.

"We've been stymied gentlemen. What's our best course of action at this point?" Louie came to the meeting fully briefed and with plenty of questions of his own. He looked at the faces in the room and there was a short burst of silence that seemed to last forever. After a round of dialogue, Louie made his decision. "Freeman has it then; I'm adding all of the UNABOM Major Case into his San Francisco operation and we will give the necessary support to run this bomber to the ground."

I glanced around the room before I spoke, knowing that I had been handed the top down support that I needed—but also realizing this was a highly perishable commodity in the Headquarters culture. The less said at this point, the better. "Louie, I appreciate your support and confidence. I've sketched out a plan that I will lay out in the next couple of weeks; a new approach from a different perspective that differs from our usual field office approach. There will be more to come on that."

I actually had quite a number of ideas at this point, but I knew they would be unpopular with most of my peers. In my mind, the traditional field office approach to FBI investigations was a hindrance to complex, fast moving, multi-jurisdictional investigations. It allowed leeway for Special Agents in Charge (SAC) of field offices to make decisions about the availability of Agents and other resources based on their own competing priorities. It simply didn't work in a complex, multi-faceted investigation like UNABOM and was akin to the old adage about too many cooks in the kitchen. I decided to say as little as possible during the meeting, but was buoyed by a comment from the Director as we were leaving the meeting.

"The status quo in this case is simply unacceptable. A fresh approach is imperative."

The Director was firm in his resolve, but midway through the meeting I had sensed what I would feel a hundred times in the coming months of UNABOM. Most of the people in the meeting just wanted to leave and get on with things they could control.

As we discussed the UNABOM case, I kept thinking about a lesson I had learned on assignment in Miami that had etched in my memory the gross failure of the old ways when victims were being assaulted and killed faster than the antiquated system of "electronic" communications could be dictated to a stenographer, typed up for approval, and then typed again for teletype transmittal from one field office to another.

In 1984 a deranged murderer named Christopher Wilder abducted and raped almost a dozen women, killing eight of them on a rampage from Florida through Texas, Oklahoma, Nevada, and California before turning back across the Midwest and finally committing suicide during a struggle with police at the Canadian border with New Hampshire. The Miami FBI office had jurisdiction in the case because Wilder transported his first victim from central Florida across the state line into Georgia.

He assaulted and tortured her, using an electric lamp fixture before she was able to escape. She bolted naked from a motel room into the cab of a trucker who was leaving the parking lot. She was lucky to avoid the fate of several victims who followed. Something had snapped in Wilder as he launched his senseless killing spree, escaping in multiple stolen cars as he sped across the country trying to avoid police detection on the highways.

I felt helpless as I came to realize that the FBI was ill suited at that point in time by culture, structure, and aging technology to handle the fast-moving case of a serial killer. The messaging system was overwhelmed and hopelessly backlogged. Telephone calls to surrounding field offices were the only recourse in trying to get one step ahead of Wilder to warn the public of impending danger as he moved from state to state.

Leads sent to the neighboring FBI offices were met with a lack of familiarity with the case making it necessary to repeat lengthy information anew with each call. My frustration escalated with the body count and then, suddenly and thankfully, it was over. I feared there were parallels to the UNABOM investigation in the Wilder experience. This strengthened my resolve to close all the loops at the outset.

In preparing to take charge of the UNABOM albatross, I was pleased that the FBI Director and Attorney General had designated the FBI the lead agency in the UNABOM investigation a year earlier. Still, we faced an inherent weakness. In practice, managing this directive was not so easy. This was a pretty unpopular notion at the ATF and U.S. Postal Inspection Service. To have a chance of success, I needed the FBI Director to affirm that I served as the nationwide FBI leader of the UNABOM Task Force, regardless of the field office territory where the investigation was taking place. Clear delegation of authority within the FBI was the only way to ensure a thorough and consistent investigation. This was an equally unpopular notion among my FBI peers and completely contrary to Bureau culture.

Besides these operational issues, there was a burning question in my mind as I left the office of FBI Director Freeh in March 1994. "How could I make a fundamental difference in this old dog of a case"?

On the flight back to San Francisco, the sprawling investigation that now rested in my hands kept turning over in my mind. A dozen or more bombings in as many venues across the nation... victims running the gamut of professors, an airline corporate officer, computer store owners, geneticists and scientific researchers, several horrific injuries and one death, bombs that were placed in the mail and some that were left at locations as disguised packages. Where was the pattern? For a fleeting minute, I second-guessed my decision to accept the assignment. The luster wore off as I came to terms with the enormity of the responsibility for UNABOM. Even my optimism over the Unabomber's decision to start communicating with the *New York Times* in June of 1993 faded, as I came to terms with the fact that he actually started communicating indirectly in June of 1980—when he sent a letter to Percy Wood, then the President of United Airlines:

"I am taking the liberty of sending you...a book...that should be read by all who make important decisions affecting the public welfare..."

"His words then did us a lot of good," I thought to myself. "Thirteen years later and we still have no idea who the socially conscious killer is!"

Once back in my office in San Francisco, a growing crescendo of telephone calls were being forwarded from FBI Headquarters with inquiries from the national media and representatives of Congress. They were all asking when the FBI was going to act to remove this menace from society. A classic dose of second-guessing and inane questions flowed.

"Who is this guy? It is a guy, isn't it? You're not sure? What has the FBI been doing for sixteen years? How long before he strikes again? Can you stop him before he kills someone else? Who's in charge of this investigation?"

Even as I deplaned from Washington, I began to receive telephonic reports of dissension and frustration among the UNABOM rank and file investigators. As I slipped into the chair behind my desk to re-tool and catch a breath from the long flight, some of the things I had been hearing were confirmed by a memo placed squarely in the middle of a pile of papers in front of me.

The memo was from Donald Max Noel, one of the FBI agents from San Francisco who had been tapped in July of 1993 by the previous team of Bureau managers to work on the UTF. I had been counting on Max as one of the lynchpins of our new effort. But it appeared from his memo that Max wanted off the task force. Well, that could wait. The new supervisor I would select to lead the investigation could handle Max. I just didn't know who that was going to be. But I knew one thing for sure; I wouldn't be getting any volunteers.

I couldn't work UNABOM alone. My first order of business had to involve assembling my own team to integrate with and then organize an effective separation from the outgoing FBI Headquarters contingent of managers that had been sent to San Francisco to organize the UTF. They had spent the previous eight months getting organized and developing an investigative response to the renewed bombings. Understandably, they were ready to put San Francisco in their rear view mirrors as quickly as possible. The departing FBI management team had achieved a level of coordination and consensus, but rumors and signs of dissatisfaction were plentiful. I would need to act fast.

I picked up the phone and called Ed Appel, the Assistant Special Agent in Charge of the counterintelligence (CI) program. For many years the San Francisco CI program had been regarded as the crown jewel of the FBI's CI efforts. The agents working the program were some of the best in the country. Since I had also been exposed to a variety of counterintelligence work during my career, I realized that their skill sets were honed by the need for patience, thoughtful analysis, the development of a strategic approach to problem solving, and the need to be diplomatic and tactful to a fault. That criteria didn't fit too many agents involved in day-to-day criminal work, but I thought it might be just what we needed to change the nature of our approach to UNABOM.

Ed Appel walked into my office as I studied the organization chart, assessing each of the CI squad supervisors as to how their individual skill sets and personalities fit into my needs for the right person to supervise the UNABOM Task Force. Ed was a refreshing blend of quirky, folksy, book smart and kind. He could recite for hours the history of the Bureau's worldwide national security program, recalling names, dates, tradecraft and the favorite pastimes of the world's greatest spies. His biggest drawback was that he could recite for hours.

"Ed, we've got UNABOM now whether we want it or not," I said. "I have to put my own team together and I'm going to need a supervisor who we can count on to manage all of these diverse agencies, people, and information. I think we need someone with a strategic vision and the capability to implement. I'm looking for your recommendation as to whether we have a suitable counterintelligence supervisor to coordinate the UTF in its day-to-day operations."

We both looked at the office organization chart and then at each other. There was only one name on it that met the criteria I wanted and whom I was willing to take a chance on, and I also knew that Ed depended upon the same person to help him manage the daily activities of San Francisco's CI program.

"Ed, you and I both know we have to get this right the first time. This is the FBI and its UNABOM; the needs of the Bureau are the only consideration that matters."

I didn't have to say another word.

"I'll go call Terry Turchie now and break the news."

Ed got up and returned to his office to make the call. I had made my first personnel move towards solving UNABOM, but I knew that it was potentially an unpopular selection in some quarters of my own office—particularly among the professional cadre of criminal agents that like Max Noel had dedicated many months and years into this investigation.

Before I intervened in his life, Terry Turchie was the Senior FBI Agent in the Palo Alto office where he was responsible for managing a team of agents engaged in a variety of national security investigations ranging from espionage to the theft of intellectual property from companies in Silicon Valley. From all accounts, he was happy and comfortable with his life until his phone rang and Ed Appel started exchanging pleasantries.

"Gosh Ed, you seem in an unusually upbeat mood today. Anything I should know about?" Terry said to Ed Appel, sensing a different tone to Appel's voice.

"How would you like to come up to San Francisco and take over as supervisor of the UNABOM squad?" Appel paused.

"Well, that's an interesting offer, but I'm fine here in Palo Alto. I sure appreciate you thinking of me though." Turchie wasn't ready for what came next.

Appel's pause was short lived.

"Terry, this isn't exactly a multiple choice question. SAC Freeman has already made the decision and you need to come up and take on this job. How soon can you get to San Francisco and get started?"

For what seemed like eternity, Turchie couldn't talk. He just stared out the window of his comfortable office. Certainly he heard wrong. But Appel was waiting for an answer, so he would play along.

"Ed, it would take at least two weeks to a month to get someone in here to supervise and do the right kind of hand-off of cases and assets, so how about four weeks from now." It was clear that Turchie was still waiting for Appel to say he was just joking.

"How about two hours from now," Ed responded and said good bye. This was no joke.

Turchie knew that Max Noel was assigned to the UTF, so he called Max to arrange a meeting. If he was going to supervise the UNABOM case, he intended to get a first hand view of what it was all about from an agent who would know. Although they weren't close friends and had never worked together, Terry knew Max from the first time they "bumped" into each other.

It was when Turchie had just transferred to San Francisco from FBI Headquarters. He was walking by another supervisor's office when he heard what sounded like a bar room fight going on inside. Swearing, cussing, and raised voices were the prelude as two FBI agents emerged. Both almost ran into him as they charged into their squad's bullpen. One of the agents was especially noticeable; his face was scarlet red, almost as if he had been holding his breath. But that wasn't the case, as his mouth was in high gear. His two hands seemed to move in three different directions as his supervisor gave chase. Turchie was lucky that the agents on his squad were docile by comparison. He learned later that the scarlet-faced agent was "Mad Max" Noel.

Turchie paced the floor in front of a pastry display case at Lyon's Restaurant on Van Ness Avenue, about a block from the San Francisco FBI office, silently practicing what he wanted to cover with the highly experienced criminal case agent Noel, several years his senior and now reporting to him as the newly designated FBI Supervisor of the UTF.

Turchie was born and raised in the San Francisco Bay Area. His FBI career had taken him to Portland, Oregon, where he spent two years working criminal cases and then east to

Washington, D.C. and New York City, where he was assigned to counterintelligence work. To my knowledge, he was the only FBI agent ever to get into a fight with a Russian spy, wrestling Soviet KGB officer Gennadiy Zakharov to the ground on a Brooklyn subway platform in 1986. In 1988 he returned to San Francisco as the supervisor of a CI squad. By 1990 he was transferred to Palo Alto, which at the time was the only FBI Resident Agency that specialized exclusively in counterintelligence investigations.

In preparing for the meeting, Terry had done a little research on Special Agent Max Noel and determined that he had a long history with the San Francisco FBI. He served as the Principal Firearms Instructor, as well as being an active participant in the development of San Francisco's SWAT Team. In 1971, Max was one of seven agents who stormed an airplane at San Francisco International Airport, while killing two Bulgarian terrorists who had hijacked the plane. Throughout the 1970s into the early 1990s, Max worked labor racketeering and excelled in the development of Top Echelon criminal informants to penetrate organized crime groups. He coordinated the use of such informants in one especially complex labor racketeering case that led to the conviction of several officials of the International Brotherhood of Teamsters and sitting Federal District Judge Robert P. Aguilar of San Jose, California. Max was no stranger to complex investigations.

Max was assigned to the Oakland Resident Agency meaning no more long commutes to San Francisco over the Bay Bridge between the city and the East Bay, where he lived with his wife and family. He had great control over his time, cases, and future. That is, until he took a call on the morning of July 8, 1993 from Assistant Special Agent in Charge Lorenzo McCrary.

"Button up your cases, Max," McCrary told him. "On Monday morning, July 12, report to Chief FBI Inspector George Clow in San Francisco. He's selected you to become a part of his newly created UNABOM Task Force. And, by the way, you have no choice in the matter."

George Clow and Max were good friends and colleagues. Clow had been an Assistant Special Agent in Charge in San Francisco until his promotion to Inspector and transfer to FBI Headquarters in Washington, D.C. I also knew Clow and had not been surprised when Director Freeh appointed him to lead the initial UNABOM Task Force. George was respected and a very competent investigator in his own right, but Max wanted no part of UNABOM and wasted little time arranging to meet with Clow to communicate his personal request.

"George, I'd like to opt out of this assignment. I've planned a number of trips this summer with my family. My son is getting married in mid-July. We're visiting with my elderly parents in Nebraska. I have much to wrap up in connection with the corruption investigation of Judge Aguilar."

As Max made his case to opt out of UNABOM, George listened politely.

"Max, the work you did on the Aguilar case has really impressed me and is why I asked you to become a part of UNABOM. It won't be like any task force you have worked on in the past. You will be assigned only meaningful work and can take your vacation time this summer. I need you to get involved with this case and bring your skills to helping us solve it."

Max reluctantly agreed and now things were changing once again. It was his worst fear. Clow was leaving. To compound things even more, word had gotten out that Terry Turchie was moving from Palo Alto to supervise the UNABOM Task Force. Down in Palo Alto and around the area, people who knew Max and Terry just shook their heads and laughed. A long time FBI employee, Diane Ambrose, who was a good friend of Max and worked closely with Terry in Palo Alto, couldn't resist calling Noel when she heard the news.

Ambrose was as sweet as strawberry jam and had the kind of cheer and kindness in her voice that made it seem like she was calling straight from Heaven.

"Max Noel, "she began, with her unmistakable laugh. "Tell me it isn't so," she continued laughing out loud.

"Diane," Max switched to his cuddly persona and smiled as if Ambrose was sitting in front of him. "What do you mean?"

"The word is out Max that you and Terry Turchie will be working on UNABOM together," her laughter subsided enough to hear Max groan about UNABOM.

"Well Max, I should be the one to tell you what we all think about this. You and Terry Turchie, it'll NEVER work!"

Ambrose was right. At first glance, Max and Terry were a study in contrasts. Max, about 5'8" with a stocky build, had a highly combustible temper and flared from quiet to red-faced, faster than Robert DeNiro in Raging Bull. But just as suddenly he could reverse course to warmhearted and kind.

At six feet and always wearing a half smile, Terry was the FBI, New York version of Mr. Rogers, according to the former Assistant Director of the New York Office, Jim Fox. Terry had worked for Fox in New York from 1980 to 1987.

Where Max was the quintessential law enforcement gun aficionado, Terry's office was a shrine to Walt Disney memorabilia— a Davy Crockett cap, stuffed Mickey Mouse, and countless family pictures of trips to Disneyland.

Max was wearing his warmest heart when he sat down in front of Terry at Lyon's.

"Terry, I know you're the right person for this job. I know a lot about you, even though we don't know one another very well and I think you'll bring an approach to the UNABOM investigation that is sorely needed."

They sat down and Max immediately glanced at and put the menu on the table. He knew what he wanted and didn't want to spend much time in his selection. He wanted to get to the point.

"Let me start with giving you a summary of what we've been trying to do in the case since last July," Max began. "I attended my first meeting of the UNABOM Task Force on July 12, as ordered. I was assigned to work on what we call Historical File reviews. Pat Webb is my supervisor. I've been working closely with a young ATF agent, Tom Atteberry. Together we were assigned to re-investigate the UNABOM explosive devices that had targeted the University of Utah in 1981 and the University of California at Berkeley in 1982 and 1985. We identified forty-four unresolved forensic issues and sixty-two unanswered questions that we posed to the FBI Lab for resolution.

"While waiting for word from the Laboratory, I started conducting leads related to the indented writing of "Nathan R" and I met with the victim of the first UNABOM attack on Cory Hall at U. C. Berkeley in 1982, Professor Diogenes Angelakos."

"In October, the Task Force established a toll free 800 phone line which was operated and staffed 24 hours a day. At the same time, FBI Director Louis Freeh, Assistant Treasury Secretary Ron Noble and Postal Inspection Service Representatives conducted a joint national news conference announcing the creation of the UNABOM Task Force, the existence of the 800 number and a $1 million dollar reward for any information related to the Unabomber's identification. The public was shown a photograph of the indented writing found on the Unabomber's recent correspondence with the *New York Times* and a Wanted Poster was featured with an artist's rendering of the Unabomber when he was seen by a witness placing a bomb in Salt Lake City in February of 1987."

"Unfortunately, the UNABOM press conference was being held at the same time that Michael Jordan was holding a press conference in Chicago announcing his retirement from the NBA and professional basketball. Guess whose press conference got the most coverage and viewers?"

"Jordan?" Turchie replied.

Max nodded. "As a result, the Director's UNABOM press coverage didn't have the desired effect."

He continued, "Bill Tafoya, who you know, began working on a Victimology project to see whether we could establish any specific connections between the victims themselves or between the Unabomber and the victims. So far, we've come up empty handed there too, although I have yet to see his assessment of where we are with that."

After his overview of UNABOM, Max turned to the business at hand. Turchie was stunned, but didn't show it, as Max continued.

"But for me Terry, I need to be back in Oakland working on the Aguilar case and with the people I have made commitments to in their own cases. I told George Clow I would work hard. I took the job without complaining, but now is a perfect time for new blood and new ideas and it is time for me to go back to what I was doing. It has nothing to do with you Terry, but I have to tell you that I sent a memo off to the SAC asking that I be reassigned back to my old squad."

As Max paused, there was only silence between them. He waited for Turchie to address his remarks. Lunch had been quite hurried and Max and Terry hadn't come close to covering the ground they should have covered. Turchie seemed surprised that Max wanted off the case, but, it was obvious that Max's passion and fiery trigger was just what was needed if UNABOM was to be solved. Terry decided to lighten up the discussion.

"Max, you may think you know a lot about me, but what you may not know is that I need a piece of one of those pies I saw when I came in here," Turchie laughed and ordered some coffee, buying a little more time to talk with him.

With his pie order placed, Turchie continued his pitch, "Max, I know how you must feel. Trust me, I can relate to the shock of being assigned to the UTF. But I have to be honest with you as well. I plan on advising SAC Freeman to disregard your request to be transferred. You are exactly the right person to be working this case and I plan on giving you all the freedom and support you need. I think this case can be solved and I think we can do it."

"Well, Terry, that's between you and Jim Freeman. If you guys decide that I'm staying, then I will stay and I won't complain and I'll give you everything I have. But I really hope I can return to Oakland and my old squad."

After his lunch with Max, Turchie walked back to the FBI office and took the elevator to the 13th floor. Stepping into my reception area, he stopped to talk with my secretary, Janet Fournier. Janet knew everyone and everything that goes on in the office. She had been the secretary to several consecutive SAC(s) and could have run the office with one eye completely shut.

"Terry, welcome back," she smiled as if she had expected him to show up unexpected. "Jim's in his office. Go ahead in. I think UNABOM takes precedence over anything else," she laughed.

I was sitting behind my desk when he approached the open outer door.

We hadn't spoken or seen each other since Ed Appel had ordered Terry to report to me.

"Come on in," I motioned to the conference table and I walked around the side of my desk to meet him there.

I explained to Turchie that I had just returned from a meeting in Washington, D.C. with FBI Director Louis Freeh and had made some decisions on how I wanted to manage the UNABOM Task Force.

"I don't aim to just maintain the case and cover leads; or post and coast as we used to say. I know it's gone on forever and everyone thinks it's an impossible dead-end, but I took this case to solve it. Terry, I want you to look at it for a few days and by the end of next week, give me your strategy to make that happen."

"Good Lord, Jim, I've been wondering how the heck I got involved in this assignment, but I suppose the answer doesn't matter. Well, let me tell you about the lunch I had with Max Noel. It's kind of the first big step I took after Ed Appel told me to close down in Palo Alto and get up here to the city to work on UNABOM. Over lunch Max told me he wanted to be reassigned back to his old squad in Oakland and that he sent you a memo. I told him I would recommend that you disregard his request and that he stay assigned to UNABOM. I think we really need him."

"I agree, Terry. Max stays. Maybe someday down the road we can revisit the issue, but now is not the time." I didn't mention that I had seen the memo from Max and had already declined his request.

With those words, Terry left my office and I reflected on the tasks that he now faced—keeping Max on the Task Force was as easy as delivering the unwelcome news, but delivering a new and viable UNABOM strategy within five working days, that I had to see! And, the way he handled it would tell me if I had made the right investment in Terry Turchie.

CHAPTER TWO

THE WONDER OF ANALYSIS: THE BOMB DIDN'T FIT IN THE MAIL

(Like most cases of its time, UNABOM lacked a systematic integration of investigation and analysis. Our plan made analysis the lynchpin of our investigative effort and foundation for our re-investigation, suspect development, and public awareness.)

RUNNING AN FBI FIELD OFFICE ISN'T A NINE-TO-FIVE JOB. MY days in San Francisco began early in the morning; sometimes breakfast with one of the Bay Area police chiefs or county sheriffs; then briefings on an investigation by a squad supervisor and his/her agents; giving a luncheon talk about the FBI to a civic organization; and spending the afternoons discussing program strategies and the impact the FBI was having on local crime problems. Throw in a few personnel issues (any organization can have them), and an occasional law enforcement crisis mandating a SWAT call-out, and any sense of boredom or routine corrected itself in an instant. Kidnappings or a child disappearance added hours to the day whenever they happened. Fortunately, they didn't happen too often.

But add a case like UNABOM, involving dozens of employees of several agencies, and ten-hour days easily grew into twelve or more. That's why I was so eager to put the right people in place to start managing the UNABOM investigation with my personal style and accountability. As I waited for Terry's strategy paper to land on my desk, the more I questioned how we would effectively confront the Unabomber. My reading of the case history up to this point had resurfaced concerns about anyone's ability to pull the case back on track before this madman downed an aircraft for real, with major loss of life or a similar tragedy. Each day, Terry and I met for an hour or two to discuss this case called UNABOM with its unique, abstract nature and a bond of respect and confidence began to emerge.

I breathed a little easier one afternoon when Janet Fornier walked into my office and interrupted my routine.

"Hey Jim," she said in her characteristic way with a half smile, "Terry Turchie came by earlier and said you would be looking for this."

She dropped his thick memo on my desk.

"He's on calendar for three o'clock, so you've got about an hour to look it over before he shows up."

As Janet turned and left the room, I realized that she relished how this UNABOM case was getting under my skin. I picked up the memo and caught the title, "Major Case #75- UNABOM, Proposed San Francisco Strategy." With more than a little anticipation, I lifted the cover page and wondered if it would hit the target. There was hardly time to read over it, as Terry showed up exactly at three. The expectation was on his face that he had hit a home run and was waiting for high fives all around. I motioned for him to sit down in one of the more comfortable chairs, adjacent to the conference table.

"There's coffee in the back if you want some," I pointed to the small room behind my office, where we kept a coffee pot and occasional donut. Then we settled into our discussion, as neither of us wanted to put UNABOM off any longer.

"So, I read over your plan. Generally, I like the approach, but I have some questions and need clarification of a few matters. Let's start at the top." Terry sat quietly and a little deflated as I continued.

"You talk about a multi-layered strategy and one of the first things you mention is a reinvestigation by the UNABOM Task Force of all the bombings up till now. But, I thought that was the focus of the task force during the past year. Are you proposing we do it over; retracing the same steps, again?" That will do wonders for our credibility, I thought to myself.

"Hold on, Jim. It's true that Clow's strategy over the past year has focused on reinvestigating the bombings. But, the devil is in the details. All FBI offices and other agencies that worked on UNABOM events over the years were directed to review their files and evidence logs with the goal of combining all of the data amassed over the past sixteen years into a centralized file system here in San Francisco so there would be one common computerized UNABOM file. While that was a worthwhile objective, we are finding that the result is more like the cliché: "garbage in, garbage out.""

I was acutely aware that a development of this type would surely raise questions at FBI Headquarters and would be immediately called to the attention of Director Freeh. That it was a problem inherited from the previous task force would make no difference back there.

Terry continued. "They've done a credible job of collecting the historical information and getting it entered into data bases so we can start working with it, but for the most part the reinvestigation has been done in the typical FBI protocol of setting leads to be handled by agents in other field offices. Sometimes it's the same agents and supervisors that are being asked to evaluate and redo their previous investigation, so you can imagine how that's going over with those folks. To truly get the job done and add an analytical component to the investigation and some consistency in quality and knowledge, we need to create our own UNABOM teams here in San Francisco, assign those teams to each of the bombings, and send them to the locales of previous UNABOM crimes to lead the investigations in those cities. That's the only way we're going to get these investigations done right. Too many leads have simply gone uncovered. And, the way it is now we have no analytical capability to manage the data."

"I like the approach, as it mirrors the new approach to investigations that I alluded to at the meeting in HQ. But, your plan introduces the concept of expanded analysis? Tell me more about that," I said.

"Yes. It's vital that our agents combine fundamental analysis along with investigative skills. In my estimation, this is the ingredient that's been missing or at least hasn't been emphasized in any formal way to gain maximum leverage from every interview and each laboratory examination over the past sixteen years. It's a hodge-podge of information without applied analysis."

Terry leaned over and propped his elbows on the table. "In time, we can move from simple link analysis to more complex assessments that will enable us to develop descriptors that match our unknown subject. Eventually, this will build into a composite description of a unique individual that hopefully we'll be able to recognize. At some point, we may even want headquarters to assign terrorism analysts to the task force, as I'm aware of some very good work they're doing."

"Terry, I've heard you speak of needing a more thorough and complete review of all of the forensic evidence in the UNABOM case. What's lacking there?"

"Jim, I've spent a lot of time with Max since you put me in charge of UNABOM. He's one of the only agents that George Clow allowed to travel into another field office's territory and actually conduct reinvestigations of specific UNABOM crimes.

When you talk with Max, it really shows that he and an ATF agent named Tom Atteberry went out and did some of their own work. They came back with a completely different level of understanding of the case, including observations that stand in contrast to those made by others who never left San Francisco and tried to do a reinvestigation by sitting at their desk and reading files.

"I have to tell you Jim, that what Max and Atteberry found out is that we need a thorough review of everything the FBI, ATF and Postal labs have done over the years because there are still so many unanswered questions about forensic matters connected to the different UNABOM crimes. We need to tie together our reinvestigations of each UNABOM crime by combining the original findings with whatever new information we can surface, add in the new forensic updates, and then develop an analytic process to identify and classify each piece of the puzzle."

"Terry, you know you're preaching to the choir on that point." And, the realization hit me that this was going to be a great partnership.

"Exactly," Terry smiled with an assurance that we were on the same page.

I nodded in return. "What're the next steps in your plan?"

"Bill Tafoya, and to a lesser extent, Mary Ellen O'Toole, have been working on something called Victimology, trying to look for common denominators that might connect victims to one another or the bomber to all the victims. A few months ago all of the surviving UNABOM victims were invited to San Francisco, participated in a round table discussion and were extensively interviewed. Nothing has come of that yet and I need to talk with Bill to see where else that might lead, if anywhere. But it brings up the issue of suspect profiling in this case and where it currently stands. We need some updating of the profile we've been working with, so I need to spend some time with them towards getting that done."

"That's something that I need to hear more about," I said with enthusiasm. "You have a working profile of the Unabomber? Based on what data, pray tell?"

I was aware of some work being done at Quantico that employed in-depth interviews and psychoanalysis of "cooperating" serial murderers on death row in a bid to describe the potential cause and effect of their aberrant behavior. But these were murderers that had personal and intimate contact with their victims; unlike bombers who place their explosives in public places or mail them in boxes to remote addresses.

"How could there be a credible criminal profile of serial bombers, since there are only two or three in the course of history?" I wondered aloud to no one in particular.

Terry was undeterred by my digression from his plan and continued his presentation to me. "This brings me to another product we can add to enhance how we use all the information we collect and establish a common baseline for UNABOM investigators."

"What's that?" I said on cue.

"Over all these years, and with so many people in so many places conducting investigation, we've sometimes lost sight of what's true about UNABOM and what's not. So, we're going to work up a fact sheet and call it *UNABOM Fact, Fiction and Theory*. We'll keep it up to date and continue to refine it to the point that it'll serve as our analytical guide and a training aide, as we assign more agents and support personnel to the investigation over time."

"I like that," I answered taking a sip of my cold coffee. "You mentioned support personnel. Are we going to give everyone that level of information?" FBI protocol was pretty tradition bound and generally agents conducted investigations and support personnel performed their specific functions and the two tracks remained apart, separated by a certain 'need to know.'

Before he had a chance to respond, I continued.

"Actually, I do agree with you. It's critical that we glue the fabric of this case together and not get lost in the details. But, the sad truth is that we wouldn't know the Unabomber if we tripped over him at this point in time. We must take steps, as you suggest, to isolate the known facts from the hunches and theories—regardless of how well intentioned they might be."

As Terry excused himself to take a phone call, I looked further into his plan and saw that one proposal was to use the UNABOM reward hotline in a more proactive way than its original intent by incorporating a media strategy to proactively engage and perhaps manage the general public in promoting the goals of the investigation. This was a controversial approach that appealed to me, but it would need careful planning and implementation to avoid a backlash. I would follow up on this idea at a later time.

Finally, there was reference to something called a massively parallel computer processor. This caused me to reflect for a moment on the FBI of 1994. Our agents were not even linked by internal email; let alone having a computer that was either massive or parallel. But, Terry was from the counterintelligence side of the house and that's one reason that I selected him—to bring innovative ideas and methods forward.

I liked most of Terry's plan, but needed a feel from him on how he intended to manage it. Some of the key elements were a distinct departure from long established FBI protocol and I agreed it would require extraordinary measures. After all, the traditional techniques and standard rules of operation had been tried repeatedly and came up empty. It wouldn't matter, if we could just move quickly and get this thing solved.

Terry walked past Janet's desk in the outer office and into the conference room after his phone call was completed and picked up where he had left off.

"Right, Jim. We'll use the 1-800 line to receive calls from the public and open suspect cases as a result. We'll use computer runs to sort suspects from geographical locations once we get the massively parallel computer loaded with information. And we'll open suspects based upon a new criteria that we'll develop from our reinvestigations of UNABOM crimes. All of these avenues will supply us with numerous suspects who fit solid criteria from the outset, rather than taking random shots in the dark."

Talk about unbounded enthusiasm! Terry and I had been talking for over an hour. Both of us were wrapped up in the moment of solving what was seemingly an unsolvable mystery—so much so that I elected to forgo my questions for another time about "what the hell is a massively parallel processor and what would it cost to get one?" I recognized that the plan called for a cultural shift and change is not a popular notion in bureaucratic cultures. But, consideration of how this would play out at FBI Headquarters or among my fellow execs in the field was not an overriding concern to me. Terry and I had come together and agreed to embrace the spirit and objectives of the plan and work out the details as we moved ahead.

As I readied my pen to put "okay" and my initials on our new strategy document, I had one more question.

"You know that attempting to manage media reports even to further specific investigative goals will be controversial in the FBI and probably also with our law enforcement partners, so it has to be crystal clear that these are official press releases and not leaks. Plus, the media will likely react negatively if they sense they are being used without their knowledge. So, against that backdrop, what if more bombs go off and people are killed before we find this guy?"

Terry was surprised and had to pause for a few seconds before answering. "I don't do media stuff. I hadn't given that a lot of thought. But what I will say is this. We need one voice and I think that should be you, not another agency and not FBI Headquarters. You should be the voice of the UNABOM Task

Force. That way, you'll always be conversant in explaining the facts and sticking with the plan. If we're going to be talking to the public, we have to be consistent and focused or they will get nothing out of it and neither will we."

I nodded in agreement. I liked what I heard and what I saw on paper. I left the chair, walked over to my conference table and picked up a plain white napkin that had been sitting on the table since morning. Terry followed me over and we both sat down. I started to sketch out a summary of what we had talked about and what he had explained in some detail in his strategy memo.

"So this is how I see it: first, reinvestigation of each event, but always under the direction of UTF members following strict priorities; second, separate the known facts from fiction and theories; and then, suspect development through event related analysis, geographic data comparisons, and media-generated leads; and finally, develop a consistent media strategy. And this is what I think about media strategy—enhance effectiveness of the 1-800 hotlines by focusing the public on the known facts about the Unabomber by giving them information that won't impede our investigation or any prosecution. That's it—that's our bare-bones strategy, right?" I looked at the handwritten sketch on the napkin and passed it to Terry as he nodded his head in agreement.

"Okay," I agreed, "Go ahead and write it up and send it on to the Bureau. Now that we've figured it out, you should be able to get this solved by tomorrow or at least bring me some good leads on subjects," we both laughed as Terry left the room. But I had a good feeling about UNABOM, as Terry left my office to prepare for his first meeting with the assembled UNABOM Task Force and an important meeting with another seasoned and experienced San Francisco FBI agent—John Conway.

Conway's favorite place for lunch was The Chestnut Street Bar and Grill in the Marina District, and Terry agreed to meet him there. It was eye-opening to learn from Conway, his perspective of the case-especially his dealings with FBI management in the lean years of the investigation.

"John, the rumor is that you're thinking of leaving the Bureau," Turchie started in as they sat down in a booth at the restaurant.

"As soon as I find out what papers I need to file, I'm ready for retirement and out of here," Conway responded in his dramatic voice, playing the role of an FBI agent having a serious conversation with his supervisor, all the while wearing a mischievous gleam in his bright blue eyes.

"What would it take for me to get another year out of you?" Turchie asked.

"Terry, it's nothing against you. I've just had so many problems with previous UNABOM Task Force management. It's left me with a real bad feeling about the case," Conway's voice almost seemed apologetic.

"Like what, what happened that was so bad?" Turchie pressed for answers.

"Just for discussion and not as an official complaint, but at one point I had asked the Explosives Unit of the Lab to take the early UNABOM devices apart and then subject them to new, more modern testing. Surely there were new forensic tests or examination techniques that might reveal new clues. I was told they had done DNA, new latent fingerprint exams, plus hair and fiber work. Later, I found out this was not accurate. The tests hadn't been completed and I was even blamed by management for not pursuing the case aggressively enough. On top of that, in 1992, a Headquarters supervisor tried to get me to close the case. So you could say I'm worn out!"

Turchie continued questioning Conway about his future plans and stressing his value to the Task Force in hopes of retaining a valuable asset to the investigation. In the end, he caved in and agreed he would give Terry another year.

"If you don't f--- with me," it was Conway who wrapped up the agreement.

With Conway also committed to staying on the task force, Terry was feeling confident as he watched the agents and analysts of the UTF gather in a classroom size conference room in the San Francisco Federal Building for the first of what would be dozens of meetings together working to solve UNABOM.

From the FBI, the investigators who pulled up chairs to sit around the massive mahogany conference table included Max Noel, Bill Tafoya, Mary Ellen O'Toole, John Conway, and Neil Oltman. Neil was a young and aggressive agent who Inspector George Clow thought enough of to be assigned as the case agent for UNABOM. Neil came into the FBI from a company in southern California, where he had been an aerospace engineer.

Inspector in charge Don Davis of the Postal Inspection Service was at the meeting. Davis had an easy going personality that hid amazing capabilities and creativity as an investigator and leader. He had mastered the art of being a calming influence and a hard charging veteran at the same time. He brought with him several talented investigators in their own right.

Among them was Paul Wilhelmus, who spoke quietly and infrequently during the meeting. But when he had something to say about UNABOM, he was directly on point. Then, there was Robin Shipman and Tony Muljat from Postal, who apparently always worked together and came across as real life partners on Law and Order. Robin was the young gun, moving in every direction at once, while Tony was obviously aware of his mentor relationship in bringing Robin up in the ranks. In fact, Tony had been assigned to UNABOM longer than any other Postal Service investigator and there was little doubt that the case had become his life's commitment.

From ATF, there was a supervisor at the meeting, Charlie Barnett, and Mark Logan, the ATF Assistant Special Agent in Charge in their San Francisco Field Office. Tom Atteberry, Joyce Seymour, Mike Grady and Jim Flannigan comprised the mainstay of the ATF contingent.

As the meeting slowly came to a semblance of order, Terry stood before the inquisitive group while the task force members, hardened by a tough case, politely gave him their time.

"Well, I've been pretty excited to get with all of you today, especially after I've had time to talk to most of you individually and read through so many files that represent sixteen years of work on UNABOM. It really looks like this is a case that we can solve." Terry paused and looked around the room to gauge the reaction to his initial comments.

If he didn't catch the occasional rolling eyebrow or hear the hopeless sigh from the crowd, he would have no chance at catching the Unabomber. Although the group was reserved and not outright hostile at their lot in life or at him, they all believed the same thing deep down. Turchie lived in a fantasyland. UNABOM had gone on for sixteen years before he came into it, and the odds were that it would continue sixteen more years after he grew tired of it, and had long since been promoted or left.

An FBI agent sitting next to Paul Wilhelmus, one of the U.S. Postal Inspectors assigned to the UTF, quietly leaned over and whispered. "I apologize for my boss. Apparently he's been smoking something if he has reviewed the case and it looks solvable,"

Paul, who spoke infrequently, but with a soft-spoken authority when he did talk, just smiled at the agent.

Terry passionately moved through his main points, "I want to go over with you the strategy that SAC Jim Freeman has approved and that we'll implement together to try and breathe new life into UNABOM. Our entire plan is geared towards an aggressive and pro-active approach to bring everything together and build a composite of who the Unabomber might be. Through meetings, conferences, analytical sessions with each other, all of us will become experts and specialists in every facet of UNABOM. And slowly but surely we will get this ship turned in the right direction."

"Up until now, there has been a kind of inconsistent approach to the media with respect to this case–and that all changes today. UNABOM will speak with one voice and that voice will be SAC Freeman. No one from any other agency is to comment on anything about UNABOM anymore. Within the FBI, no one other than Jim will talk to the media about this investigation. This arrangement has been worked out with the Director and at the highest levels of the Justice Department and if anyone deviates from this policy, they won't be working on the case any longer. It's very important from this point on that everyone understands this. It is an important part of our strategy going forward," Terry paused and looked around the room.

He understood that veiled threats to remove malcontents was dangerous policy, as it held the risk of encouraging everyone to act up so they could get transferred off this dead-end assignment. But everyone seemed to be on their best manners and somehow he guided the group through their first formal analysis under the San Francisco management team.

"So now, let's talk about the first two UNABOM crimes from 1978 and 1979," Turchie glanced from one face to another in the group, and John Conway looked at Paul Wilhelmus and spoke first with the deep and authoritative voice of a British actor and the demeanor of an Irish boxer. He immediately caught the attention of those in the room.

"Terry," Conway said, realizing that he had the stage and all eyes were focused on him, "Paul Wilhelmus and I have already spent some time working together so we'll be a team and we can brief the first two UNABOM events and Paul will start us out."

Wilhelmus said on queue as he exchanged glances with John

Conway, "I'll talk about the first bomb,—UNABOM, Event Number One started in May of 1978 when an individual in Chicago named Mary Gutierrez was walking through a parking lot next to the Science and Engineering building at the University of Illinois Chicago Circle Campus. She saw a package on the pavement next to a parked car and reached to pick it up. The package had ten one dollar Eugene O'Neill stamps on it, but had never been mailed. The stamps hadn't been cancelled. The package had red and white mailing labels with a handwritten destination address and a return address and the words, 'First Class' were also printed on the package."

Paul stopped talking, got out of his chair and walked to the classroom's white board where he carefully wrote the names on the package exactly as they appeared printed on the mailing labels: "From: Professor Buckley Crist, Jr. Northwestern University Tech. Institute Evanston, Il 60201, To: Prof. E.J. Smith, School of Engineering, Rensselear Polytechnic Institute, Troy, New York, 12181."

Paul returned to his seat and resumed telling the mystery of UNABOM Event Number One. "Gutierrez arranged to get the package returned to Professor Buckley Crist at Northwestern University, forty miles north of the UIC campus in downtown Chicago. Because he knew he wasn't the originator of the package, Crist was suspicious of it and contacted the university Public Safety Department. One of their officers, Terry Marker, met with Crist and attempted to open the package. That's when it ignited."

As Paul stopped to look around the room for any questions or reactions from the assembled group, Bill Tafoya jumped in, exclaiming, "We need to know if the device was found lying face up, exposing the mailing label or face down with the mailing label obscured to passers-by."

Paul and John looked quizzically at one another—neither

knew the answer and they both shrugged off the question. Others in the room seemed equally as puzzled.

Tafoya pressed ahead, emphasizing his interest one more time, almost using the same words as the first time.

Having enough of Tafoya's issue, John Conway cleared his throat loud enough to get everyone's attention back and picked up where Paul left off. Tafoya stayed quiet as John gave every impression he would kick the crap out of him if he interrupted again. The room was tense.

John continued, "The actual bomb was made from a galvanized pipe about nine inches long and an inch in diameter. It was encased in a homemade wooden box about twenty-two inches long. Two kinds of smokeless powders and match heads were the main charge inside the pipe, sealed on one end with a wooden plug. The bomb had an improvised mechanical firing system, consisting of a nail and heavy rubber bands held under tension. A small door was cut into the box and sealed closed with black electrical tape. A black Sharpie marker was used to draw an arrow pointing to the door, with the words, 'open.' When the box was opened, the tension was released, the nail struck the match heads, and the strike ignited the smokeless powders, causing the detonation."

Paul jumped back into the conversation, "Fortunately, Officer Marker had only minor injuries from the blast."

"That's a great summary to get us started," Turchie looked back out at the group.

Then, Max entered the discussion while reading from the notes he recorded on his yellow legal pad, proclaiming, "I think it's good to remember here that from the very beginning, it was obvious that whoever this bomber was, he made his own devices from scratch. None of us should forget that Chris Ronay at the FBI Lab Explosives Unit started calling this guy the 'junkyard bomber.' All of the components of his bombs are hard to trace because he builds his own parts, sands serial numbers off of batteries, and gets the pipes, wood, nails and screws for his bombs from a variety of places. He completely builds his own bombs from carving the wooden switches to everything else. These early devices showed that right out of the gate."

"Yes! Max is right. Someone took great care with the making and assembling of this first bomb. The carvings on the wood are intricate and the assembly was done with care and precision. The way the bomber worked with and used the nails, screws, epoxy, and tape show somebody who took his time, and was neat and patient as he put everything together," John added his authority to the assessment Max had provided.

"Totally agree with Max and John," Paul Wilhelmus added.

"So let's look at the investigation that's been conducted over the years on this bomb," Turchie stayed by the white board, using the chalk like a conductor's wand.

"Every name that's come up in connection with this event we've checked against the UNABOM database. We haven't come up with any relationships between this and any other bombs," John paused for a minute and then added, "there were several fingerprints on the package. They belonged to Buckely Crist, except for one. We still need to compare that print to Guttierrez' kids."

"I think we all know who the Unabomber is and that's Buckley Crist!" Bill Tafoya's voice boomed as if out of nowhere, from across the room and everyone turned to look in his direction. He sat with his arms crossed, showing a certain defiance.

"What do you mean?" Terry asked Tafoya, who had been trying to assert his role as a profiler on the UNABOM Task Force, but in reality was a Bureau "futurist" who had served a stint at the FBI Academy at Quantico while researching potential issues that law enforcement would confront in the year 2000 and beyond.

Without hesitation, Tafoya launched into the slippery slope of who-dunnit and stepped beyond the credible role of a profiler by sharing his personal hypothesis with the team. Investigators want

profilers to tell them the behavioral characteristics of the perpetrator—not attempting to put a name to the suspect.

But Tafoya pressed ahead with his case, "Crist came out to San
Francisco to participate in our Victimology conference at a time
that his wife was very ill. Instead of staying home and caring for
her, he came here. I think he may have wanted to see what kind
of progress we were making on the case. As soon as the bomb
came back to Crist, he feigned suspicion as he stepped back in the
room while Officer Marker opened the package. I think he was
mad because previous to this Marker had given him a traffic tick-
et. He could have been trying to get even with Marker, knowing
that if he placed this bomb somewhere else on campus with his
name on it as the return address, it would be found, returned to
him and then he could ask the Public Safety Department to open
it for him. He could have done this when he knew Marker was on
duty and would be the responding officer."

"Stop for a second," Turchie tried to keep himself calm as well
as everyone else, finding Tafoya's analysis somewhere between
ridiculous and highly offensive. With Max's face starting to light
up like a Christmas tree and John Conway's Irish boxer demeanor
replacing his British actor persona, it was time to move on with
the meeting before trouble erupted.

"Let's come back to that when we talk about suspects," Turchie
dropped the topic and the group moved on to discuss further
points of the investigation.

With the discussion winding down, Turchie launched one
more issue at the group, by posing a question to them all, "This
package with all the un-cancelled stamps—do we know if it would
have fit in the nearest mailbox to the Circle Campus parking lot
where it was found?"

Paul Wilhelmus rubbed his beard while pondering a possible
answer to the decades old question of why the first package bore
ten dollars worth of stamps, but had never been mailed. Paul

looked around the room at the others, whose expressions made it clear that they couldn't field an answer to the question no one had ever asked before now.

"We will certainly check that out, Terry," Paul responded on everyone's behalf.

Without prompting, John Conway then moved on to discuss the circumstances of UNABOM Event Number Two.

"It happened almost a year later to the day. A box had been sitting on a table in a room on the second floor of the Northwestern University Technological Institute. The room was near the university's civil and mechanical engineering departments and was used mostly by graduate students, faculty, and visiting scholars. A graduate student named John Harris found the box and opened it. When it detonated, he suffered burns and lacerations. The box turned out to be a Philly's cigar box of the 'Blunt' variety, wrapped in brown polka dot paper. Match heads used in the device were set off by two circuits composed of C-cell batteries wired to homemade loop switches and improvised wooden dowel initiators. The device was designed to explode upon the pulling of a piece of tape marked "tab" located on the top of the box. Several types of tape, solder, epoxy, copper wire, fishing line, and wooden initiator assemblies were found among the remnants of the crime scene."

Since there were no interruptions or questions, John continued telling the story— "The FBI in Chicago found similar brown polka dot paper at a Montgomery Ward store, and checked all the parking lot citations issued at Northwestern in the timeframe relevant to the detonation and the first sighting of the package. The registered owners of all the cars in the parking lot at the time of the blast were interviewed. ATF put together a list of all the gun shops and ammunition dealers in the area where smokeless powder could be purchased. Nothing unusual came from all that work."

Max abruptly interrupted John Conway's story to tell the group that the campus police had mistakenly referred these cases to ATF, instead of to the FBI, where they were assigned to a couple of young, inexperienced agents. They didn't develop any suspects and closed the investigations a short time later."

Max added with passion in his voice, "It's important to understand that the first two bombs weren't known to anyone outside ATF until after the third bomb. Everyone seems to think that we were aware of these bombs in chronological order, which we were not, and I believe strongly that this was one of the contributing factors to the case not being resolved earlier."

Max was hitting full stride and launched into a broader dissertation. "The public often misunderstands why there are three different Federal agencies investigating these bombings. But, back in that time any bombs on college campuses and aboard airlines were the jurisdiction of the FBI, and bombs going through the mail were the responsibility of Postal, while generally all other bombs in public places were the jurisdiction of the ATF. In fact, this same problem came up later with the bomb device at the University of Utah. It was inappropriately referred to ATF, whose lab examined it and arrived at the conclusion that it was designed to be a dud. The FBI and Postal authorities didn't learn about the bomb in Utah until a year later following the device at Vanderbilt. These multi-jurisdictional problems have impeded the investigation from its earliest days and it's time we put a stop to it."

Max sat down amid a lull in the room, as if all were digesting the wisdom of his thoughts, that is, until Tafoya again jumped into the fray, this time with the support of his protégé, Mary Ellen O'Toole.

"I think we need to look at Crist and that we should open a suspect investigation so that we can dig a little deeper than normal," Mary Ellen calmly stated.

O'Toole's voice was soft and knowledgeable. Unlike Tafoya,

she had received formal FBI profiler training at the Behavioral Science Unit at Quantico and was the only Bureau approved "profiler" to be assigned to an FBI Field Office. O'Toole correctly recognized that the FBI could only take a limited look at Professor Crist in the absence of an official suspect investigation.

"No, I don't think I'm ready to do that right now," Turchie made clear. "I think the three of us—me, you Mary Ellen, and you Bill, should discuss your thoughts later and then we'll decide what to do. I also have more to ask you about profiling as it relates to UNABOM, but we can also do that away from this meeting."

The day's discussion had drained everyone and Turchie saw the debate about profiling as a good stopping point. "Let's continue tomorrow with the next two UNABOM events and that way we'll be finished with the first four devices that were all placed or mailed from Chicago. Then, we can look at any suspect information we have connected to them. And John and Paul can decide how they're going to approach the riddle we developed from today's conference—could the package containing the very first UNABOM device have been too large to fit in the mailbox? That certainly would explain a lot of things and put water on a certain conspiracy theory at the same time."

Bringing the meeting to its conclusion, Terry made a final point. "I'd like all of you, when you leave here to pick a partner. You'll be working with this person from now on, so make sure you get along. I don't care if an FBI agent and ATF agent team up, or whatever, I just want you to work as teams.

"There are two reasons for this. First, if you have a partner, you'll be more inclined to bounce ideas off one another and I believe you'll end up being more creative and pro-active. Second, you'll keep each other energized. Usually, people aren't likely to both get depressed at the same time, so having a partner will keep you moving through the good and bad days of UNABOM. There'll be lots of both, I'm sure.

Some days later, Terry returned to provide me with an update from his first meeting with the UTF. He found out I wanted more than a high-level summary. I wanted details at the grass roots level of the investigators and analysts. But I knew that my attendance at the meetings would have a chilling effect on discussion. So, at my express direction to be specific about all important aspects, Terry settled in for a blow by blow account of his first meeting.

We relaxed over cups of coffee and looked at a map depicting all the various sized groups of personnel across the country that were also engaged in the UNABOM investigation on a daily basis, interacting with the UTF team in San Francisco by working on a variety of potential suspects and projects. We didn't know it at the time, but within months the UNABOM Task Force would triple in size. But for now, this was the group that faced into the head-winds of our new investigative strategy.

Members of the UTF took seriously the information they were digesting at the many conferences that became the analytical thread stitching UNABOM together.

John Conway and Paul Wilhelmus flew to Chicago to meet with their local FBI counterparts-FBI agents John Larson and Joe Dorley. Away from the confines of the Chicago FBI office and tucked away in a quiet corner of one of Larson's favorite eateries, Wilhelmus reported the results of the first San Francisco strategy meeting and then turned to Larson and Dorley.

"Our profiler, Bill Tafoya wants to know which way the package bomb faced the ground," Wilhelmus stated in a sort of dead pan manner.

Dorley responded with his usual unguarded manner, lacking any hint of self-censure, exclaiming, "Face up or face down, what the f---difference does it make?" Doorley made clear he'd had enough of UNABOM.

Larson was every bit as tenacious as Conway, but a little less intense. He accompanied Conway and Wilhelmus to the

University of Illinois Chicago Circle campus, where they did a walking survey of the area where the first UNABOM device was found sixteen years earlier. They toured parking lot number five and found the exact spot near the southwest corner of Taylor and Morgan Streets.

From an employee, they learned that the parking lot had been gated to control access at the time. It held about thirteen hundred cars in unassigned spaces, with the first two rows usually taken up by employees of the University's Physical Plant operation or University of Illinois Police Department, both of which were located directly across the street.

They quickly ascertained that the nearest Postal Service collection box in 1978 was across the street and around the corner. A maintenance supervisor for postal mailboxes confirmed that the current collection box was a replacement for the one that had been there in 1978, but that it had the same dimensions.

Wilhelmus pulled out the mock-up of the original package bomb that he had constructed in his garage at home. He and Conway tried to drop the exact replica into the postal collection box—but it wouldn't fit. With a bit of sheepishness, they realized that an obvious and plausible explanation had been overlooked since 1978. The wily Unabomber had carefully constructed a bomb and then wrapped it and stamped it for postal delivery to an unsuspecting victim—only to discover, it didn't fit in the mail box.

* * *

Like sunshine slowly breaching San Francisco's mid-morning fog, it was becoming clear to those of us attending the UTF leadership meeting that the bomber became stuck with a problem of his own making—a live bomb in his hands and no Plan B! I had a visual image of the Unabomber crouching between the parked cars to conceal his furtive movements, or maybe to hide a red face. That made me smile.

Conway and Wilhelmus didn't fully understand the extent and scope of their discovery at the time and it was Turchie who immediately tagged this as the first step toward eventually unlocking the mystery of the Unabomber. It was a satisfying moment—to relish in the realization that this serial bomber was capable of such a blunder. The package didn't fit. The Unabomber had done it then and human nature was such that he would blunder again. It was a moment—a UNABOM moment to be savored.

It was a starting point. I would eventually tell the public in a series of press conferences and media interviews that we believed the Unabomber originated in the Chicago area, lived or visited there in the 1970's and early 1980's, migrated towards Salt Lake City in Utah during the early 1980's to mid-1980's; and then spent a great deal of time in, and might have moved west to the greater San Francisco Bay Area in the mid to late 1980's.

The bomber's familiarity with Chicago, Salt Lake City and the San Francisco Bay Area illustrated a definite migration pattern. Repeated numerous times between 1994 and 1996, the message about the Unabomber's origin in Chicago and his westward migration focused the media and galvanized the public. Thousands of calls came into the UNABOM hot line per our plan, and numerous solid-appearing suspect investigations were opened as a result of these reports.

Looking ahead, it was only months later that Max, Terry and I along with a select team of Task Force agents descended upon a small mountain cabin in the Montana wilderness. After we arrested the hermit-like occupant and painstakingly searched among the cabin's contents, a member of the FBI evidence team brought me a thin stack of documents from within the cabin. They were written in meticulous handwriting with the title of "autobiography" scrolled across the top.

I found Terry and we started reading through the early life story of the cabin's sole occupant, Theodore John Kaczynski. I was struck by Kaczynski's description of the first UNABOM device:

"I came back to the Chicago area in May, mainly for one reason: So that I could more safely attempt to murder a scientist, businessman, or the like. Before leaving Montana, I made a bomb in a kind of box, designed to explode when the box was opened. This was a long, narrow box. I picked the name of an electrical engineering professor out of the catalogue of the Rensselear Polytechnic Institute, and addressed the bomb package to him. I took the package to downtown Chicago, intending to mail it from there (this was in late May, I think around the 28th or 29th), but it didn't fit in mail boxes, and the post-office package drops I checked did not look as if they would swallow such a long package, except in one post office...but that was where I had bought stamps for the package a few days before, so I was afraid to go there again because, going there twice in a short time, my face might be remembered. So I took the bomb over to the U. of Illinois Chicago Circle Campus, and surreptitiously dropped it between two parked cars in the lot near the science and technology buildings. I hoped that a student—preferably one in a scientific field...would open the package himself and blow his hands off, or get killed."

We were speechless and awed by this discovery—a direct intersection of Terry's intuition about the mailbox and an identical account contained in the bomber's diary. It was intuition such as this, captured through our newly "institutionalized analysis" and coupled with solid investigative skills that kept us in the game. The "plan" was paying off better than we had realized at the time.

CHAPTER THREE

LEARNING TO SHARE INFORMATION WAS JOB #1

(We encouraged everyone on the UTF—agents and support employees alike, whether they had been on the task force two years or two days, to engage in debate and information sharing with each other. It was the only way to achieve a high level learning curve, separate fact from fiction, and implement our version of the Silicon Valley corporation, growing out of its garage based on its own creativity).

MID-MORNING ON NOVEMBER 15, 1979, AMERICAN AIRLINES Flight # 444 left Chicago's O'Hare like it had a hundred times before, destined for National Airport in Washington, D.C. As it climbed gently to its cruising altitude, no one on board was aware of the package that had made its way into the plane's cargo hold, via the United States mail. Thirty minutes into the flight the plane jolted in mid-air. Sensitive instruments on the plane reflected fluctuations in the cabin pressure. Passengers became alarmed as the floor underneath their feet became hot. The flight engineer hastily walked through the cabin and inspected every inch of the plane, but could find nothing wrong. None of the cockpit instruments reflected any problems.

With just twenty minutes left in the flight, and as the plane readied for its descent into National, smoke suddenly billowed into the main cabin through the floor and air conditioning vents. Oxygen masks dropped down automatically for the passengers to use. The pilot calmly reported his emergency to air traffic controllers and was immediately diverted to Dulles Airport in suburban Virginia, outside Washington, D.C. As passengers evacuated the plane, the fire department raced to extinguish a fire raging inside the forward baggage compartment of the cargo hold. One of the cargo pods, in close proximity to the plane's fuel crossover lines, had caught fire during the flight. The pilots told a grim story as the fire was brought under control. Ten more minutes in the air, and some of the passengers would have died from smoke inhalation, to say nothing of what would have happened had the fire burned through the fuel lines.

As additional details emerged, the situation turned more ominous. Someone had placed a bomb in the U.S. mail and it ended up on the airplane. The FBI and investigators from the U.S. Postal Inspection Service launched an extensive investigation. Forensic evidence collected at the crime scene was sent to the FBI Laboratory, where Chris Ronay, the Bureau's head explosives examiner, made some alarming discoveries.

The bomb was mailed in a box made of cottonwood. It was about ten and a half inches deep, ten inches wide, and a little over seven inches high. The box top was hinged at the rear and the front was secured with tape. The bomb contained an aneroid barometer, an atmospheric pressure sensitive electric fusing system, altered and set to detonate when the plane descended to an altitude of about thirty-three hundred feet. Four Eveready "C" batteries provided energy to activate the charge, which along with the initiators was contained in a metal can holding the main explosive charge, consisting of several types of smokeless powder.

The builder of the bomb had tried to confine the main charge by wrapping the tin can with layers of tape, including monofilament fishing line. After an initial "mild" detonation inside the plane's cargo hold, the tin can burst and the fire started. Inside the tin can were traces of potassium chloride, barium sulfate, and varying amounts of aluminum and magnesium.

Barium sulfate is a common ingredient of combustion fireworks, where it is used to achieve a green colored flame. Yellow grain smokeless powder found in the device and grains of ball type powder most likely came from mixing powders that had been removed from the propellant of many different rifle cartridges. Excessive use of solder, five types of tape, three kinds of nails, and tool marks found on some of the screws had emerged as the bomber's individual "signature."

Much of the brown wrapping paper concealing the wooden box was burned in the fire following the explosion, but still visible was a partial delivery address with the letters "R LINES," and "NW." The FBI Lab and investigators looked at all of the airlines located in Northwest Washington, D.C. and compared the number of letters in their company name with the space measurements on the package that would allow for twelve additional letters in the space available. This allowed for the package to have been addressed to any one of several airlines at the time—American, Continental, Delta, Eastern, Pan Am, Trans World, or United.

As he examined the bomb components and the remnants of its packaging, FBI Lab Examiner Chris Ronay noted the postage on the package. It included three $1 "American Light Fueled by Truth and Reason" stamps, two $1 "Eugene O'Neill" stamps, five half-dollar "Lucy Stone" stamps, and six quarter-dollar "Frederick Douglas" stamps.

From the way the bomb was built, Ronay could review the evidence from prior bombings to see whether any were made in the same way or with similar materials. And, future bombs built by the same person would immediately give themselves away as their bombs are as individual as fingerprints, handwriting, and DNA to the eyes of a trained explosives expert.

Ronay hadn't seen these particular construction techniques before, even though he had examined the remnants of thousands of bomb parts over the years. Yet, he was convinced the bomber had struck before. Ronay prepared a detailed description of the bomb and its packaging and circulated it to other agencies and crime labs, hoping that he might discover other bombs built by the same person.

In the meantime, Postal Inspectors fanned throughout the Chicago suburbs and painstakingly put together the trail of the package that would be labeled as UNABOM Event Number Three. Incredibly, they found a postal carrier at the Elgin, Illinois post office who remembered a similar package. He had picked it up at a postal contract station at Gromer's Supermarket in Elgin. Other employees of Gromer's market also recalled seeing the package on the floor of the contract station on November 14. Since the package had been collected towards the end of the day, it wasn't cancelled at the Elgin Post Office, but was sent on to the North Suburban Illinois Postal Facility (NSIPF) in River Grove, Illinois, for processing.

The postal inspectors found an employee at the NSIPF who believed she handled the package. Their work was nothing short of remarkable, since the NSIPF handled 2.3 million pieces of mail every day from over one hundred post offices in the area. The parcel was then transported to the airport from the NSIPF, where it was loaded at random into a cargo pod, and eventually placed onto American Airlines Flight #444.

Just as the work of the postal inspectors yielded results, Ronay's instinct also paid off. An ATF bomb examiner who worked on the 1978 and 1979 bombs with Northwestern University connections saw Ronay's bulletin and contacted Ronay immediately. After gaining access to the ATF Laboratory materials and conducting further examinations of the Northwestern University bombs, Ronay concluded the bomb on American Airlines Flight #444 was constructed by the same individual or individuals who had constructed the first two devices.

This was a highly significant finding. There was a serial bomber on the run and he had tried to bring down an airplane.

The placement of the bomb aboard Flight #444 was a significant violation of Federal Criminal Statutes as a crime aboard an aircraft. The FBI assumed primary investigative jurisdiction and the three bombings linked to the same unidentified subject that targeted universities and an airline became known as "UNABOM," the FBI's designation for University and Airline bombings. No one knew in 1979, but UNABOM would become the longest, unsolved serial bombing investigation in the history of the Bureau. The newly dubbed "Unabomber" wasted little time before he struck again.

The President of United Airlines, Mr. Percy Addison Wood, lived within the safety of a quiet, tree-lined neighborhood in Lake Forest, Illinois. On June 3, 1980, just seven months after the bomb that exploded on the American Airlines flight, Wood received a letter in the mail at his residence, signed in green ink by an "Enoch Fischer." The letter read, in part:

"I am taking the liberty of sending you, under separate cover, a book which I believe to have great social significance. I am sending copies of this book, "Ice Brothers," by Sloan Wilson, to a number of prominent people in the Chicago area because I believe this truly to be a book for our time, a book that should be read by all who make important decisions affecting the public welfare."

As promised in the letter, Wood received a package seven days later at his home bearing the return address of "Enoch W. Fischer, 3414 N. Ravenswood, Chicago, IL 60657." The package was wrapped in brown paper. Wood noticed that it bore his middle name, which struck him as odd since "Addison" was known only to his close friends and family.

Wood cut through layers of paper and packaging tape, shoving aside sections of the June 3, 1980 Chicago Sun Times, newspaper used as packaging material. One section of the Times contained an advertisement for the hiring of new college students at Morton Thiokol, Incorporated, in Brigham City, Utah. Another section included front and back panels of a Bugles snack food box. There was a cutout of a political cartoon which featured a disheveled, unemployed man sitting on a park bench with an open lunch pail beside him—a pigeon was eating crumbs from the lunch pail.

As he sorted through the packaging, the novel Ice Brothers was revealed without its jacket cover. Wood tipped the book upright, placing one of his hands on the top. As he opened it, the bomb built inside the book exploded. Mr. Wood suffered third degree burns and lacerations from the resulting explosion. Among the debris was a small metal tag with the letters "F.C." stamped into the metal. The investigators didn't know it at the time, but "F.C" would become the calling card for the Unabomber.

It would take sixteen years, twelve more bombings, and three dead before the FBI would serve its only search warrant and make its only arrest in the case. The conclusions reached from the reinvestigation and analysis of the first four UNABOM events by the Task Force in 1994 and 1995 would play a prominent role in unlocking the mystery of the identity of the Unabomber.

* * *

"Okay, look, I realize all of you have lots of work to do and these analytical sessions seem to be taking more and more of our time, but let's try and concentrate for a few hours and focus on the first four bombings as one UNABOM event," Turchie announced.

He started yet another weekly UTF analytical meeting in the late summer of 1994. The time had been moving quickly and he was moving the task force at the cadence of a marching band as agents conceived of and created a variety of investigative projects, traveled to other jurisdictions to test their theories, and continuously uncovered leads that had previously all but disappeared in reams of paper and the passing years.

"I'll go ahead and give the results of the 'address project' to get us started."

Postal Inspector Paul Wilhelmus had gained confidence over the months since the task force had been assembled. He was always ready to share his latest findings as his FBI partner John Conway looked on. The address project had become an important and constant basis of fact for the investigation. Wilhelmus scoured open sources and searched the names of all the victims and their addresses, as well as those for the return addressee on UNABOM mailed devices in an attempt to determine where the Unabomber was getting the personal address information for his mail bombs. Everyone on the task force was aware and hopeful that a breakthrough in identifying the bomber might come if a pattern could be found in the address information.

"For the return address used in the first device, I could only find Professor Buckley Crist, Jr. with an address of Northwestern University Technological Institute at Evanston, Illinois, 60201 listed in their Graduate School catalog for 1977-1978. There wasn't any reference to him in any of the *Who's Who in America* editions between 1978 and 1993. For the address of the intended victim, Professor E.J. Smith, School of Engineering, Rensselaer Polytechnic Institute, Troy, NY 12181, I found his name and address information in the *Undergraduate* and *Graduate Bulletins* for RPI for 1976-1977, and in the *Graduate Catalog* for 1977-1978. I couldn't find any record of Smith in the editions of *Who's Who in America* from 1978 to 1993," Paul said:

"Thanks," Turchie looked around the room. "What else do we know about Crist and Smith?"

Max added, "Well, I don't know if you want to get into the

Utah events yet, Terry, but I think people need to be reminded that Professor Smith did a one year sabbatical at the University of Utah between 1975 and 1976. He was taking part in some post-doctoral studies in connection with a research grant of some sort."

Max Noel was responsible for the reinvestigation of the UNABOM events that had a Utah nexus in the early to mid-eighties and had done his homework, pulling together potential connections involving players from other UNABOM events.

UNABOM analyst Alexandra Jacobson stepped in after Max finished talking to give the results of a project she completed identifying the special interests and hobbies of UNABOM victims and other individuals connected to UNABOM events.

"Buckley Crist, Jr. liked boating, card games, chess, music, photography, reading, and small appliance repair. Professor E. J. Smith was into computer hardware and software modification and development, electronics, building models, shooting firearms, skiing, and operating remote control model airplanes. To contribute to what Max said, investigation we've done recently determined that Smith belonged to a remote control model airplane club while he was in Utah," Alexandra offered.

The sheer volume of information developed and shared among the investigators was diverse and sometimes without immediate relevance, as the team worked toward clarifying a composite view of the Unabomber. Fortunately, as each day passed, more and more of the team members seemed to be getting caught up in the chase and changing their attitudes about the odds of eventually identifying the subject. Wilhelmus cheerfully continued sharing his analysis about the partial mailing address for the package that was placed aboard American Airlines Flight #444 and then moved onto the package sent to the President of United Airlines, Percy Wood.

"As you might expect, I haven't been able to identify anyone named Enoch W. Fischer. However, North Ravenswood Avenue is a legitimate street in Chicago. It's in an area that's a mix of businesses and houses. There's no 3414 N. Ravenswood and the location where that would be is a vacant lot. In the entire 3400 block of North Ravenswood, there's only one real address and it's a commercial building that doesn't seem to have any relevance to UNABOM," Wilhelmus told the group, then pausing to look around before finishing.

He concluded his assessment with his findings about how the bomber might have obtained the information on where to send a package to Wood. "In December of 1978, Mr. Wood was promoted from Executive Vice-President and Chief Operating Officer of United Airlines to president of the airline. I could only find his name and address in the 1978 and 1980 editions of *Who's Who in America*. Wood wasn't listed in any editions after 1980. The information had the same home address and zip code as that used by the bomber and included Wood's middle name of Addison,"

"Here's what I find interesting about Percy Wood," John Conway's clear, booming voice had everyone in the conference room turning their attention in his direction. As if on cue, he paused for a minute and then continued. "When all this first happened back in 1980 and agents did interviews of Wood, he told them he couldn't think of any reason why someone would want to send him a bomb in the mail. He was adamant that he never made any decisions or took any actions that would cause employees or anyone else to want to kill him."

Everyone knew that there was more, but Conway added another pause for suspense.

"When we returned to Chicago to reinvestigate this case several weeks ago and coordinate updated interviews of Wood and others, we developed a completely different picture of the environment back in the 1970s and early 1980. For example, thirty-nine days before the second bomb was placed at Northwestern in May of 1979, United Airline employees began a fifty-eight day strike. Sometime between 1979 and 1980, Percy Wood gave a speech at Northwestern University. He was in the middle of restructuring United Airline's workforce—over five thousand employees lost their jobs as a result.

"Paul and I and other agents were told that many of those people who lost jobs migrated to Salt Lake City where a new airline—Western Airlines was forming in the early 1980s. Eventually, Western was bought out by Delta. At some point, United Airlines recalled some of the employees to work and assigned them to the airline's maintenance centers in San Francisco and Oakland. Perhaps the political cartoon depicting an unemployed man had some significance! In 1993, United Airlines let go of almost three thousand more employees. Interesting too, since the Unabomber came back to life in June of 1993 after a seven year hiatus."

The task force members were intrigued. This information had the potential to uncover motive and, if nothing else, mandated a focused avenue of investigation on the Wood bombing that had gone unnoticed for fourteen years. If Wood and United Airlines had a connection to Northwestern University, if thousands of employees had lost their jobs because of Wood's restructuring of the airline, and if the migration of those employees took them to Salt Lake City and the San Francisco Bay Area, the "hubs" of UNABOM attacks from 1982 until the present, then the task force had to have an aggressive program to find out if any of the employees who had lost their jobs had become a rogue bomber. That was a lot of "ifs," but there weren't any shortcuts. It was a mind numbing moment to contemplate the added workload.

Neil Oltman, the young UNABOM agent who had come into the FBI from his job as an aerospace engineer in southern California had long believed that the forensics of UNABOM devices appeared to connect the bombings to the airline industry. Neil had conscientiously read and reread UNABOM crime scene reports a dozen times. He worked closely with the FBI Lab

Explosives Bomb Unit and National Transportation Safety Board (NTSB) to find proof of his theories and he flagged a report of the NTSB in the early summer of 1994 that seemed to validate his suspicions.

"Terry, this is what I've been saying," Oltman started "The information John, Paul and others gathered when they went back to Chicago is totally consistent with the forensics of the case and pointed out by the NTSB in their report. For example, the wooden box the subject used in the American Airlines bombing is the same type used to ship heavy parts in the airline industry. The bomber solders his batteries in place, very similar to how airline mechanics solder batteries in a series for battery packs to operate overhead lights.

"The bomber had the correct address for and knew about the Boeing Fabrication Division when he mailed a bomb to them in Auburn, Washington. When we interviewed the Boeing liaison manager who deals with research and development and relations with universities, he told us that a person would need to be familiar with Boeing or worked for Boeing to know of the existence of the Auburn Fabrication Division. He also said that Boeing had relationships with several universities and this included BYU in Provo, Utah and RPI in Troy, New York."

Oltman didn't talk much during the analytical sessions—but when he did, his command of facts and authority that came from personal knowledge of the aviation industry and how the Unabomber might be part of that industry, carried substantial weight.

Turchie cast an approving nod at Oltman. "We'll have to take a closer look Neil at whether we need to ramp up an aviation investigative project and put more resources into resolving the possible leads."

No one in the room questioned Turchie's observation, but it was obvious that the task force was overwhelmed at the thought of even more work than before, with scant resources to follow all of the new facts and theories that they were uncovering in the reinvestigation of UNABOM.

"Is there anything else we need to cover today?" Turchie was an untiring optimist, but even he admitted that he felt widespread bewilderment at how the task force was ever going to follow up on so much new information in a timely way.

"I know we've been here a long time this morning, but we probably should go over one more avenue of unresolved leads," Paul was almost sheepish as he introduced yet another dilemma. His audience was polite, but beginning to be stretched thin by yet another story spawned by the reinvestigation.

"I'll keep it short. One of the students of Professor E.J. Smith at RPI came from Evanston, Illinois. The student's mother was a secretary at Northwestern University, working in the vicinity of the office of Buckley Crist, Jr. The student supposedly had a beef with Smith and had returned to Illinois about two weeks before the first bomb that was intended for Smith. The student and a number of his friends played a game called *Dungeons and Dragons* in a room at the NWU Tech Institute between 1978 and 1980." Paul hesitated.

The entire room groaned, but largely from the intrigue of inquisitive minds. "How many students were playing Dungeons and Dragons in these groups, Paul?" Turchie asked, looking bewildered at what would obviously be a growing suspect list.

Conway jumped into the conversation again. "At least seventy players were involved in the games, with about ten of them frequent and key players throughout the NWU Tech building. In around 1980 or 1981, after the first four bombings happened and after some of these people were interviewed at least once by the ATF, the FBI did some trash covers at a residence of the main *Dungeons and Dragons* players. The results were kind of surprising. Among the things found in the trash was a scrap of paper with the name Enoch Fischer written on it and a bookstore bag containing a receipt from a store called Kroch's and Brentano's at 1711 Sherman for fifteen dollars. During that period of time the book Ice Brothers was a military book-of-the-month club selection and available at the K and B bookstore at 1711 Sherman."

Someone chimed in, "Have you personally seen the scrap of paper with the Fischer name?"

"I'm almost afraid to ask—have we eliminated the *Dungeons and Dragons* players as suspects in UNABOM?" Turchie stood up as he asked the question, implying the meeting was over.

"Not really," Paul and Conway joined in near unison, as the noise of chairs shoved back under the long conference table amid even greater sounds of sighing all around the room, nearly drowned out Turchie's final words.

Turchie raised his voice to be heard, "Alright then, John and Paul, if that Fischer story checks out I need you to figure out an investigative strategy that takes on and confirms or eliminates these D&D players. We'll just add it to all the other things that need to be prioritized for completion. Neil, if you are proposing a viable aviation project, I need to receive the details on paper with your recommendation for next steps and resources needed. Based on budget realities, Freeman will look very closely at requests for more manpower."

"Don't forget though Terry, we haven't eliminated Buckley Crist, Jr. as a suspect," Bill Tafoya's voice rang through the crowd of people leaving the conference room.

Turchie merely shook his head and rolled his eyes as Tafoya kept talking and followed him out of the conference room.

As was becoming routine after UNABOM Task Force meetings, Turchie came to my office to brief me on the high points. This time around he emphasized the aviation angle and the tale of *Dungeons and Dragons*, including the amazing intersection with the Fischer name and a potential relationship between early victims in this case. In a sense, it was a common refrain that I had heard before—everybody's an expert and has a personal theory. But, it was impossible to discount all of these theories. I pressed Turchie for a better means to separate myth from fact.

"Terry, our challenge is to balance their enthusiasm for problem solving with an occasional dose of realism. We can't afford to over-invest in anyone's pet theories; unless they're mine." But, my attempt at humor was lost amid Terry's intensity.

"Jim, there's no doubt the work we've done on the first four bombings will tell a story. The Unabomber was and is very familiar with Chicago and what was going on there in the 1970s and 1980s. Many of us are convinced that he's from there originally," Terry seemed confident and left me with some thinking to do, as he quickly moved on.

"You're going to tell me we need more people?" I responded half laughing.

"Well, yes, but not right now. On the brighter side, I'm convinced that all of this new information we're developing every day will help us shine the light on the Unabomber in a new way, and when the puzzle finally comes together in the right way, we'll know we have our guy. It's going to take lots of hard work and a few personnel adjustments here and there to get the right mix of people we can count on to pull all of this together."

As Terry left my office, he gave me a look that signaled there was more to say about moving toward the right mix of people, but there would be time for that. I knew he had a lot on his plate and my prodding about multiple theories wasn't making the load any easier for him. As time went on, we ended up interviewing dozens of these Dungeon and Dragon players from the late 1970s and early 1980s. One case at a time, each was eliminated as a UNABOM suspect and the project entered the book as one big dead end.

We even launched an aviation investigative project, combining analysis, forensics, and interviews. In the end, I fully supported both projects. Each blind alley looked as good as the real thing. We badly needed help from Quantico or somewhere in sorting out the false positives from the real thing.

The emphasis on the aviation aspect of UNABOM did ultimately prove to have relevance to the case, but not in the expected way. We had worked so hard to determine any connection between the Unabomber and the aviation industry, only to discover a new twist and the real meaning among his written words.

After Ted Kaczynski was arrested and removed from his cabin early on the afternoon of April 3, 1996, Terry and I went on to study thousands of pages of material in Kaczynski's own handwriting. The connection of the Unabomber to the aviation industry and those people who comprised it was simple, direct, and had been there all along.

"...Actually, during the last few months (except at a few times) I have been troubled by frustrated hatred much less than usual. I think this is because, whenever I have experienced some outrage (such as a low-flying jet or some official stupidity reported in the paper), as I felt myself growing angry, I calmed myself by thinking —'just wait till this summer! Then I'll kill!'"

Most of us ignore the sounds of passing jets and the other noises that invade our everyday space. For Theodore Kaczynski, it was motive for murder.

CHAPTER FOUR

WHEN IS THE PROFILE REALLY THE PROFILE?

(There was a broad-based institutional problem in the way behavioral profiles were integrated with FBI investigations. Profilers trained at the FBI Academy in Quantico, Virginia were assigned to field office cases at the discretion of Quantico. This didn't work for us! I assigned an agent from San Francisco with a PhD in clinical psychology to provide behavioral support for UNABOM. This decision was foreign to the FBI at the time and highly unpopular).

I COULD TELL FROM THE LOOK ON HIS FACE WHEN TERRY WALKED into my office that something was wrong. Without saying much, he sat down at the small conference table a few feet away from my desk and rested his head on his hand. I finished a phone call, got up from my desk and walked over to the table.

"So what's going on, have we identified the UNABOMBER yet?" I joked sarcastically.

I wasn't much for letting potential problems get me down. I usually didn't spend a lot of time and effort trying to be warm and fuzzy. UNABOM was my top tier business priority at this point, but I had an office to run with a full plate of additional programs and investigations. Following the Polly Klaas kidnapping in 1993 I had launched a Crimes Against Children Task Force—which was totally outside any of the programs funded by FBI Headquarters, but my introduction to the high incidence of unsolved child kidnappings in Northern California had impressed upon me the need for FBI leadership in this area.

I felt compelled to devote a portion of our already scarce Agent resources for re-investigations of some of the cold cases—in exactly the way we were doing with UNABOM. The fact that Terry had entered my office with some trepidation about raising another problem and likely asking for more manpower was not surprising to me, but he also knew of my high regard for his hand-picked UNABOM team. They were making reasonable progress and had my full support.

"Jim," Terry got right to business, "I think the worst part of this job is what I mentioned to you the other day. Sometimes it's going to be necessary to move people off the UNABOM Task Force if they can't get with the program. And I'm here to tell you that Bill Tafoya and Mary Ellen O'Toole just can't get with it. Each of them poses a different kind of problem, but as long as they're taking up two slots on the task force, we're never going to get the kind of behavioral support we need."

"So, what are the issues that would move me to reassign these two?"

I had my own ideas, but I wanted to hear Terry explain to me why we should move agents off the task force, especially with Mary Ellen being a Quantico trained profiler and Bill having attained recognition in academia as a "futurist" in the study of where law enforcement was going in the next decade. I had always wanted to ask Bill if he envisioned UNABOM remaining as an unsolved case in the next decade, but that was just my mind at play. And, Terry was proposing a serious realignment of UTF personnel that would definitely impact sensitive egos and send signals all the way to Quantico and Headquarters. Terry knew it too and thus, it was a heck of a problem that had just become my problem.

"Its part personality, but also disagreement over their role in providing behavioral profiling support. To be honest, I don't think either of them has actually investigated a case. Everyone else on the task force is picking up on it and that's really damaging their credibility with the other FBI Agents, ATF Agents and even with the Postal Inspecton Service. I just can't get on the same page with them, which means there isn't any useful   work being produced by them to assist the investigators—that's the bottom line. And believe me I've sat down with them, written memos to them and tried hard to get my expectations across, but nothing is working."

"Let's take a step back a minute. Is this a problem of two individual agents not getting it or might there be a broader institutional problem in the way profilers are being assigned to assist the UTF?"

I didn't continue immediately, as I didn't want to put words in his mouth. To me, some of the profiling gurus in Quantico sounded better in front of a camera and microphone than in their real life interactions with investigators. And, they frequently overlooked the knowledge gap when it came to profiling serial bombers. There had been some excellent profiles constructed by FBI profilers on the basis of serial murderers who had confronted their victims personally, butchered them to order with an array of killing instruments, and displayed their remains in unique ways. Serial bombers, on the other hand, inflicted their brand of mayhem from afar. Mostly, they were unable to target a specific individual because they lost control over their bomb as soon as they mailed it or placed it in a public place. Bombers seemed to be a different animal entirely.

I wasn't reluctant to remove Agents from a case, if that's where this was heading. And, the advantage of an FBI field office is the variety of priority investigations and span of expertise requirements that present opportunity for one to move between investigative programs.

But I still wanted to hear some solid justification for it and also wanted to know how Terry planned on filling the gap in obtaining relevant and current behavioral assessments when asked. Although it was unspoken between us, Terry and I both understood the political implications with Quantico and FBI Headquarters if we squandered valuable talent that on paper had potential to solve this old dog of a case.

"A few weeks ago," Terry continued. "I took them both over to Lyons Cafe for some breakfast and to go over some things we needed. I asked for them to work on an updated profile of the Unabomber, based on all of the recent developments."

"So how'd that go?" I asked.

"Not well. And it's gone downhill since then. I was greatly surprised that they used identical reasoning in telling me in no uncertain terms that the profile is the profile. In their view the behavioral profile that Quantico had provided is relevant and hasn't changed, nor should it. They won't budge on their philosophy that the 'profile is the profile.' In effect, this leaves us standing still as we develop additional information about the Unabomber from our reinvestigation of the bombings. Jim, for a profile to be of any value to the UTF, it has to incorporate new concrete findings that arise from the investigation and the profilers themselves must assist in interpreting all possible variations in the type of suspect we might consider and eventually encounter."

"Terry, I seriously doubt their viewpoint would pass muster at our Headquarters or the Behavioral Science Unit. But, I am mystified—this is Major Case 75, right? It has the personal attention and support of the Director. Why in hell aren't the most experienced profilers at Quantico crawling all over it? I don't recall any high profile volunteers calling to join us; how about you—no calls from Douglas or Van Zandt? Could it be that UNABOM has a rookie profiler assigned because the big names don't want their reputations soiled by a potentially unsolvable case?"

"Jim, I hesitate to even speculate on that. I don't really need to start a war with Quantico or Headquarters, but what I do need is someone that can give aid and support to our investigators. Let me throw out an idea. Kathleen Puckett is a PhD clinical psychologist with extensive experience in counterintelligence and espionage cases.

"Although it's not referred to as profiling on the counterintelligence side of the FBI, there are many similarities. I think she'd be fantastic for UNABOM. She's worked with me before and she has the confidence of Joel Moss and other key supervisors on the UTF. She's exactly what we need, as I know she would fit right into the team. The only trick might be getting acceptance and approval at FBI Headquarters by the Criminal Division to allow her to function as a criminal profiler and by the Counter-intelligence Division to free her up from her current work."

As I was building my team to solve the UNABOM case, Terry was building his. Soon after taking over the task force, Terry approached me and asked that Joel Moss be assigned to work on UNABOM, adding that Moss had volunteered. I knew that Moss and Turchie had several years of history together and wasn't surprised when Terry requested that Moss become his "principal relief supervisor" on the UTF- the agent in charge during any time Turchie was absent. I approved Terry's request because the chemistry between the two was remarkable. Besides, they were always together anyway! And Kathleen Puckett was usually not far behind.

"That's a novel idea," I responded. "I've a healthy respect for the work performed by our psychologists on the counterintelligence side of the house and the way they get into peoples' heads. How do you know she would even want to jump disciplines and get into something like UNABOM?"

"I already kind of asked her. I tracked her down one day last week and agreed to discuss it with her over a lunch at some vegetarian place a few blocks from here. The lunch was terrible, but I did it for the team. Anyway, she loves the idea of coming to work on the UNABOM case."

"OK, I like where this is going. Bring Kathy in for a chat, so I can get to know her better. And write this up for Appel, as I'd like to have Ed's agreement on taking Kathy away from her current assignments and also his buy-in that she would be the right addition to the UTF. As for moving Bill and Mary Ellen to another assignment, I'll speak with Ed myself and we'll decide on how and when to handle it."

Some weeks later, I approved the transfer of Dr. Kathleen Puckett to the UNABOM Task Force. I was convinced by Turchie's argument that her background in clinical psychology and proven track record in both interviewing and assessing suspects in espionage and counterintelligence investigations would provide a substantial boost to our overall approach to UNABOM.

I moved Dr. Bill Tafoya and Mary Ellen O'Toole to new assignments in the San Francisco Office where their talents could be of better service. Mary Ellen was assigned to assist the Crimes against Children squad, where she served on a full time basis and made valuable contributions in an area more suited to her considerable talents and skills. Dr. Tafoya decided to retire from the FBI shortly after his reassignment.

Before announcing Kathy's designation to the UTF in the role of a behavioral profiler, I called Turchie to make sure there was clear understanding by all. "She'll need to hit the ground running. I expect that you are going to reassign some heavy lifting to her in the way that we discussed earlier—like the study you had asked for on George Meteksey, the guy they dubbed the 'Mad Bomber of New York," and the other two historical serial bombers, the 'Alphabet Bomber' and the 'Ink Bomber.' It's incredible at this stage of our investigation that we haven't been able to get a comparison of behavioral characteristics between the very few serial bombers in the history books with that of our Unabomber. This is where Kathy needs to shine."

Puckett didn't disappoint. She quickly showed her worth as a valuable contributing member at the weekly UTF analytical sessions and Turchie gradually introduced her participation at the management team meetings held in my office. Soon, she was reaching out to Quantico's National Center for the Analysis of Violent Crime in a determined effort at networking where she received a favorable response from Jim Wright, who was newly assigned to support UNABOM. I saw Wright's assignment as an obvious counter to my assignment of Dr. Puckett, but it ultimately worked to the UTF's advantage as Jim Wright himself became a valuable mainstay in our growing line-up of contributing professionals.

* * *

The morning management meetings in my office were growing more interesting by the week. With Max stopping in when he wasn't traveling on assignment and with Joel Moss and Kathy Puckett joining in, we were not at a loss for new and interesting topics of discussion. Max was quick to join Terry's refrain about the conflicting profiles that had been directed to the UNABOM investigation over the years in direct contradiction of the maxim— "the profile is the profile."

Max was so adamant on the subject that he produced a spreadsheet to summarize the pronouncements of behavioral studies from various profilers dating back to 1980. There were some attributes of similarity about the Unabomber's likely personality traits that were not in dispute among the multiple profilers, nor the investigators for that matter.

There was universal agreement that the Unabomber was

white, male, and a loner motivated by anger and perhaps revenge. The areas of disassociation among the five distinct profiles between 1980 and 1993 were mostly in the potential age ranges of our suspect. In 1980, the age range was believed to be between 18-22 years. Just five years later, in 1985, the senior profiler of the team that said the suspect was 18-22 years old in 1980 said he was between 28-35 years old. Another profiler expanded this range in 1986, saying the bomber was in his late 30s to early 40s. And, for the record, O'Toole and Tafoya claimed a probable age range of 43-53 in 1993. The profiles had little agreement on the highest level of probable education to look for in a suspect, as the various profiles went all the way from a high school education; to some college or technical school; to possibly a Bachelor of Science degree or a failed PhD candidate.

Max intoned repeatedly, "Which one is The Profile? What can an investigator use in any of this?"

To that latter question, Terry answered in unison with others joining in the mantra that we had come to accept as truth. "The Unabomber is most certainly a white male since virtually all serial bombers in history have been white and male. And, he once lived in Chicago and has since migrated westward as far as Utah and California. He's likely a loner, but with a familiarity with universities and their environment."

On these points, we felt secure—not because they were contained in profiles, but because these were clear and obvious deductions based on years of investigation and reinvestigation. We were solid in this assessment, which played a prominent role in our continuing plan of sharing "what we knew" about the Unabomber with the public in a series of news conferences and interviews where I engaged the topic with as many media outlets as were interested and repeatedly asked readers and viewers to report any potential matches or relevant suspicions to the UNABOM Hotline.

We had no idea during this time of searching for any shred of evidence or a clue to the possible personality traits of the Unabomber, that he might be huddled under the poor light of a single, small window in a remote one-room cabin with little separating him from the cold winds and snows of winter except for a curious obsession with assessing his own psychology. But, a scant two years later, when Terry and I had the opportunity to delve deeply into Theodore Kaczynski's own written words taken from that same forlorn cabin in the snow-covered mountains of Montana, we were treated to the Unabomber's own assessment of his personality:

"My motive for doing what I am going to do is simply personal revenge. I do not expect to accomplish anything by it... These days it is fashionable to ascribe sick-sounding motivations (in many cases correctly, I admit) to persons who commit anti-social acts. Perhaps some people will deny that I am motivated by a hatred of what is happening to freedom. However, I think I know myself pretty well and I think they are wrong."

"...Of course, the term 'sick' in such a context represents a value judgment. I am not very concerned about the negative value-judgments that will be made about me, but it does anger me that the facts of my psychology will be misrepresented."

CHAPTER FIVE

Have Agents, Will Travel— A Botched Bomb in Utah

(The FBI's normal practice was not to send agents from one field office jurisdiction to another to conduct investigations. This infringed on the prerogatives of the local Special Agent in Charge. This never worked in UNABOM, and had the potential to undercut our strategy and eliminate our ability to integrate analysis with investigation. I approved sending UTF agents to other field offices, to coordinate and conduct investigation if necessary).

BEFORE LEAVING THE OFFICE LATE ONE AFTERNOON, TURCHIE picked up the phone and called Joel Moss. Turchie had a proposal for Joel and wanted his input before floating the idea with Max. "I'm going to talk to Max on the way home today and propose that you and Max travel next week to Utah. I want Max to walk you through all the UNABOM events that have a nexus to Utah so we can widen the circle on our next step which is to seek similarities and whatever else is available between the first four Chicago bombs and the ones that came after in Utah." (Max had been the exception to the general rule that Agents from one field office don't travel to another field office to conduct investigations. Inspector Clow had allowed him to travel to Utah on a number of occasions to conduct investigation on behalf of the UTF).

"Then, we can add on the California connection and try to put all the pieces together. If Max can show you the venues and talk through the reinvestigation he conducted in Utah since he first came to the UTF with George Clow in 1993, it will benefit your grasp of the case and give Max some back-up so that at least two of you will be intimately familiar with details of the UNABOM happenings in Utah. I'm going to have you guys call in to Jim and I while you're away to keep us both up to date on things as well. It's time to get you onboard and start up the old analytical engine like we did in the old days."

"Sure," Joel smiled. "I think that's a great idea. I look forward to working with Max."

Terry and Max lived in the east bay towns of Danville and San Ramon, just a few miles apart. Despite the misgivings of some people in the San Francisco Office about them working together on UNABOM, their temperaments made for an interesting mix and they were soon commuting to and from work together. Several hours in heavy traffic to and from San Francisco extended their day and allowed unlimited discussion of UNABOM—the only case for either of them at this point. Max was slow to charge his batteries in the early morning hours, so Turchie drove into the city.

Every morning they stopped at Rudy's Donut Shop in Castro Valley for pastries and then drove a few blocks further and stopped at the Starbucks where Max bought his first coffee of the morning—a double espresso. By the time they headed home each night, Max was fully caffeinated and ready to do the driving and most of the talking. It was no different on the day Turchie brought up the idea of traveling to Utah.

"Max, before you go on with your story, I have an idea to run by you. I'd like you and Joel to go to Salt Lake City next Monday and spend a few days. You're the expert on the Utah investigations and I want Joel to see the locations of the crimes, meet some of the investigators, and get up to speed on what happened up there."

Max chose his words carefully before answering. "Well, that's fine and I'm happy to do it. But, you and Jim should know that I had a run-in with a couple of agents when I went up there last year. I got into a big pissing contest with their main tech agent, who had assured me that some important work had been carried out when it hadn't. It was a wasted trip for me and I didn't hold back in telling them so. In fact, I sort of lost it in the office in front of everybody. The SAC at the time, Gene Glenn, was traveling, but they got word to him real fast. Even though Gene and I had shared a previous assignment together, he listened to their side of the story and put the word out that I was to get out of his office by sundown."

"Max, just like in the Old West—get out of town by sunset. So, you made it out in one piece?"

"Yeah, we can probably laugh about it now. I just wanted you and Jim to be aware in case something was said." Max sounded confident that this little episode was behind him.

"Get your tickets; talk to Joel and head on over to Salt Lake City. I'll call you over the weekend to finalize what I would like you to cover as you revisit the crime scenes. I'll schedule time with Jim for you guys to call in to update us."

The next week, upon his arrival in Salt Lake, Max was surprised by the big changes in that office in the months since he had been there. SAC Glenn and his primary back-up had both moved on and an interim management staff was running the office. Although most of the agents and support personnel who had witnessed his altercation were still around, the feelings had calmed and there didn't appear to be any lingering impact from the disagreements that had prompted Max's outburst.

Joel quickly found that Max was an encyclopedia of UNABOM

knowledge and trivia. Max was determined that they should review every page of the case file and then retrace every known step of the Unabomber. He started his tour at the University of Utah, walking to the Bennion Business complex that was almost in the center of the large campus. Max guided Joel through the bombing that occurred there on October 8, 1981. Walking down a third floor hallway of the Business Classroom Building, Max recited names, times, and pointed to room locations as if he had been present along with the Unabomber on that day.

"Two students, a man and a woman, came out of room 306— a typing classroom. Across the hall here is Classroom 302A, which was a Computer Lab for the Economics Department." Max had pointed to the door of the classroom as he continued walking down the hall. "The students had finished taking a typing test and left the classroom early. Normally they wouldn't have exited the classroom until 11:00 am, when students from all the surrounding classrooms would be pouring into the hall. It was 10:45 am and they saw a package right here." Max had stopped and pointed at a space on the floor beneath a hallway clock.

"Neither student recalled seeing the curious package when they had entered the class at about 10. The man picked up the package and felt how heavy it was and saw that it had no writing on it. Then, he went on full alert when a wooden stick fell out of the bottom and he quickly put it back on the floor.

"They were concerned and looked around for someone to tell their concerns to. Finally, they found a graduate student down a hallway who listened to their story about a suspicious package and called the Campus Police. They responded a short time later and concluded that it might be a bomb. Army EOD technicians from nearby Fort Douglas were called in for assistance with their portable x-ray equipment and upon arrival they wasted no time in confirming its potentially dangerous contents. The devise itself was carefully moved into a nearby restroom where they 'rendered it safe.'"

Joel and Max were quiet as they took a few minutes to picture the scene as it must have looked thirteen years earlier when the bomb was found. They observed the windows on either end of the long hallway and noted the position of elevators and stairwells, staring at them as the bomber had done years earlier.

"Max, what in the world would motivate someone to put so many innocent students and faculty at risk of such violent injury or death?" Joel asked, stunned as he pictured how much worse the scene could have been had the bomb worked properly.

"Just a sick and demented mind, but I will say this—anybody who would carry a bomb to the center of a large campus and expose themselves to the risk of being identified had to feel comfortable and knowledgeable about this environment. He had to fit in or at least feel like he wouldn't stick out like a sore thumb." Max said while shaking his head at the idea that this person—the Unabomber—could have escaped notice.

"I know. I agree with you Max. It's another university target similar to Northwestern in 1979, when he put the bomb in the graduate student room on the second floor of the Technological Center. What the heck is the point of all this?" Joel asked again, trying to bring any semblance of logic to the year's long bombing spree.

Moss and Noel walked outside into the clear, cold winter day and found a place to get some coffee. They sat down outside, hoping the combination of cold and coffee would enliven their thinking and energize them for the long day ahead. Max later told me he was thinking that UNABOM was the most enduring disease they had ever faced, except for the news that had hit him a few weeks earlier—his wife, Kit, had been diagnosed with breast cancer. Now, in addition to dealing with the long and uncertain days of UNABOM, Max knew that every day and every night he and Kit would be enduring a long and uncertain war with cancer. Despite this sad turn of events, Max had made it clear to Terry and

I before leaving for Utah that he no longer wanted off the case and would see it through to the end—or at least until he was forced out at retirement age.

"Max," Joel had looked at his watch, "I almost forgot to remind you it's time to check in with Jim and Terry." They walked back inside the university building where they had arranged to call us from a conference line in one of the offices.

"Hey, calling in right on time," I answered when the phone rang, "what's the weather like out there?"

"Cold, very cold," Max blew into his hands and sipped on his coffee.

Terry and I both laughed as we glanced outside my office to see the sun shining across the tops of nearby buildings. "It's beautiful here, but I won't rub it in too much."

"So Max, take Jim and I on a tour of the scene at the university's Business Building," Terry brought us back to the purpose of the call. After bringing us up to date on the scene, Max turned his attention to describing the actual device.

"The bomb was an innocuous looking, odd shaped package, about ten inches tall and six inches wide. It was wrapped with plain brown paper and tied with string. Inside the wrapping was a wooden box holding a gallon gasoline can. A metal pipe sealed with wooden plugs was suspended in the gasoline."

"So Max, let me stop you there," Terry paused. "Was it similar to the one placed at Cory Hall in Berkeley the following year?"

"Yes, it was built along the same lines, but the Cory Hall bomb worked and this one didn't. This was a botched job, a dud that didn't ignite or explode. He was using a newer, improved model when he got to Cory Hall," Max answered, suggesting what we had surmised—the bomber was experimenting and improving his ordinance as he went along.

"The pipe had three types of smokeless gun powder and the usual Unabomber signature materials were used in the construction. There was something different in the electrical wiring—a wire from a lamp cord was leading to a common household 'on/off' switch. It allowed the bomber to arm the bomb at his convenience. Another wire led to a wooden dowel that served as an anti-movement device, so when the package was picked up the dowel dropped down and pulled two bare wires together, completing an electrical circuit that was supposed to initiate the explosion. Had the bomb worked as it was designed, the explosion would have sent a fireball raging down a hallway filled with students. It was an insidious bomb! Fortunately, the dowel assembly got bound up when the student lifted it and didn't properly complete the electrical circuit!"

Max added an important point: "The lab report also describes a thin piece of metal which had the letters 'FC' punched into it by a series of punch marks." The Unabomber had left his calling card.

"Max, did the lab report give a technical description of why the bomb failed?" I was wondering about the bomber's reaction to producing a dud.

Max had the report at his fingertips. "Whoever made the bomb was careful to get rid of any tool marks by filing and sanding the surfaces. He seems knowledgeable and concerned about forensic examinations, but despite his precautions a reddish blond Caucasian hair was discovered between two layers of tape. Obviously, this is a critical piece of evidence that they're keeping for future lab comparisons."

Max's tone was far from happy as he continued. "But, get this. The University Police mishandled the referral to the Feds. They sent it to the ATF when it should have gone to the FBI, since crimes on college campuses were prime FBI jurisdiction at that time. And, to make matters worse, the ATF Regional Lab reached the conclusion that it wasn't a functional bomb. They decided the device was a hoax that couldn't function because there looked to be an intentional break in the electrical circuit."

"Max, you're telling us the ATF Lab said this bomb was a hoax?" Terry jumped in.

"They think the bomb was intended to be dysfunctional? And, their examiner could tell this—how?" I was incredulous at such a notion.

Max continued. "Well, that's just part of the story. The bomb debris was returned by ATF to the University of Utah Police, where it remained in their evidence locker for the next seven months. No further investigation was conducted and there was no connection made to the work of the Unabomber. The bomb's existence was not even known to anyone in law enforcement outside of Utah and the Regional ATF Lab. When the next UNABOM bombing occurred at Vanderbilt University in Nashville, the investigating Postal Inspectors traced the origin of that mailed bomb to Brigham Young University in Utah. While interviewing a BYU Campus Police Officer, they mentioned that the Vanderbilt bomb contained a small metal tag with FC punched into it and he remarked 'that's just like the bomb last year up at the University of Utah.' Their response was 'what bomb last year in Utah?'

"Postal Inspectors went to the University of Utah and retrieved the remains of that first bomb and their Lab concluded it was a functional bomb and not a hoax. Then, I guess as a tie-breaker, they sent it to the FBI Laboratory to resolve or confirm the disputed findings and guess what? It was confirmed to be a dangerous firebomb that simply had failed to detonate. It was not a hoax and was finally identified as the work of the Unabomber." Max could be heard muttering in frustration as he closed the book on his account of the University of Utah bombing.

"Good enough, Max and Joel. That will make for interesting discussion at the UTF meeting when you return to San Francisco. Jim, do you have anything else right now? These guys are heading on to Brigham Young and will check in again after they have something to report." Terry caught my headshake, "no" and we both said goodbye and ended the phone call.

* * *

Provo, Utah is forty miles south of Salt Lake City along Interstate 15. The city of 116,000 is the third largest in the state and the home of Brigham Young University (BYU). With Utah Lake to its west and the Uinta-Wasatch National Forest to the east, Provo's scenic views and apparent serenity make it appear as an unlikely place for Unabomber activity. But the mysterious killer was confirmed by the Postal Inspectors to have been on the BYU campus on April 23, 1982, where he placed a package containing a bomb into the drop box at the Postal Station inside Brewster Hall, the home of the BYU Student Union.

While waiting to hear back from Max and Joel, Turchie and I decided to catch lunch at the nearby Max's Opera Café and he used the time to brief me on the odyssey of this mail bomb that traveled from BYU to Penn State University and finally ended up in the office of Patrick Fischer, a computer scientist at Vanderbilt University in Nashville, TN.

"Jim, the package mailing label was addressed to 'Prof. Patrick C. Fischer, Computer Science Department, Pennsylvania State Univ., State College, PA.' The return address was 'Prof. LeRoy W. Bearnson, Electrical Engineering, Brigham Young Univ., Provo, UT 84602.'"

Between enormous bites of sandwich, Terry continued to speak. "Professor Fischer had been a professor at Pennsylvania State University in the Computer Science Department until December, 1979, when he moved to Vanderbilt University in Nashville. Although the Penn State address was out-dated, the package was delivered to the Computer Science Department. And, since Professor Fischer was no longer there, someone forwarded the package to him at Vanderbilt. It was opened by

Fischer's secretary on May 5, 1982. It exploded as the Unabomber had intended. The force of the blast and resulting shrapnel caused severe injuries to her face and upper body."

Later that afternoon, Terry and I fielded our second call from Max and Joel with an update on their reinvestigation of the Utah bombings.

It had been a long day and Max was not making small talk beyond commenting about the frigid Utah temperatures. "Jim and Terry, you already know the circuitous route of the package bomb from BYU and reaching its final destination at Vanderbilt, so I won't describe that journey. But, it's worth noting that the Postal Inspectors found yet another employee who remembered the package in the mail stream. Any little deviation stands out I guess when you see letters and packages all day that conform to an established process. In this case, the stamps on the package had been 'lined out' with a pen rather than by other means of cancellation. At any rate, two employees at Penn State recalled seeing the package come through, including the one who readdressed it and sent it on to Professor Fischer at Vanderbilt."

"The bomb was constructed in a homemade wooden box and the investigators' report indicated that the bomb shared many of the features of a UNABOM device—multiple types of smokeless powders; D cell batteries; wooden dowels; and homemade triggering assembly. A thin metal tag affixed to the device bore the stamped letters, FC."

"Apart from the FC tag, was it pretty easy to tell this was a UNABOM device?" Terry asked.

"Terry, this was a classic UNABOM device. It didn't need 'FC' to have Unabomber written all over it. The red, white and blue mailing labels, the $1 Eugene O'Neill stamps, and even the intended targets whose backgrounds are in computer science and electrical engineering—these are repetitive elements of his bombs.

"Fischer graduated from the University of Michigan with a computer science degree and went on to teach at places like Harvard and MIT. Bearnson was mostly associated with Utah and got his electrical engineering degree from the University of Utah and then went to Syracuse and Auburn where he got his PhD in 1970. And, if you want to engage in more UNABOM trivia about the possible relevance of aviation among UNABOM targets, Fischer is a private pilot and Bearnson is into remote controlled model airplanes."

I groaned at that reference, but didn't pick up the conversational thread. And, thankfully, Terry also let it pass.

"Max, what more do you have planned for Joel to see back there?" I asked, again showing a degree of frustration with the slow pace of these reinvestigations.

"We're going to drive downtown so that I can show Joel where the Unabomber mailed the McConnell device and then we'll call it a day. Tomorrow we'll head over to CAAMS Computer store and do exactly what we've been doing the past couple of days," with that Max concluded the fact finding tour at BYU and we all got off the phone.

Moss did the driving as Max gave directions to the last stop. It was getting dark outside and their conversation had shifted to where they should go for dinner and how did they go about finding a beer or maybe wine in Mormon country.

"We need a Mormon agent with us Max, they'd know." Moss glanced at Max and gave a brief smile.

"Yeah, but it'd probably be their private stock," Max shot back.

Max motioned for Joel to pull over while pointing in the direction of one of several buildings in downtown Salt Lake City.

"All we know is that UNABOM Device Number Ten was mailed from a drop box here in the downtown area to Dr. James McConnell in Ann Arbor, Michigan. I really don't know a lot of the details of where we are with this investigation, but I wanted you to see the location and general environment of where the bomb package was mailed. For a detailed description of the bombing, I'm going to defer to Tony Muljat and Robin Shipman. They're all over the McConnell device. Besides, Squatter's Pub and Brewery is just up the street and I'm starved." Max was signaling the end of a long day was near.

In San Francisco, Terry and I were on Pacific Time and Terry had more to say.

"So Jim," he ventured cautiously, "I think you will be quite interested in Kathy Puckett's initial impressions after she has begun to wade through the mountain of UNABOM materials that I have given her.

"What? She is already reading UNABOM reports?" I pressed him.

"Well, kind of. I knew we would be getting briefed on the Fischer Device, but was surprised you asked as much as you did about the 'botched' bomb at the University of Utah. I had already asked her to take a look at the Utah bombings and the Fischer bombing in particular and to address them in the context of UNABOM overall. Knowing her as I do, I was sure that her observations would be interesting." Terry knew that his vagueness was getting to me.

"So let's hear Kathy's behavioral analysis," I sat back in my chair while Terry turned to entries among his notes.

"Kathy believes that the 1978 bomb at Circle Campus in Chicago and the 1981 bomb at the University of Utah Business Classroom Building were exceptions to what she calls the 'environmental fit' of the Unabomber."

"What does she mean by that?" I interrupted.

"All of his bombs have been designed to fit carefully into their environments, but not those two. The Business Classroom Building is apart from the technical and engineering focus and the location of the device in a hallway is inconsistent with the other devices placed in student areas. The hallway was open to any passerby. The bomb wasn't tailored to fit the environment."

While I was very supportive of bringing Kathy to work on the behavioral analysis, I had not expected a work product this sudden and Terry picked up on my skepticism.

"Kathy simply believes that the Unabomber didn't end up delivering the University of Utah bomb to its intended location or victim. He may have been on his way to make the delivery and was forced to abort by some set of circumstances out of his control. Just like at Circle Campus, he may have abandoned the device in a location it was not intended for."

Terry stopped there, knowing I was fully engaged, intrigued and anxious for more. But, that's all that he or Kathy or anyone had at the moment.

Months later, Terry and I would have the opportunity to read Theodore Kaczynski's diary and to learn of his own frustrations at his failed University of Utah bomb. In his words, it was a "firebomb" meant for maximum mayhem and destruction:

"For instance, last fall I attempted a bombing and spent nearly three hundred bucks just for travel expenses, motel, clothing for disguise, etc aside from cost of materials for bomb. And then the thing failed to explode. Damn. This was the firebomb found in U. of Utah Business School outside door of room containing some computer stuff."

CHAPTER SIX

PEOPLE ARE DYING—
SO WE'LL DO IT OUR WAY

(We tried our best to gain everyone's cooperation for our strategy by setting an example of hard work and leadership. But as time passed between bombing events and the trail appeared to some to be cold, resolve in other field offices to prioritize UNABOM dissolved. So when we had to, we cut to the chase with people—"it's our way or the highway," we told them, regardless of agency. Some people were offended at our approach—so be it; people were getting killed).

IT WAS ONE OF THOSE OVERCAST, NONDESCRIPT SAN FRANCISCO mornings as I ended my commute from Half Moon Bay, passed the security checkpoint with a nod of the head and grabbed a waiting elevator to my office. The first order of business was to make my own coffee; a task that Janet often reminded me is not in her job description. Not to worry, I was thinking, what could be better than landing as Agent in Charge in San Francisco, my office of choice; and then having some of the best—actually the best—work that existed anywhere in the Bureau? And, if that didn't cheer my gloom away, I could always call upon thoughts of my previous assignment in Honolulu—all sunshine and palm trees. Life is good.

A clinking coat hanger and the familiar creak of a chair outside my office signaled Janet's arrival and returned my thoughts to the business at hand.

"Janet, give a call to Terry and have him stop in to decipher that report he dropped off yesterday. Let's do it by 11:00, as my fairway seminar at the Presidio starts at noon." For some reason, I continued to use this old euphemism for golf with Janet as we both knew it was unnecessary. "Oh and good morning! How about a cup of strong coffee?" knowing full well that she was a tea drinker with no appreciation for a good cup of joe.

Turchie arrived almost immediately armed with facts and figures, as he had begun to anticipate my questions and clearly enjoyed holding back tidbits to spur my interest even further. This morning, he couldn't miss on that score—as my eyes were already focused on the thick binder in his hand, with the caption "1985—The Year of the UNABOMBER."

"Hi Terry, grab a cup of coffee and sit down. We've got a busy day so let's get it started."

He nodded, poured a cup of coffee and took a seat.

"Last night, I scanned this thing and I get the general drift that not everything about the FBI response back then was completely up to snuff. But, this guy—the Unabomber—he placed or mailed four highly lethal bombs that year. Each one had a connection to Salt Lake City, Sacramento or the SF Bay Area and surely this must have rung someone's bell in the FBI or elsewhere that maybe this geographic area had turned into his personal playground." I said it as half statement, half question; and for a moment Terry left it hanging. It was obvious he was gathering his thoughts.

With an audible sign, he responded. "It's true that the task force of today is light years away from the mind-set of the team back in 1985. I'm not going to make excuses for them or to say that today's UTF has the magic formula. If we did, you and I would be at the courthouse right now indicting the Unabomber, whoever he is. All I can say is that I'm working very hard to avoid the forces and frustration that splintered those earlier teams of Agents."

"Look, Terry, don't turn defensive on me. I don't question the integrity or dedication of our men and women back in 1985 or now. In fact, I'm hopeful that a 'eureka moment' will come from our reinvestigation of the earlier bombings; a new scrap of evidence or a lead that might make the difference for us today. Got any of those in that report of yours?"

"That's the goal. To get there, we have to actually experience these bombings from the 1985 perspective. With assistance from our analysts and with added contribution from Kathy on the psychological end, Max and Joel and I have sorted through a mountain of interview reports and lab documents and gained some insight into what makes our guy tick—no pun intended."

"Now, there's a hopeful sign of progress," I interjected, while looking at my watch and simultaneously motioning out the door for Janet to cancel my appointment at the Presidio. No golf for me today.

"OK, I'm almost on board here. But, this sudden flurry of UNABOM activity in '85; it was right in our backyard. It begs the question that we have asked over and over ourselves—and a question that I often get from the media. How and why was there no break in this case? Four bombs in 1985: one mailed from Oakland and another placed in Cory Hall at UC, Berkeley within a week or so of each other. And, this was even the second go-around for Cory Hall—an almost identical targeting back in 1982. Then, there was the mailed bomb from Salt Lake City in November; followed by the placed bomb in Sacramento that killed Hugh Scrutton in mid-December. It's a very valid question. How the hell did he get away with this without being tripped up?"

Terry shrugged his shoulders, but there was a lilt to his voice. "That is precisely the point of our reinvestigation and we have lined up a couple of presentations that should be of interest."

"I look forward to it. But, during the 'show and tell,' keep in mind that in the end there will be this simple question asked of us: Are we any closer to a solution today than our fellow Agents back in '85? And, if 1985 was the year of the UNABOMBER, when's it going to be our turn to get the bastard?" With that pithy comment, I grabbed my car keys and left the office with a determination to get in an hour or so at the driving range.

I had taken up golf in Hawaii and found it to be a great device for networking and schmoozing with my friends and associates in law enforcement. In my usual headstrong way, my approach had been to avoid professional lessons and learn golf on my own in the same way I had taken up downhill skiing. But, in attempting golf, I found no benefit whatsoever from being athletically inclined as one's body has too many moving parts that uniformly balk against acquiring a consistent golf swing. Absolute unison of will and muscle memory are required to reliably drive a tiny white ball in a straight line. I mused about the similarities of golf and life in general—and UNABOM in particular. Had there been an inability to control all facets of those four investigations back in '85?

It was a day or two later when Turchie invited Tony Muljat of the Postal Inspection Service to brief us during our morning management team meeting about his investigation of the bomb mailed to Dr. James V. McConnell, a professor of psychology at the University of Michigan. It was the third UNABOM device of 1985 and in preparation Terry had passed me excerpts from the reinvestigation package that recalled the composition of the mailing package and the bomb itself.

The package had been mailed from downtown Salt Lake City on November 12. Like other UNABOM devices, it was wrapped with brown paper using both masking and filament tapes to keep it sealed. "Priority Mail" was stamped on the package and it bore two kinds of U.S. Postage Stamps. An envelope taped to the package had a red, white and blue mailing label with Professor

McConnell's home address in Ann Arbor, Michigan typed on it. The return address was carried as "Ralph C. Kloppenburg, Department of History, University of Utah, Salt Lake City, Utah."

I read quickly to refresh my recollection, as Muljat made small talk at the conference table. On the afternoon of November 15, Nick Suino, McConnell's teaching assistant, had opened the package, causing the bomb inside to detonate. The explosion burned his forearms and abdomen and hearing loss resulted from the force of the blast.

The explosive material of aluminum powder and ammonium nitrate had been packed inside a galvanized steel pipe. A small metal disc containing the letters "FC" was attached to one of the metal end plugs by a small nail. The detonation was powered by D-cell and AAA batteries which had their outer casings removed.

If that wasn't enough to conclude this was the work of the Unabomber, the cover letter from Ralph Kloppenburg and the addresses on the envelope and mailing label were all typed on the same L.C. Smith Corona typewriter that had been used in other UNABOM attacks. It had Pica style type, with 2.54 mm spacing. The bomb itself was concealed within a black three ring binder that Kloppenburg's letter had represented as containing a draft of the dissertation that he wanted Professor McConnell to read.

Tony faced an expanded group of attendees to the morning management meeting. Mark Logan from ATF was present along with Don Davis, Tony's boss at the Postal Inspection Service, and Steve Frecerro, the Assistant U.S. Attorney assigned almost 100% of his time to support the investigation. Kathy, Terry, Joel and Max sipped on their coffee armed with yellow legal pads, listening to Tony as if they had never heard him discuss his topic before. In reality, they'd heard it a dozen times, like so much else with UNABOM. But there was little choice.

Without further ado, Tony began his presentation. "Jim, I'm

really honored to be talking to such a distinguished group so early this morning," Muljat began with deliberation and sarcasm that was met with both snarls and laughter around the table.

Muljat was fond of saying that he had worked the UNABOM case longer than any other investigator, having been assigned to it almost a decade earlier. No one disputed his statement, including the FBI's long time UNABOM case agent John Conway. Personally, I considered it a dubious distinction given that the case remained unsolved during their tenure on the case, but I left that unsaid with the realization that someone might be saying that about me in future years.

Muljat's voice had only one volume setting when he talked—loud. Along with an air of self-confidence that came from a combination of age, passion and experience, I had been forewarned that Muljat was seldom interrupted when he started talking about UNABOM. On the UTF he was sometimes called "Hollywood Cop," and with his thick white hair and golf-tanned face, he did look as if he stepped right out of Central Casting.

"First off, let me tell you I've worked on a lot of UNABOM Task Forces but this is the best one ever. I've never felt so positive that we have a shot at solving this case. I can feel it. And I want to thank you and Terry for letting everyone speak up and feel a part of things." Muljat stopped, nodded at both Terry and me and continued after we smiled in acknowledgment.

"Our investigation has turned up some pretty interesting stuff," Muljat looked across the table at his partner Robin Shipman making sure he shared the credit.

"Professor McConnell was a long time member of the Psychology Department at the University of Michigan. He had a reputation for dancing to a different drummer than many of his colleagues, but was very popular with university students. He used to spend time talking to students informally in their dorms."

"What do you mean used to?" Terry asked.

"Well, McConnell died in 1990. But his legacy will live on for a long time. McConnell wrote a textbook called 'Understanding Human Behavior' a few years back that made him a wealthy man. The book is still being used all around the country. No doubt there are plenty of people who know about his work and opinions and I guess someone out there got so offended by McConnell they ended up sending him a bomb."

"Tony, do we know where *Understanding Human Behavior* was actually used?" Terry asked, and I groaned inwardly knowing that Terry was likely thinking about yet another investigative project with additional drain on manpower.

"I have that information right here," Robin Shipman read from notes in front of him, as Muljat gave him an approving nod.

"The first edition of his book was used in a number of schools in the Chicago area from 1975 to 1977, including Lake Forest College. It was also used at Brigham Young and the University of Utah. The third edition was used at a number of community colleges in California."

"There's something else—a month before he received the bomb in the mail, Professor McConnell wrote a marketing letter to about 160 professors all over the United States hawking the upcoming Fifth Edition of *Understanding Human Behavior*," Muljat added.

"Is he known for anything else?" I asked Muljat, still processing the information on the psychology book, and I soon regretted asking the question.

"I'm glad you asked. McConnell wrote a paper called *Memory Transfer through Cannibalism in Planarians*," Muljat paused as he looked at a few sets of puzzled eyes around the table.

"Planarians," Muljat repeated for impact, "flatworms."

Sensitive to his audience and desirous of holding their attention until he made his final points, Muljat responded to the collective, "What does any of this have to do with UNABOM?" groans.

"McConnell believed that learning and memory transfer could take place when planarians were ground up and fed to other planarians. Research he and his students conducted involved worms being educated to respond with a conditioned reflex after being exposed to light and electric shock. His research was pretty much discredited when it first came out. But he went on to put together two satirical publications, the Journal of Biological Psychology and the wildly popular, *Worm Runner's Digest.*"

I utilized the interval of laughter to move the discussion back on track to the bomb and its letter. "So Tony, what's your assessment of the letter that was on the package bomb?" I prodded him along.

"Two things stand out about the return address and the letter, as Ralph Kloppenburg says in the letter that he is a doctoral candidate in the History of Science at the University of Utah. We've conducted a lot of investigation and so far haven't identified any Ralph Kloppenburg who wrote the letter. We did find a Kloppenburg family in Sacramento where the elder Kloppenburg worked for a computer firm. He has a daughter who married a fellow named Ralph and they live in Salt Lake City. She is an employee of the University of Utah. Her husband works at a medical device company located near the University. But, these are just weird connections to other UNABOM events. We washed the family out as potential suspects."

Turchie jumped in quickly with a question of his own, for which he undoubtedly already knew the answer. "Tony, are we still sending out leads to identify any other individuals named Ralph Kloppenburg and do you feel pretty certain it's just a pseudonym?"

"We're trying to identify every Kloppenburg we can get our hands on, but yes, we think it's a phony name, just like Enoch Fischer on the Percy Wood bomb. We've found several other Kloppenburg types, including one who attended Northwestern

University in the mid-seventies. We don't think they're relevant to this case, though."

"So, the letter writer claimed to be a doctoral candidate in the History of Science program. Talk to us about that, as I'm unfamiliar with the discipline." And, by a look around the room, I wasn't alone in that regard.

"Robin, go ahead and give that part of the briefing, I think you have the information they're looking for," Tony took a break and turned things over to his teammate.

"About a month after the McConnell package exploded, one of our Postal Inspectors received a letter from Professor McConnell. He told us there are probably only a few hundred people across the country knowledgeable of the History of Science. We've done some checking and found out he's pretty much correct. The 1983 edition, for example, of the *Guide to the History of Science* only had forty-four colleges offering graduate programs in the discipline. About four hundred students were enrolled in all of them combined when we checked."

"What about the colleges and universities that were the sites of UNABOM attacks—did any of them offer History of Science programs?" Terry asked.

"University of Illinois, Chicago Circle Campus, RPI, University of Utah, Northwestern, Brigham Young, University of Michigan and University of California at Berkeley—all of them have History of Science programs and all had experienced UNABOM attacks," Shipman rattled back.

Terry summed it up and brought this portion of the briefing to a close. "The History of Science, a graduate school discipline with highly limited distribution and availability, and yet these eight universities that were the sites of UNABOM bombings also had such a program? I want to thank both you and Robin for the great briefing and we will be talking soon about how to exploit any new leads that might come of this."

As Muljat left the room, he could hardly hide his emotions. Tony spoke of trying for years to convince previous task force managers that taking the case to college campuses might produce substantial new trails. But, he says that he was continuously rebuffed. Now, he had found an attentive and receptive audience.

After everyone but Max and Terry had left my office, Terry turned to me and could hardly wait to get out the words. "Max and I'd like to go over UNABOM Event Number Eight with you. It's the first intended bombing by the UNABOMBER in 1985, but it was delayed in its delivery and never actually exploded. Max has done yeoman's work in coordinating all aspects of the case with the reinvestigation team to find out why."

Max took up the discussion at this point, as he had firsthand knowledge of the investigation. "The bomb was mailed to the Boeing Fabrication Division in Auburn, Washington from here in Oakland, CA. Although it arrived at Boeing Fabrication in early April, it wasn't opened until June 13, 1985. It turns out that Boeing Fabrication is a large multi-building complex and the package address did not name a specific person, building or room number. So, when it arrived at the Receiving Department, no one knew where to direct the package and clerical workers placed it on a shelf, where it sat for over a month. Finally a Supervisor took it upon himself to try and determine whom the package was intended for.

Max continued. "The Supervisor called Oakland information and requested the telephone number for the name on the return address—Weiberg Tool and Supply at 16 Hegenberger Court. The information operator said there was no such listing. Next, the Supervisor attempted to open the package to determine its contents. After removing the outer, brown wrapping paper he discovered a solid wooden box from which two small wooden sticks popped up. The Supervisor was very lucky, but not deterred, as he then proceeded to chisel a hole in the wooden box and finally exposed wires and a metal pipe inside. The Auburn police were called, who in turn called the King County Sheriff's Bomb Squad. They arrived a short time later and rendered the bomb safe."

To no one in particular, I mumbled, "So, they blew it up and scattered any useful evidentiary material all over the place." Surely in this day and age, I thought to myself, the FBI Lab or military contractors can build a device to safely disarm bombs without blowing them up. I made a mental note to run this request up the flag pole the next time Headquarters asked if the UTF needed any special equipment.

Max continued to report on the make-up of the package, "In retrospect, everything about the device spelled UNABOM. It had a red, white and blue mailing label. The address and return address had been typed on the same L.C. Smith Corona typewriter, as before. Both end plugs of the steel pipe used in the bomb's construction had "FC" stamped on it. Traces of ammonium nitrate and aluminum powder were found by the FBI Lab on some fragments."

Terry added, "Max and I drove by the return address on Hegenburger Court the other day. There is a Hegenburger Court about a mile from the Oakland Airport, but there isn't now and hasn't ever been any Weiburg Tool and Supply. There's a Mechanics Tool and Supply and several other businesses, but no one has ever heard of Weiburg."

"The Postal Inspectors did a lot of work on the address used at the Fabrication Division and helped figure out the delivery issues," Max continued.

"They found that the bomber wasn't that familiar with the facility, as the mailing address indicated 15th Street when it should have been Avenue. It turns out that the mailing address for Boeing's Fabrication Division is not well publicized to the general public. But, the biggest problem with the address was simply the lack of a specific building, room or person. To make matters worse, the zip codes are different depending on if one uses the street or avenue address and the mail can end up miles down the road from where it was intended to be," Max finished up as I was about to ask a question.

"Besides the Supervisor that tried to open it and was lucky not to have his head blown off, were there any witnesses who described seeing the package when it first arrived? I'm curious about the long delay from when the package arrived and whether the bomber himself might have attempted anonymous contact to see what happened to it. Not likely, but you never know."

Max was on it. "It turns out there was a couple that recalled seeing it. One said the paper wrapping had an oily backing, like that used to prevent the buildup of moisture and condensation on military surplus equipment. But, I didn't turn up any reports of someone trying to reclaim the package or inquire of its where-abouts."

Terry began, "There are similar intersections here with other bombings. BYU and RPI interacted heavily with the Boeing Fabrication Division at that time. Boeing was recruiting on cam-pus at UC Berkeley over a period of several years in the early 1980's and in May, 1985 they offered jobs or accepted resumes from Berkeley students. Boeing has over two thousand sub-con-tractors in California, with five hundred of them in Northern California and just about all of them are connected with the avia-tion industry in some way. We've also linked a number of Boeing suppliers with UC Berkeley, so there is overlap there."

"So at least at this juncture, there's some credence in the the-ory of an airline connection to the Unabomber," I agreed. "But, isn't that thread lost at the point of considering motivation. It might be revenge of a current or former employee. Or a family member that believes they were wronged in some way. Or perhaps it involved a financial angle by a contractor that was cheated. Or, someone that lost a loved one in the crash of an airliner." As I spoke, my thoughts were mired in the many thousands of mathematical possibilities buried in all of the information we were collecting as to motivations and possible characteristics of the Unabomber. And, wanting to get out of the doldrums and put this discussion back on track, I abruptly changed direction.

"Terry, there's only so much that you and I can get on paper or from a conference room briefing. We've got two Berkeley bombings at nearby Cory Hall and the site of the Rentech computer store bombing that killed its owner, Hugh Scrutton, is only another hour or so up the road in Sacramento. And, who's better to lead the excursion and interpret the 1985 investigative landscape than Max?" I saw smiles break out and then said, "Clear your calendars for a fresh start in the morning. Tell Joel to hold down the fort for a day."

The next morning, I met Max and Terry at the University exit from I-580 and they climbed into my car. As I hoped, Max produced cups of coffee and Terry had a bag of pastries in his briefcase. We decided to remain parked for a while and plan our day while partaking of breakfast.

After a swig of really hot coffee, I spoke to Max. "Alright, the podium is yours Max. Make it worth our while."

Max was up to the task, beginning with the University of California bombing in 1982.

"The Unabomber showed up at UC, Cory Hall on July 2, 1982. At around 7:45am, Professor Diogenes Angelakos who was the Director of the Electronics Research Lab, walked into Room 411 to make a pot of coffee. This was his daily routine, since he was usually the first to arrive each morning. The small room served as a faculty lounge at that time and a computer 'clean room' was being built directly across the hall. The construction work was being done at night when no faculty or students were present and those workers used the lounge to take their rest stops during the night.

"Upon his arrival that morning, Dr. Angelakos observed a one gallon gasoline can that had its metal handle replaced by a handle made of wood. The can was completely covered with double layers of filament tape and black plastic tape, giving it an appearance of having been made of wood. A crudely made paper numerical dial and two wires with alligator clips were attached. Because of the nearby construction work going on back then, Professor Angelakos said that he thought this strange looking device was a piece of electrical testing equipment left behind by the construction workers the night before. Just as he attempted to lift the device by its handle, the explosive detonated and splashed gasoline over him. Fortunately for him, the gallon of gasoline failed to ignite.

"He was very lucky," Max continued. "A galvanized steel pipe was suspended in the gasoline can and attached to a handle built into a wooden box that sat on top of the can. Picking the can up by the handle was the trigger—and that should sound familiar. Also, the component built on top of the device served no purpose other than to look like a piece of test equipment. The real puzzler that remains unidentified as to its intent is a note that was found in the room following the explosion that said, 'Wu—it works! I told you it would. RV.' The note was typed on a L.C. Smith Corona typewriter, Pica style type, having 2.54 mm spacing. Our Lab reported it was the same typewriter used to type the mailing label on the bomb sent to Patrick Fischer at Vanderbilt and now we know of others."

"So we have two typewriters used by the Unabomber?" I wanted clarification.

"Yes, there was a different older typewriter used in the Percy Wood bombing. However, the Fischer bombing, this Cory Hall note, and the mailing labels of other bombs were all typed on this same Smith Corona typewriter," Max explained.

"One thing's for sure—we find that typewriter and the

Unabomber is toast in a court of law. Can we put a bounty on that Smith Corona?"

"In a way, we have done that," explained Max. "The UTF has put notices out to all the crime labs in the U.S. and internationally to search their crime records for typing samples that might match the UNABOM typewriters. We have mailed flyers to pawn shops, second-hand stores, and are leaving no stone unturned to find the Smith Corona typewriter in particular. Unlike most of our lead material, this is solid forensic evidence that can someday hang the bastard that's doing this."

With a lull in my questions, Max moved deftly on to the second bombing at Cory Hall. "This bomb was placed in Corey Hall sometime during the week leading up to May 15, 1985. It was the only time that the Unabomber has returned to the same location to place a bomb."

I interrupted with a question. "So, this was damned close timing to when he was in Oakland to mail his bomb to Boeing Fabrication. It was mailed on May 8, a week before the Cory Hall bomb was placed. Has sufficient attention been given to the fact that the Unabomber spent the better part of that week in and around the Bay Area—if indeed he doesn't live here full time?"

Terry responded to me that this was a topic for another time and place, while motioning for Max to bring his overview of the 1985 Cory Hall bombing to an end, so we could visit there and see for ourselves.

"Room 264 was used by graduate students in the electrical engineering program and secured by a punch key lock. The pipe bomb was built into a black three-ring binder held together with rubber bands. The binder was left on a table, where it easily blended into the setting, and it was designed to explode as it was opened. Several people we interviewed had noticed the binder lying there over a few days, but left it undisturbed on the table for its owner to recover. A graduate student named John Hauser eventually opened the binder and the bomb inflicted horrific damage to his right hand and arm. He lost four fingers on his right hand. Again, one of the end plugs of the pipe bomb had been stamped with the calling card, FC."

As I pulled into a parking garage across the street from Cory Hall, Max was finishing his summary. "Mr. Hauser, an Air Force Academy graduate, was days away from learning that he had been accepted into the space program. The Cory Hall bomb ended his potential career as an astronaut."

We had that thought to ponder as we stepped lively from the car and into the very university environment where the Unabomber seemed to move in and out with relative ease and anonymity. As we walked off the busy street into Cory Hall, we were conscious of standing out like typical FBI agents in suits and I commented that it was a good bet that the Unabomber didn't dress this way when on campus. Max had been here many times and he led us down a hallway beyond bulletin boards laden with thumb tacked announcements, and assorted pictures and advertisements. We climbed a flight of stairs to the fourth floor and took a couple of turns down a long and sterile corridor. We finally came to a dead end facing a computer lab, with a classroom across the hall. And, to our right was a small, unremarkable room, # 411, which was still serving as a break room for members of faculty.

"Take a look. Professor Angelakos went to make a pot of coffee here and tried to pick up the device on the floor over there—and boom." Max illustrated a mushroom shape with his arms.

"This is amazing," I added. "It feels like a stranger would be a dead giveaway up here, and especially in the confines of such a hallway and a room like this. It's easy for an investigator to conclude that the bomber must feel absolutely at home in a college environment like this. What do you think Max—'the profile is still the profile'? Yes? No?"

Max gave me one of his looks and said, "Boss man, you haven't seen anything yet. Wait 'til we go back downstairs and you get a look at room # 264. You won't even believe it," Max spat out.

We returned to street level where the volume of students, faculty, and a variety of workers were moving about with more intensity. Max led us up to a second floor landing, through double doors and into a narrow hallway. Glancing at the numbers marking the doors on each side of the corridor, I could tell we were closing in on room #264—the scene of the 1985 Berkeley bombing. It was difficult to imagine the Unabomber stalking the same area years earlier, walking past countless students and yet no one was suspicious as he walked into the computer room, carefully placed the black three-ring notebook on the table, and walked away.

We looked inside the room quickly as a student exited into the narrow passage way. We said nothing while in such close confines and continued our walk down the hall. Max pulled up and pointed to the name on the door across from the computer room. It was the office of an individual who headed the History of Science program—the scholastic program that was referenced in the bombing of Professor McConnell at the University of Michigan. I shook my head in wonderment at the twisting and turning plot lines of UNABOM. With some relief, we returned to the openness of the main floor and felt like we could talk again.

"No question that our guy had to feel secure in the knowledge that he blended in up there. There's no way anyone who hasn't moved around a university environment would ever risk just strolling in and carrying a bomb into that hallway!"

"That's what I meant Jim," Max jumped in. "It just boggles the mind to think this guy moves around in places like this, and they're all the same, whether at Northwestern, the University of Utah, or here on two different floors of Cory Hall. And, here's another amazing tidbit that I learned in speaking with Professor Angelakos. After the first bomb at Cory Hall in 1982, he moved his office from the 4th floor, near room #411, so guess what?

When the second bombing went down in 1985, there was Professor Angelakos' new office on the second floor and very near room #264." Max posed the question, "Was Professor Angelakos the intended target of both bombs? He is obviously concerned that he was targeted, but he says there is no one he knows that would want to hurt him."

Terry said it was time to eat and we found a place to grab a quick sandwich. During lunch, we discussed the variety of investigative projects and extensive number of leads that were swirling around the two Berkeley bombings and the three additional ones that occurred in 1985. The case had a vastness that was difficult to fully grasp and it helped immensely to become directly involved in viewing these old crime scenes and interacting with Max and Terry.

I thought back to the first conversations I had with Director Freeh and my trepidation on the flight back to San Francisco about taking on this investigation. If I had any lingering concern, it was washed away after the experiences of this day—and we weren't finished yet. There was still the sprint up to Sacramento to spice up the afternoon.

Soon, we arrived at the site of the former Rentech Computer Store in Sacramento and walked the area while Max verbally recreated the scene on the day when the Unabomber mutilated and killed the store's owner.

"By all accounts, Mr. Hugh Scrutton was a hard working and caring young man who had built Rentech Computer Store from nothing into a highly successful business years before the computer age had fully sprung to life. When he walked out of the rear door of his store at the Century Plaza strip mall near Howe Avenue at noon on December 11, there's little doubt in my mind about what he was thinking when he saw an object lying on the ground near his car in the parking lot behind his store."

Max continued with the solemn story. "Not wanting to see anyone hurt or a car damaged by this thing that a bomb technician later labeled as a "road hazard," he likely intended to pick it up and toss it in the nearby dumpster. As Scrutton stood directly over the misshaped wooden object and reached down to lift it off the ground, the first tiny movement set off a tremendous explosion. Among the remnants of the device strewn across the parking lot, there was the telltale end cap of the pipe bomb stamped with the letters 'FC.' This bomb had been concealed in two hollowed out Douglas fir and redwood two by fours, and shiny nails protruded from the top making it visibly appear as a very dangerous hazard for a car tire.

"To the bomb examiners arriving at the crime scene and also to investigators experienced with the UNABOM investigation, the tell tale signs were everywhere—not only the 'FC' signature, but the same types of solder; wires; D-cell batteries and a nine volt battery with the outer casings removed. All being unique and familiar materials that led to a single forensic conclusion—this was UNABOM Event Number Eleven. But, even more importantly for the Unabomber—he finally had achieved his first kill."

Mr. Scrutton seemed an unlikely target for such a crime. Popular, with a wide range of hobbies and interests, he was a quiet and law-abiding citizen living and working in a safe part of town. He liked cooking, music, rebuilding old automobiles, ceramics, research and reading. Three of the four bedrooms of his suburban home had been converted into libraries. But he never had a chance to escape once he touched the device.

Terry was saying that Mr. Scrutton died almost instantly from the devastating results of the blast, just as I was reading the much more graphic summary in the UTF report about the extent of physical damage to his body. There was a feeling of sadness and revulsion, but at the same time a passion for getting the job done.

In Sacramento, a task force was formed and a massive investigation was launched. A single drop of red paint on a piece of the tape used in making the device was preserved for analysis. Over a thousand Rentech customers were identified and interviewed. The owners of almost one hundred cars parked at the strip mall at the time were located and asked whether they saw anything suspicious on the day of the bombing. Over three thousand individuals staying at hotels in the surrounding area during the time span of the crime had been identified and their names entered into a database for suspect comparison purposes and potential follow-up.

As each day passed in 1985, the intensity of the investigation grew until there was a diminishing supply of credible leads to logically follow. Gradually at first, but then accelerating with the passage of more time, the task force followed the path of least resistance and dissolved itself as the trail grew cold. The savage killer had escaped and seemed to disappear back into the ether. It would be fourteen months before he would reappear; and that would spark a new chapter in the hunt for the Unabomber.

* * *

Eleven years later in 1996, after his writings had been decoded and then translated from Spanish to English, Terry and I had the unique opportunity to read Ted Kaczynski's admissions about the Hauser and Rentech bombs. It was every bit as chilling as that wintry day in Montana when we had stood outside his cabin after Max and his small team had removed him forcibly from his wilderness home. In reading his words, we shook our heads and found it difficult to speak of this personification of Evil.

On the bomb that ended John Hauser's astronaut aspirations, the Unabomber wrote:

"May 8 I planted a small bomb...in the Computer Sci. Dept. at Berkeley. This is device No. 2, Exp. 83 in my notebooks...It was sprung by Airforce pilot, 26 yrs old, name-Hauser, working on Masters Deg. In Electrical Eng. He probably would have been killed if so positioned relative to bomb as to take the fragments in

his body. As it were, mainly his right arm was hit. Witnesses said, 'whole arm was exploded' 'blood all over the place.'...Later, further search of newspaper yielded...Hauser's arm was severed or severely severed. Tips of three fingers torn off. Use of arm and hand will be permanently impaired... Hauser father of 2 kids...He was afraid his 'dream' was ruined. Dream was to be an astronaut... I am no longer bothered by having crippled this guy... I laughed at the idea of having any compunction about crippling an airplane pilot."

On the murder of Hugh Scrutton, the Unabomber was equally cold blooded:

"Experiment 97. Dec. 11, 1985 I planted bomb disguised to look like scrap of lumber behind Rentech Computer Store in Sacramento. According to San Francisco Examiner, Dec. 20, the 'operator' (owner? manager?) of the store was killed, 'blown to bits' on Dec. 12. Excellent. Humane way to eliminate somebody. He probably never felt a thing. 25000 dollar reward offered. Rather flattering."

CHAPTER SEVEN

DEAL WITH THE MEDIA—BUT DON'T EMBARRASS THE BUREAU

(The FBI long advocated public awareness in fighting crime, but all public statements on high profile cases were vetted and issued from FBI Headquarters to avoid embarrassing the Bureau. Director Freeh delegated unprecedented authority to me to manage UNABOM and I accepted this as authorization for an aggressive media strategy. My UNABOM media strategy was intended to draw out reluctant witnesses or trigger identification and/or recognition of the Unabomber by the public).

OVER A FOGGY AND DAMP WEEKEND AT MY HOME IN HALF MOON Bay, I had been studying Turchie's compilation of "Known Facts, Fiction and Theories about the Unabomber" and I had a few questions and ideas of my own—especially about the attack on February 20, 1987 at CAAMS Computer Store in Salt Lake City. This was called UNABOM Event Number Twelve and it was significant for so many reasons. I wanted to know how the investigators at that time and in the years since 1987 had taken advantage of the only eyewitness sighting of the Unabomber. Often, a break on this order of magnitude would blow a case wide open— but not so with UNABOM. After grabbing a snack, I settled in to read Max's first-hand account of his reinvestigation.

CAAMS was a small family-owned computer store on the

southeast edge of downtown Salt Lake City. Max had taken Joel to the location while they were in Utah and recreated what the site must have looked like on the day of the bombing. In the previous months, Max had spent countless hours in sifting through the prior reports and talking to some of the original investigators; and he spoke at length with that eyewitness on multiple occasions.

On the morning of February 20, 1987, CAAMS employee Tammy Fluehe had been working inside the store as she watched a man she had never seen before walk into the rear parking lot. Her car was parked up against the building directly under the window where she was working. She watched intently as he removed an object from a white canvas bag. The object looked like two short and narrow boards joined together with sharp and shiny nails, some of which were visibly protruding from the top. As Tammy watched intently, the man very carefully placed the strange looking object down next to the left front tire of her car.

"Hey! Come and look at what this asshole is doing!" Alarmed and disturbed by what she saw, Tammy yelled loudly to her boss and CAAMS owner, Gaye Wright.

The man, only a few feet away, appeared to have heard Tammy through the window as he looked up and stared into her face. Undeterred, he left the thing on the ground next to her car, closed up the white bag and calmly walked away. Tammy had started to go out and confront the man, but Wright dissuaded her.

"One of the boys will go out and move it before you leave," Wright assured her.

Less than an hour later, Wright's oldest son Gary drove into the parking lot and noticed the object lying on the ground. Thinking it was a piece of construction debris, Gary knelt beside it to pick it up and throw it into a nearby dumpster. He reached to touch it and caused it to move slightly. A violent explosion chewed into his face and upper body severing a nerve in his arm and he was left lying on the ground—severely injured.

After the responding medical personnel had removed Gary to the hospital and the police had searched and cleared the area of any remaining sign of the bomber, the bomb technicians began their work of sifting through the debris that was scattered in the parking lot and embedded in nearby cars and walls. Most prominent among their findings were metal end plugs from the pipe bomb. Stamped into the end of one of the plugs were the letters "FC." Without question, the attack was the work of the Unabomber—confirmed by the "FC" calling card, but also by his signature construction techniques and habits that made this an unnecessary affirmation of his craftsmanship.

Even though he was severely injured by the Unabomber's device, Gary Wright was lucky on the day of the attack. Had he not knelt down beside the bomb as he reached out to pick it up, he would have suffered the same fate as Mr. Scrutton. The bomb's construction and the wooden fragments of maple, pine, yellow poplar, and Douglas fir showed it to be an almost exact replica of the device that viciously murdered Scrutton in Sacramento, California less than two years earlier.

Up to that point, the Unabomber had operated for nine years without anyone observing him as the bomber. At last, an eyewitness account. On that February day in Salt Lake City, new life was breathed into the hunt to find the Unabomber. Now, he became an elusive prey, wrapped in a gray hooded sweatshirt and wearing aviator style sunglasses.

Tammy Fluehe told police the bomber she saw from her vantage point inside the office was a white male, about twenty-five to thirty years old, with strawberry blond colored hair, a light strawberry blond moustache, standing anywhere from five feet ten inches to six feet tall and weighing one hundred sixty five pounds. His complexion had a reddish flush and was rough looking in appearance. His hands were whiter than his face. As she watched him through the window, she was only four feet away from the

Unabomber. The Salt Lake City police sat her down with one of their artists and the resulting composite drawing became an instant piece of American crime lore. From *Reader's Digest* to television news channels, the full color composite was shown across the world.

I contemplated the immense value and opportunity that this eyewitness account had meant to the investigators back in 1987. Except for the following—Max's reinvestigation of the CAAM's bombing and re-interview of the eyewitness revealed a big problem that proved to be a gaping hole. There was an artist's conception of the Unabomber and it had been exhibited to the world, but someone had overlooked the fact that Tammy Fluehe was never satisfied that it was a good rendition of the man she saw.

Tammy Fluehe told Max she had never been happy with the 1987 composite. She didn't like the coloring or the heart shaped face in any of the artist's versions. When Max reviewed the file on the CAAM's bombing he noted that there were several versions of the artist's composite drawing based on Fluehe's description. Each was done on a different date and Max wondered why.

On one of his early trips to re-interview Fluehe, Max asked her why there were different versions of the composite drawing of the Unabomber. Tammy answered that the artist was never able to capture what she was describing to him. The shape of the face was incorrect and the complexion not an accurate reflection of what she saw. When Max asked Tammy how she could be so certain, her response was both surprising and mind numbing! She had simply reviewed the notes that she had written down of the incident on February 20, 1987. Unbelievably, Tammy still had her original notes from the day of the bombing. She had diligently followed the police instructions to write down what she saw, but then no one (police or Feds) had ever returned to ask for her notes.

* * *

Before I assumed responsibility for the UNABOM investigation, the San Francisco FBI had just wrapped up our lead role into the kidnapping and murder of twelve-year old Polly Klaas from her home in Petaluma, California, in October, 1993. Multiple witnesses gave descriptions to a noted, forensic artist, Jeanne Boylan, who prepared a composite sketch of the subject from their information. When Richard Allen Davis was identified and arrested as Polly's killer, his real life photograph bore an eerie resemblance to Boylan's composite. I was impressed with Jeanne's drawings that were based on her in-depth interviews with eyewitnesses. They looked like real-life images of people.

When Max first told me of Tammy Fluehe's dissatisfaction with the Unabomber sketch done in 1987, I gave him Jeanne's telephone number and suggested that he talk with her about what might be possible. You don't know if you don't ask. He contacted Boylan and set up an interview with Terry, Joel and himself. She then agreed to attempt a new drawing, although she had never done a drawing from interviewing a witness almost seven years after the incident.

Max and Jeanne Boylan flew to Salt Lake City where they met with Tammy Fluehe in her suburban home. In order for Tammy to give Jeanne her undivided attention, Max was called upon to go the extra mile by entertaining Tammy's two year old son. During the next few hours, Max got down on the living room floor and watched a video of the "Lion King" with the two year old. In the next room, Jeanne was busy pulling memories from Tammy, who was greatly assisted by the contemporaneous notes that she had saved. Besides being a first rate artist, Jeanne proved to be an outstanding listener. She created a new, black and white composite drawing of the individual that Tammy saw place a bomb near her car in February, 1987.

Although Tammy assured Max and Jeanne that she was now satisfied that this new drawing closely resembled the man that she knew to be the Unabomber, I wrestled with the decision of whether or how to go to the public with a competing image of the bomber. Seven years had passed since the original drawing and it would be going far out on a limb for something that was probably unprecedented in law enforcement—and certainly so in such a high profile case. And, our reinvestigation of the CAAMS bombing was wrapping up, so it was getting close to decision time. First, I needed to close the loop on how this development would factor into our UNABOM strategy and I was curious about receiving input from our resident clinical psychologist.

I asked Kathy Puckett to join me in a scheduled meeting with the UTF leadership team as we were rounding out discussions of the reinvestigations—and specifically the CAAMS bombing. She had been formally assigned to the UTF for only several weeks, but had already completed her behavioral assessment of the book *Ice Brothers,* and put many of her thoughts about the Unabomber into a preliminary written assessment.

It was time for key members of the UTF to hear and vet her observations prior to unleashing the behavioral information on the entire task force. I liked what Kathy had to say, but almost as important was the way she said it. I could see how proud Terry was as he gave a formal introduction to the small group surrounding Kathy at my conference table.

Terry began with a little history. "Kathy and I have worked together since I first arrived in San Francisco back in 1988. She played an instrumental role in breaking up a Soviet bloc illegal operation through the behavioral support she provided our squad. She helped us out on many occasions down in Palo Alto with espionage and technology transfer cases where we needed her assessments to best determine how to move forward with suspects in our cases. I have nothing but confidence in her ability and think she will be a fantastic asset to the UTF."

"Well, it's about time we had some first class psychological support if you ask me," Tony Muljat jumped in to the welcome party with his loud and definitive voice. It was clear that he approved of the selection.

Kathy let out her distinctive laugh, which was a mix of 'I approve of that joke' and 'let's get right down to business.'

"I can see I'm going to have to work real hard here to earn all this admiration and trust," she fired at us.

"Kathy?" It was my turn to get serious. "You've already completed some yeoman's work and I want you to give everyone here a view of your preliminary conclusions." I glanced at each assembled UTF player as I spoke. Given the problems the UTF had experienced with behavioral analysis and support, I wanted to emphasize Kathy's rollout as a big and positive development.

I continued with my introductory comments. "Terry has briefed me about your feelings surrounding the early bombs, so just start with those and give us a blow by blow of your key findings. And, anyone should feel free to jump in at any time with questions."

"Oh, definitely, please stop me whenever you have a question. This is a lot of material and we'll definitely need breaks in the monologue," Kathy laughed at her own presentation style.

"Safety, security, and secrecy are of paramount importance to the Unabomber. He has a strong sense of self-protectiveness. Take the first bomb back in 1978 as an example. The subject put ten dollars in stamps on the package. They were never cancelled and the bomb was found in a parking lot at Chicago Circle Campus. I believe it is reasonable to assume the device was too big to fit in a mailbox and out of concern for his own safety from an active device and security from detection, he simply dropped it off in the lot." Kathy was confident in her conclusions and in her delivery, as she slowed and looked at the faces of her audience leaving an opening for the question she wanted to hear.

"Dr. Puckett," it was Tony who took the bait, "what does that tell us about the addresses on the package then?"

Kathy cast an approving smile in Muljat's direction. "Tony, that's a great question, consistent with the bomber's actions in leaving the bomb behind in the parking lot. His self-protectiveness would indicate he had no direct connection with either Buckley Crist, Jr. or E.J. Smith. Otherwise he would have risked exposure, which is counter to his need for safety, security and secrecy."

"Why did he choose Crist and Smith?" Terry asked, already knowing where Kathy was headed, but wanting to keep the discussion moving along.

"Crist and Smith were both engineering professors at different universities. The Unabomber chose them as representational targets and likely came across their names in a safely incidental manner. He chose them because of what they represented to him, probably in the field of engineering."

"Kathy, the targets started to change to airlines after the first two bombings involving universities so what do those changes tell us about his motivations?" Don Davis, asked a complex question that fit perfectly into Kathy's flow.

"Don, that's important. Motivation in human behavior is not clear cut and not wholly consistent over time. His rationalization for his bombings evolved over time as did the physical and technical evolution of his explosive devices. His early bombs were less planned and more vulnerable to detection than his later ones. His rationalization for selecting targets and sending bombs has evolved as well."

Everyone became engaged in the conversation, scribbling notes, asking for clarification and mentally applying Kathy's principles of human behavior to specific UNABOM events that they were working on. After a short break everyone returned with more questions gleaned from their active sidebars around the room. I appreciated the enthusiasm and momentum the behavioral discussion was generating.

"What can we say, then Kathy, about the early UNABOM events?" I prodded. "I want to take the UNABOM attacks between 1978 and 1987 because I think we can make some key observations. With just a couple of exceptions, the early bombs were built to fit into the environment where they were found or from where they were mailed. There were enticements to the victims to open the packages. In the case of Percy Wood and James McConnell the enticements were the letters that preceded the bombs. The first device had the word 'open' printed on it. The Hugh Scrutton and Gary Wright bombs were disguised as road hazards. The bomb at Northwestern in 1979 and the bombs at Cory hall in 1982 and 1985 were supposed to generate a curiosity that would encourage someone to open them."

Tony Muljat began his question. "I suppose Kathleen that you are omitting the Chicago Circle Campus bomb and the University of Utah Business Classroom bomb because those are the two exceptions to the environmental fit?"

"Yes, Tony, that's right where I am heading," Kathy jumped in before Muljat could finish his thought.

"But what are we to conclude about those bombs? Why did they not fit in? Was it because he didn't want them to? Was it that he made them that way? Or was it something else?"

Tony's non-stop probing and the many ways he asked the question reflected his excitement at the potential answer.

Kathy picked up on the excitement and didn't want to leave everyone hanging. "Tony, by leaving the device in the hallway at the University of Utah, it was open to any passerby and apart from a technical or engineering focus would indicate that our bomber was forced by circumstance or worry to abandon his bomb. The University of Utah event is an echo of the Chicago Circle Campus event," Kathy paused.

I watched Terry write a full page of notes as he listened to our new psychologist. I could tell that he was already thinking how to best utilize this new information that was awakening the behavioral component of our investigation.

Kathy continued emphasizing her point. "The early direct relationship to the environments lends itself to our analysis of the early return addresses on the packages. The North Ravenswood return address on the Percy Wood bomb is a manufacturing neighborhood very similar to the area surrounding Hegenberger Court, which was the return address on the Boeing device. He had to have been comfortable and familiar with engineering departments at universities to repeat their mention through his bombs. And yet, he never returned to the location of Circle Campus—possibly because it was too close to his own daily environment and simply too risky to mention again."

"Kathy, Jim," Terry looked at both of us. "Our investigation has already confirmed some of these points that Kathy is making from a behavioral analysis and now she is making a credible case that the Circle Campus might have been too close to his own daily environment. Aren't we very close to being able to tell the public that we think the origin of the Unabomber is in Chicago? We have to start somewhere to focus our message and I say his roots are in Chicago."

I had been thinking the same thing, although I wanted to refine the message to avoid painting us completely into a corner with the media—and with FBI Headquarters. I waited for the others to add their piece to the conversation, but there weren't any eager takers to pick up the theme.

"Let's hold onto the discussion we just had, hear more from Kathy about the bombings up to and after 1987, and then come back to this idea of how best to use the information to refine our strategy and finally solve this case. I glanced at Kathy and she continued.

"By 1993 the bomber was separated from the environment where he sent his bombs. His targets have become representational. In his letters, the Unabomber now wants to present his self-image as a rational revolutionary attacking the industrial-technological system that he opposes for the good of the public. In reality, he is simply seeking attention for himself.'"

"Fine, then our opening salvo to the public is this—when you think of the Unabomber, think of someone who was likely born and raised in the Chicago area and was active there through at least 1980." Terry was ready and determined to make the leap.

I intervened. "Terry, hold onto the thought. We're not there yet, but we're close. Let's come back to this in a moment." I wanted to slow down to make sure we were ready to rely on this new blend of operational and behavioral assessment as a focal point of our strategy. And, if I would be going out to the public with broad new conclusions and descriptions about the Unabomber, there was the matter of introducing the new composite drawing from the 1987 eyewitness.

"Kathy, putting aside for the moment the motivational aspects and environmental fit you discussed, what can you tell us about the personality we're dealing with?" Don Davis always delivered his questions with significant forethought around every word.

"I think all of you already know that the way he constructs his bombs is illustrative of an obsessive-compulsive personality. They're meticulous and reflect a real pride in the manner in which he assembles them from all the forensic descriptions I've read. People with an obsessive-compulsive personality are very organized and pre-occupied with details. They are perfectionists. They're also rigid in their ideology, unlikely to risk injury to themselves, and polite. An obsessive-compulsive is unlikely to appear very emotional and may be very cold in their appearance to others. Above all, they must be in control at all times."

"How important is control to him Kathy? Does he understand that he must be in control?" Joel asked what turned out to be the last question.

"Look, control is everything to him. In an obsessive-compulsive, while the subject might appear on the outside to be calm and rigid, that's nothing more than a defense mechanism to prevent deep anger and anxiety from spilling over into his life and ruining everything. Take the example of the event you've been discussing—the sighting by an eyewitness at CAAMS in 1987. The Unabomber wore sunglasses and a hood and clearly was trying to disguise his appearance to protect his safety and security. At the same time, while he could control internal actions, he couldn't control external events. The result was his disappearance from the scene for seven years after the witness encounter at CAAMS. His careful and cautious nature drove him underground." Kathy used the question and her answer to put an explanation point on her description of our elusive prey.

Terry stood to signal that time was an issue. "Jim, we're going to need to stop now. The UTF is assembling in the main conference room for our monthly analysis and discussion. Are you ready to roll this out again Kathy?"

Terry was pushing his chair under the table as our meeting adjourned and he was already moving toward the next brainstorming session; this time with the expanded UTF group. Hashing and rehashing had become second nature to him. I assumed it was like this in the scientific world of discovery, where theory was always just one step away from a major break-through. I hoped it would be the same for the UTF.

I asked Terry to stay behind for just a minute as everyone else left the room.

"So Terry, we have the new composite drawing and Max reports that the witness is happy with it. We have an operational reason to go to the public with the composite and now, with Kathy's clinical observations, we seem to have a behavioral confirmation of key points that we've developed operationally. Obviously, you were eager to pursue that discussion during our meeting. What are your thoughts?"

"Hey, I know I'm thinking what you're thinking. It's time.

You should personally go to the public and announce that we believe the Unabomber was raised and attended school early on in Chicago. And, by the 1980 time frame he may have left for Utah, and by the mid-1980's he made multiple appearances in Sacramento and around the San Francisco Bay Area. That message will resonate with the public and help people that unknowingly have been in contact with the Unabomber in any capacity to wake up with the realization that they actually do know this guy or have known him in the past. Going public with the new composite drawing of the suspect will add another facet to draw public attention and will increase the chances that someone will recognize him. And, in follow-up, I will be proposing that we apply the same geographic criteria and timeline to our computer runs on possible suspects based on public data of where they have lived, worked or attended colleges during the relevant time frames. There—that's my updated version of the UNABOM strategy in one big mouthful. Now, I've gotta go."

"Okay, we're on the same path here." I nodded and Terry left. It was the decision-making mode we would employ countless times in the coming months as we closed in on the Unabomber. We would always seek broad input and even look for consensus on occasion, but for a specific change of direction Terry would state his case and the buck would stop with me.

This was to be my final decision alone, as I was not comfortable in putting the Director on the spot by requesting permission for something that you really had to be there to understand. From 3,000 miles outside the Beltway and knowing the increasing pressures being generated there by UNABOM, I knew that the answer would be a resounding 'no.'

I had confidence in Terry, Max, Joel and the dedicated people on the UTF—and, as a recent addition to that UTF class of 1994, Kathy was closing fast. I was swayed by the potential that someone might actually recognize the Unabomber from Jeanne's new composite drawing or that Kathy's behavioral portrait might jog a memory.

After weeks of planning for the likely onslaught of calls to the UTF hotline and carefully timed notifications to key executives at FBI Headquarters and to our UTF law enforcement partners, I conducted a nationally-viewed press conference and released the new drawing and provided an update on recent behavioral assessments of the Unabomber. The reaction from FBIHQ and the Department of Justice was grudging silence until it was clear that the sky had not fallen. This I viewed as a win-win.

The public did not disappoint. There was a huge wave of telephone calls with speculation on a variety of look-alike and sound-alike types—but it was not to be an easy resolution. And, yes—we were second guessed mightily by the media and also by past members of our FBI brethren who were quick to lend their voice and face on national television, criticizing our methods, techniques and conclusions as irrational, immaterial and naive. My philosophy—if you aren't doing enough to be criticized soundly by wannabe's and has-beens, then you aren't moving forward fast enough. This was added motivation that would make the reward all the sweeter if we somehow were able to spring the UNABOM trap.

We would find out months down the road that our operational and behavioral conclusions about the Unabomber were correct and on-point. In fact, he was following along as we put our findings and conclusions out to the public. He offered his thoughts about the CAAMS' sighting and he certainly shared Kathy's beliefs about the anger that raged inside him:

"...The device was placed Feb. 20 and worked the same day; it exploded and probably detonated but the results - as far as we could find out—were not enough to satisfy us. Description (several versions)... The 'composite drawing' did not show any beard, although it did show a small moustache.

"As you know, I have a good deal of anger in me and there are lots of people I'd like to hurt.

"...when I have experienced anger from sources other than technological progress, invasion of wilderness, etc., I often have made a conscious effort to turn this hatred against organized society, technology, etc., because I regard organized society, technology, etc. as my greatest enemy...

"Since committing the crimes reported elsewhere in my notes, I feel better. I am still plenty angry, you understand, but the difference is that I am now able to strike back, to a degree."

CHAPTER EIGHT

EXPLOSIVE PERSONALITIES AT THE FBI LAB

(Bombing investigations were a rarity and are typically run by forensic experts at the FBI Lab Explosives Unit out of FBI Headquarters. This long tradition was counter-productive and didn't work to solve UNABOM. I insisted that the UTF was going to manage all facets of the UNABOM investigation—not the FBI Explosives Unit. It was a painful comeuppance for all).

THE FBI'S UNEQUALLED SUCCESS AS THE WORLD'S GREATEST AND most effective law enforcement agency was foremost in my mind, as I stood at my window and gazed at the bustle of people and vehicles on the streets below my office at the San Francisco Federal Building. On this day, I had been reviewing segments of the historical account of the FBI's original series of UNABOM investigations and I was at once impressed and disappointed. There had been excellent work over the years that stretched back to 1978, especially the early recognition by Agents that this was a serial bomber that possessed hatred, or at least great anger, toward persons associated with universities and airlines.

My frustration stemmed from the lack of any visible organizational plan or strategy over 16 years of start-stop investigations, and it concerned me that little value was given to maintaining continuity of professional leadership in the field or at FBI Headquarters over any appreciable span of time or geography. With some amusement, I imagined that a list of Case Agents, Supervisors, Special Agents-in-Charge, Assistant Directors, Section Chiefs, and Unit Chiefs that were affiliated with the UNABOM case would fill a small town telephone directory.

I wanted to not wallow in excessive 20/20 hindsight, but I had a nagging realization that the FBI culture of management and leadership had not kept pace with the changing face of crime in America. In my thoughts, I quickly backtracked from this assessment as being too broad and settled on a narrower version based on my prior experiences and our recently completed reevaluation of UNABOM. The characterization that I settled on was that the organizational culture of the FBI was practically speaking incapable of dealing with the phenomenon of the lone wolf serial murderer. Make it a serial bomber and the odds against were stacked even higher.

And I count myself as a participating and enthusiastic member of FBI culture for three decades, so I am leery of casting stones. It's just that now, with the shoe on the other foot, I either had to challenge that culture or risk being relegated to the scrap heap of UNABOM history—sixteen years and counting without a solution.

Soon, it was time for the Wednesday morning huddle and Terry stuck his head into my office with the usual reference to coffee and a pastry. He knew where to find the coffee, but I knew that he had missed out on the last morning bun by a mere three minutes—a testament to my own sugar cravings. He found me in an introspective mood and ready to begin without small talk.

"Terry, my priority this morning is to get agreement on a timetable for wrapping up our analysis of the previous bombings and move to a point where we aren't bogged down by the past."

The examination of previous bombings was extremely important, but there had been weeks going on months of reviewing the old cases.

"Let's change the agenda and take control of the game, so to speak."

Terry replied right back, "We are in the game! We've been in the game since last April when you accepted the challenge. But, we do have two additional bombings remaining to review with you. They occurred last year just before you arrived in San Francisco from your cushy assignment in Hawaii."

"Whoa, not everything about Hawaii equals cushy assignment. But, it's a hard point to argue. We can talk about that another time. Anyway, I've already read your summaries for all of the reinvestigations. What else have you got?"

Terry thought for a minute and said, "Fundamentally each of the 1993 bombings are included in the report, but not in the same way. John Conway was our investigator of the first bombing that occurred just across the bay in Tiburon. You know the general details, but John was the first FBI responder to the crime scene and I'd like for you to hear his first-hand account."

"OK, I'm good with that. Set it up and invite the right people to cover the material."

"You got it," Terry answered as he walked out to Janet's desk to calendar the meeting.

Conway gave his presentation in the office conference room during a specially called meeting. Terry invited Postal Inspector Davis and ATF Assistant Special Agent in Charge, Mark Logan to join most of the UTF, Kathy, Joel, Max, he and I to hear what Conway had to say. Agent Conway was on-stage and moderately theatrical as he presented his story. For a complete theatrical experience, John could be seen as an actor at the Marin Playhouse; but today he was all business with his somber account of the time leading up to that day on Thursday afternoon, June 22, 1993.

John began with some background of a UNABOM meeting

some years earlier that he attended with his supervisor, Patrick Webb. There hadn't been any bombings for almost six years since the 1987 CAAMS bombing in Salt Lake City, and the meeting topic was centered on this burdensome investigation that had been passed on to these unholy participants via the back burner. A few in the audience voiced speculation that the Unabomber was dead—killed accidentally while constructing another bomb or perhaps imprisoned for an unrelated crime. In the course of the conference, FBI Laboratory supervisors gave presentations on the forensic evidence, while adding their personal views on the type of psychological characteristics the Unabomber might possess based on the materials used and his workmanship skills.

Of course, they had no professional or academic standing to provide any psychological assessment on the Unabomber. John said that everyone voiced theories about the case, but then the UNABOM supervisor from FBI Headquarters introduced himself and proceeded to direct pointed questions at John and Pat Webb, Conway's squad supervisor and the individual responsible for UNABOM in the 1980's until the establishment of the UTF in 1993, about the lack of progress in the case.

John had long ago been tagged as the FBI 'case agent' for UNABOM and conferences like the one he described had become routine in handling this 'old dog' of a case. Every two years or so, the usual suspects had gathered and discussed its status. Chris Ronay of the FBI Laboratory Explosives Unit usually chaired the meetings, while Tony Muljat from the Postal Inspection Service and Ray Biondi of the Sacramento County Sheriff's Office were perennial attendees. Ray was the senior detective investigating the Unabomber's murder of Sacramento business owner Hugh Scrutton.

John abruptly lowered his tone while portraying this FBIHQ supervisor, who to the surprise of everyone present at that conference, insisted that the UNABOM case should be closed.

Conway mimicked for all of us what the FBIHQ supervisor had said, as we gave him our collective laugh. "After all, he hasn't been heard from in almost six years. I agree with those of you who think he is dead," Conway concluded with emphasis and rolling eyes.

Using the refined techniques of the amateur actor he was, Conway explained how Detective Biondi from Sacramento wouldn't have any of it and interrupted with a stinging comment.

"And Biondi shot back at the Bureau supervisor, 'Sir, since 1985, I've received a telephone call the first Monday of every month from the mother of Hugh Scrutton wanting an update on the progress we're making in finding her son's killer. What do I tell her if the case is closed?'" Conway's mocking tone reflected the anger and passion that had characterized Biondi's own words at the time.

Conway related that he and Webb took the Headquarters supervisor to dinner that night in an effort to reach common ground. The upshot was that Conway and Webb fought off the bureaucrat's directive to close the case, but paid the price of now having to compose and send detailed daily summaries of the investigation to FBIHQ. The tactic was less than subtle and Webb later learned from personal contacts that the Unit Chief responsible for the case was just tossing their daily summaries unread into a box in the corner of his office. In the succeeding months, Conway found himself increasingly isolated while trying to come up with fresh leads and by mid-1993 he was resigned to working UNABOM virtually alone.

Next, Conway turned his story up a notch. He described in great detail where he was and what he was doing the day the Unabomber returned to life with a vengeance. It began for him at the baseball field on the property of the former Hamilton Air Force Base, close to Conway's residence. It was a half hour drive from Tiburon, a small town directly across the bay north of San

Francisco that resembles a small Mediterranean village with hill-sides extending into the sea.

John described the comfort of being with his son, hitting baseballs and running in the open air. But his day off and his moment away from UNABOM was short-lived, as he felt the annoying pulse of his pager. It was the FBI duty agent telling him that a bomb had just exploded at the Tiburon home of Dr. Charles Epstein, a geneticist at the University of California at San Francisco (UCSF). The Unabomber was believed to be responsible.

Conway spoke of being stunned by the news. He quickly gathered up the baseball equipment and drove his son home. Without delay, he turned the car in the direction of Tiburon while still dressed in tank top and shorts. As the FBI's designated UNABOM case agent, it was vital that he get to the scene as soon as possible. While racing south on Highway 101, Conway was notified by radio that Pat Webb was also on his way to Dr. Epstein's home. Webb had been returning home to Marin County from another Bay Area location when he received a call from a radio dispatcher for the Mill Valley Police Department, a former FBI employee, who called to say there had been a serious bombing incident and she thought he'd like to know about it.

Conway was the first FBI agent to arrive. An hour earlier, the Epstein home had been a beautiful location of emerald gardens, a strategically placed hot tub, and an endless view across the bay to San Francisco. Instantly, the idyllic neighborhood of quiet trees and peaceful streets was turned into a crime scene that over-flowed with the lights and sounds of emergency vehicles and the images of first responders moving to secure the premises and offer protection.

Conway told of his deliberate approach through the crowd to the front door, holding his FBI credentials in his hand in hopes of offsetting the sight of his casual attire. While walking past Dr.

Epstein's vehicle, he made a mental note of the license plate—"DNADOC."

Upon reaching the front door, a young redheaded Postal Inspector called out and stopped him abruptly. "This is a crime scene, who are you?" the youthful investigator was serious about his assignment.

Conway knew most of the Postal Inspectors, but he hadn't seen this one before. "Can you get Terry Fail for me?" Conway had dropped the name of a ranking Postal Inspector in San Francisco and his insistence paid off, as he was allowed into the house.

Conway related what he saw—a vicious scene of blown out walls and windows, destroyed countertops, and small fragments of a kitchen table that had been blown throughout the house. As he glanced around the room, Conway reached the painful conclusion that the hiatus of more than six years was over—and the Unabomber sure as hell was not dead.

Inside the kitchen, fragments of a brown mailing envelope were strewn across the kitchen. Partial strips of a mailing label colored red, white and blue were visible, as well as remnants of copper tubing, small metal end plugs, a wooden dowel, an improvised switch and bracket, and nine volt batteries with their outer jackets removed. For a seasoned UNABOM investigator like Conway these were telltale signs of the elusive Unabomber.

Apparently, when Dr. Epstein tugged on the padded envelope's pull-tab to rip open the package, the spring tension was released by the anti-opening switch and battery power was supplied to the improvised hot wire initiator which ignited the explosive charge.

Later, when Dr. Epstein was able, he described what happened. He had arrived at his house and looked at the mail on the kitchen table like a hundred times before. He walked around behind the table, picked up the package, pulled the tab, saw a flash and heard the loud explosion. Fortunately, a chair between his abdominal area and the package absorbed much of the blast or his mid-section would have been torn apart.

Turchie added that the bomb debris had contained a redwood box with a narrow thickness about the size of a videocassette. The same L.C. Smith Corona typewriter used in previous UNABOM attacks had been used to type the mailing label.

Almost immediately, the pace of the resurgent 1993 investigation changed once again. There had hardly been time to digest the Lab forensics report of the Tiburon bomb, when calls from FBI Headquarters flooded in that there had been a similar explosion in the office of a well-known computer scientist at Yale University in New Haven, Connecticut.

Max stood up in the San Francisco office conference room to remind the task force employees that he had handled the UTF interviews of two New Haven FBI agents who had responded to a call from the Yale police during the mid-morning of June 24, 1993. Upon arriving, they found the site of a horrific explosion. Professor David Gelernter of the Computer Science Department had been rushed to the hospital after the blast.

Max related that Professor Gelernter was in his office at Yale on Saturday morning and was opening the mail that had accumulated during his travel the previous week. He came across a package bearing a return address of Mary Jane Lee, Computer Science, California State University, Sacramento, CA 95819-6012. It was addressed to Professor David Gelernter at Box 2158, Yale University, New Haven, CT 06515, and bore a postmark from Sacramento, California dated June 18, 1993. Like the Epstein device, it exploded upon opening.

Max quickly described the similarity in the packaging and bomb debris to that found at the Epstein residence across the continent. Again, the outer package was a brown Jiffy padded mailing envelope containing a homemade redwood box about the size of a videocassette. The fragments from a red, white and blue mailing label with typed addresses, remnants of copper tubing, an impro-vised wooden switch and other debris at the scene made the mes-sage crystal clear that the Unabomber was back in business. While still at the crime scene, the agents received the news that Professor Gelernter had lost several of his fingers as a result of the explosion.

Terry concluded that morning's meeting with a reminder that there was more, much more. Even though we had all heard the account before, there was a highpoint in an otherwise depressing account of the resurgence of the Unabomber. *New York Times* edi-tor, Warren Hogue, was in contact with the FBI in New York City and reported receiving a letter prior to the bombings of Dr. Epstein and Professor Gelernter. He recalled that it had been postmarked from somewhere on the west coast and it said, in part:

"We are an anarchist group calling ourselves FC. Notice that the postmark on this envelope precedes a newsworthy event that will happen about the time you receive this letter...This will prove that we knew about the event in advance, so our claim of responsibility is truthful...Right now we only want to establish our identity and provide an identifying number that will ensure the authenticity of any future communications from us. Keep this number secret so that no one else can pretend to speak in our name. 553-25-4394."

This was a game changer–finally some physical evidence beyond the debris of exploded bombs that might be traced back to the Unabomber. The letter had been turned over to the FBI in New York and then it was forwarded to the FBI Lab to be exam-ined. The letter had been typed on the same L. C. Smith Corona typewriter having Pica style type and 2.54 mm spacing. The Lab then made a fascinating discovery of indented writing, invisible to the naked eye, on the letter. When chemically processed, it bore a cryptic message: "Call Nathan R Wed 7 pm."

What followed was a massive investigative effort by the FBI and law enforcement partners in pursuit of the identity of 'Nathan R' as a possible conduit to the Unabomber.

About a week after the simultaneous 1993 attacks on the west and east coast, Webb and Conway traveled to Washington, D.C., for a meeting on the UNABOM investigation held in one of the many conference rooms at the J. Edgar Hoover Building on Pennsylvania Avenue. By their estimate, about eighty of the FBI's higher ranking officials were in attendance, including Larry Potts, the Assistant Director of the Criminal Investigative Division and George Clow, the FBI's Chief Inspector. The attendees were told that Attorney General Janet Reno directed that a UNABOM Task Force was to be assembled under the direction of the FBI and Inspector George Clow was to be its leader.

Terry halted the meeting at this juncture, providing a brief reminder of the difficulties faced by Inspector Clow and the contingent of FBI Headquarters supervisors that he brought with him from Washington, D.C., to San Francisco to run the UNABOM Task Force. They made their offices in the San Francisco Federal Building and began a serious effort of developing a new strategy that made sense and seemed logical.

Continuing the wrap-up, Terry explained, "The framework of their strategy had a lot of promise, but after a few months dealing with getting the right mix and balance of people from several agencies became as important as the strategy itself. As 1993 turned into 1994, the same problems that had plagued other task forces crept into this newest one. The 'Nathan R' campaign had identified thousands of potential 'Nathan R's' across the country and was a primary focus."

"But one by one, they were all eliminated as being relevant to UNABOM. The offering of a one million dollar reward with much publicity and fanfare had stimulated a huge response from members of the public, who called the toll free number giving information that they hoped would qualify for the reward. But other FBI field offices became burdened with the press of their own workload and Nathan R and other UNABOM leads were considered by some SACs to be make-work projects. Valuable time began to elapse, as other Divisions of the FBI failed to turn around the requests for investigation coming from the new task force in a reasonable time. The result was an investigation that severely slowed down in the execution of its strategy," Terry concluded and another of our exhausting UNABOM meetings had finally come to a close.

On this note, I stood up and thanked Conway and others in the conference room for the detailed briefing. Finally, I could celebrate that we had reached the end of the reinvestigations of every UNABOM event from 1978 to 1993, which had begun as a worthwhile initiative by George Clow and his group of Bureau supervisors. Now, with their departure in early 1994, the fate of UNABOM had come to rest on my shoulders and that of my leadership team.

I spoke quietly to Turchie as I left the room. "It's time to put the full scope of our UTF plan to the test. We're moving beyond the reinvestigations into a new chapter of our choosing."

He responded confidently, "Good. We're ready."

Upon reaching my office, I cracked open a notebook with a stack of memos and notepapers with inked comments that I had jotted down over the course of multiple briefings and discussions with Max and Terry. One was Terry's assessment of the intended strategy of Clow's task force. The initial 1993 Task Force had conducted a historical file review and the re-investigation of each bombing; had initiated new forensic examinations of the evidence; had established the 1-800 Hot line; had assembled a comprehensive UNABOM file with documents from all three Federal investigative agencies; had entered into contracts with various entities securing the $1 million Reward: had conducted an extensive

Victimology project and had begun the Nathan R Project. I sat down to consider the contrasting plans and options that were available to us.

First to think about was whether to continue efforts to track down 'Nathan R,' whoever he might be. The origin of the indented writing on the letter to the *New York Times* could mean nothing or it could be a clue accidentally left behind by the Unabomber when jotting a reminder on an overlying paper. In the end, this UTF project might be a wasteful fishing expedition, as it had already consumed enormous energy and resources. But on this point Terry and I shared a common view—the UTF must retain this project as a top priority in our media announcements. This mysterious puzzle had captured public attention, and was serving our goal of finding help from anyone who might have the memory jogged, by adding 'Nathan R' to the equation. We'd keep this in our plan.

Reading on in Terry's paper I was reminded that Clow's team had begun the reinvestigations of some of the previous UNABOM crimes, but had little to show for it before their departure. Our approach was undertaken with the view that mistakes were always made in fast moving cases and some productive new leads could be found by methodically examining and redoing what had been done before. And, we were firm in asserting that the chance of success was greatly improved by assigning our investigators to travel and personally handle the key interviews and documentary reviews. Nothing put a stamp of approval on this tactic more than Max's persistent re-interviews of the CAAMS eyewitness, which led to a more accurate artist's depiction of the Unabomber.

On the next item, Turchie had made a notation that the FBI Laboratory must take a leadership role in forensic examinations of all of the bombs and their shipping containers. Max had made another big find here—it turns out that no single laboratory saw

100% of the UNABOM materials. What's up with that? We wanted the FBI Lab to take another look to discover anything that investigators might exploit using shoe leather and good police work.

Then, there was the inadequacy of behavioral information about serial bombers in general and regarding the Unabomber in particular. We had seen this as a hindrance to the investigators' ability to perceive the qualities of the person being pursued. The Victimology project initiated by Clow was a step in this direction, focusing on finding a common dimension among the victims as to how or why they were targeted. The investigators needed reliable and ongoing profiling that is updated constantly with each new investigative finding. Surprisingly, we had to build out this capacity on our own volition.

And, looking back to the initiation in 1993 of George Clow's original task force, there was an announcement of a one million dollar reward for information leading to the identification, arrest and conviction of the individual known as the Unabomber. To assist in this effort a toll free number was established to receive information from the public and the response of people from all walks of life was almost overwhelming before a basic computer system was implemented to help manage the data.

A huge challenge that Turchie inherited from the previous task force was receiving, analyzing, and developing an appropriate investigative response to thousands upon thousands of these telephone calls. And, adding immensely to that task, our team was moving forward with planning to add a series of computer-driven initiatives based on a geographic strategy of locales where the Unabomber was believed to have lived, worked, or attended schools of higher learning. The assumption was that someone in the bomb-building business for sixteen years that traveled periodically in Illinois, Utah, and Northern California, who showed skills in craftsmanship, and also typed letters in standard business format to professors—this was someone that likely had paid taxes, owned a car, home or business, or attended colleges in one or more of these States. I tried not to show it too much, but of all the ongoing UTF projects this one held my attention for having the highest potential to produce a winner.

Before leaving for the day, I inked some comments onto Terry's memo and tossed it on his desk with the expectation that this would stimulate a torrent of conversation during our next encounter. And, I welcomed it. We had finally broken clear of the reinvestigation stage and were taking the initiative.

The next morning, as I was tending to my daily routine of field office management I saw that Max had made time on my calendar. He arrived a little after the appointed time and said that Terry and Joel were attending to a personnel issue at the task force and wouldn't be joining our meeting. That struck me as a good opportunity to get to know Max a little better. In meetings, he was an excellent listener and always ready with factual information to add to our discussions. But, one-on-one was a new experience for us. He was often quick to the point, so I made an effort to temporarily direct our conversation to areas that we have in common.

"Max, let's take a load off and have some coffee or a soft drink. There's something I've been meaning to discuss with you—I see from your profile that you're SWAT-trained and a Principal Firearms Instructor, as well as references to some heavy-duty arrests. I'm not asking about how many you might have shot that were evading arrest and attacking you. Those are bang, bang— pure reaction. I know how that works. But, I'm interested in the training and the planning that you have experienced in the most dangerous situations—those involving a subject that is known to be armed and dangerous, someone who may be surrounded by innocents in a public place or barricaded in a building."

Max connected immediately with recent events. "You mean like Waco or Ruby Ridge?"

"That's exactly my point. We're in a massive project to identify the Unabomber, but guess what? We find him and we might not have time to sit down to plan an arrest strategy. Let's talk about 'what if' for a second. I recalled, but didn't mention how circumstances had honed my risk management skills the hard way in Miami during the 1980s. The notorious cocaine cowboys with their automatic weapons routinely and hopelessly outgunned brave FBI agents yelling, 'Freeze FBI' and waving puny Government-issued revolvers in response. It was no longer an effective arrest technique. I knew what it was like to lose two Agents in a gun battle and did not ever want a repeat of that experience.

"Yeah, I get where you're going with this." Max responded. "The Unabomber might be recognized while boarding a plane or the Postal guys might get lucky and run into him while mailing a suspicious package. These things happen all the time and arrest plans are made on the fly—you've done it and I've done it."

I was preaching to the already converted, but I continued anyway. "This case is too big to handle the arrest on a shoestring. Terry and Joel and the other UTF project leaders have their own burden of identifying the Unabomber and I'm certainly not relieving you of that task either. But, I'm giving you a specific assignment now—24/7 to always be planning for every arrest scenario and eventuality.

"Although we don't know who, what, when, or where, I can assure you of the why. If fortunate enough to have a chance at an arrest, we will avoid a confrontational arrest scenario at all costs. I am personally accountable for my own people—and any mistakes will be my own. I will take steps to keep the arrest strategy and execution in our hands—not in the hands of a Headquarters supervisor thousands of miles away. If special personnel and tactics are needed, we have highly qualified Agents in our SWAT team in San Francisco."

I stopped for a breath and could see that Max was on-board with accepting the role of arrest planning. "OK, Max, let's have it. Why did you come to see me anyway?"

He settled into an easy pace of discussing his time on UNABOM and what was important to him personally. "I've been talking to the Agents about the reasons for delays from other offices in getting our leads handled within deadline. For the most part, those leads are being assigned in other offices to Agents with no prior knowledge or experience with UNABOM crimes. We can specify priorities such as the 'Nathan R' project all we want, but the reality is that supervisors in those offices are putting their own case priorities first. I understand the conflicts, but come on—we're trying to solve a major case here.

"As much as time allows, we are having UTF agents travel to these other jurisdictions to coordinate and handle some of the more important and complicated leads ourselves. But, we can't do that for the volume of leads that are coming out daily from the hotline calls or the analysis projects. We need to get the attention of the supervisors in these other offices."

I withheld comment, waiting for Max to finish. While he had the floor, Max picked up on his next point. "And, I have been surprised in learning that bombing investigations—not just UNABOM—have been routinely directed by the FBI Lab's Explosives Unit. They are directing investigations, not just processing the bomb evidence. I've seen documents where bomb examiners have set investigative leads for field offices to handle and others that suggest behavioral characteristics of the perpetrator. These are forensic experts, not case agents."

I interjected a comment here. "That's likely a carry-over from the Hoover days when FBI Lab examiners were required first to serve as Special Agents to become grounded in the conduct of criminal investigations and then they received their Laboratory assignments later. Perhaps they took on a bigger role in directing bombing investigations when most of these cases were solved by forensic examinations and it might have been an easy transition to place increased reliance on the bomb techs to direct an investigation."

I reminded Max of his previous frustration that there was not a centralized FBI Laboratory coordination and that not every shred of UNABOM-linked bomb debris had received a uniform and consistent examination. "To me, these are also serious issues where the Laboratory needs to change—at least for UNABOM. It's difficult to imagine the possibilities that might have been, but our job lies before us and we do have a solid strategy. I know Terry is working constantly to correct all of these issues and he and I are committed to making it work this time."

* * *

Throughout the spring and into the summer of 1994, Turchie and the UTF resurrected every piece of information that could possibly breathe life into the UNABOM investigation. Working with the Postal Inspectors, it was conclusively determined that the Unabomber had physically been in Sacramento on Friday, June 18 and on Monday, June 21, 1993, when the bombs had been mailed to Epstein and Gelernter. The message from 'FC' had been mailed to Warren Hogue of the *New York Times* in the same interval.

The study of postmarks and other postal markings on all of the UNABOM parcels was paying off by confirming the specific dates when the Unabomber was physically in a given location. This was the foundation for our separation of case data into the "Known Facts, Theories, and Fiction of UNABOM," which was designed as a tool to eliminate potential suspects from further consideration if their whereabouts on key dates were in conflict with known Unabomber activity on those dates.

The Postal project that studied the minutiae of addresses on the explosive packages enabled us to understand where the Unabomber was likely getting his mailing addresses. The unique way that Professor Epstein's name and address was applied by the bomber onto his package appeared in only one public listing—the 1992-1993 edition of *Who's Who in America*. It was the only public reference located that described the address as Tiburon-Belvedere, just as the Unabomber had done on his mail bomb. It turns out that the post office facility lies astride the boundary of Belvedere and Tiburon, where it serves both suburban communities under the shared name.

Similar work led to the UTF implementing a survey of libraries and determining the distribution of some books and manuscripts quoted by the Unabomber in his letter bombs, which he had used as an inducement to open the accompanying package. There was a theory advanced that somewhere in America the Unabomber was curled up in a library conducting research for his next attack; and perhaps he'd acted suspiciously or asked questions of the librarian that might give away his identity—if only we could find that person. The theory proved correct! We found the librarian we were searching for working in a small double wide trailer that served as the town library for Lincoln, Montana.

The utilization of computers was rare for FBI criminal investigations in the early 1990's, but quickly became integral to our UNABOM strategy out of sheer necessity. With some 85,000 investigative documents in the rapidly growing UNABOM files, all UTF personnel were trained in the use of a complete text retrieval program ZyIndex for key word searches and this was hailed as a major improvement over card index files and even better then the FBI's Rapid Start computer deployment.

Exclusive to the UTF and not available elsewhere in the FBI, the task force had use of the Sunsparc 10 Computer System that could process upwards of seven million names at a time. The UTF assembled massive lists of individuals relevant to the locations and dates of UNABOM crimes for comparison with driver's license and property records from the states where the crimes occurred. The ultimate objective was to find the one individual with multiple points in common with the Unabomber's movements and activities. Armed with the known geographic migration of the subject from Chicago to the western states and our growing catalogue of "Known Facts," we were moving quickly with a sense of mission and strategy.

* * *

Soon, we would learn just how devious the Unabomber was back in 1993 as he penned in his own words the contempt that he held for his victims:

"I sent these devices during June, 1993. They detonated as they should have. The effect of both of them was adequate, but no more than adequate.

"...In a letter say that, 'scientists consider themselves very intelligent because they have advanced diplomas (advanced degree) but they are not as intelligent as they think because they opened those packages. This will make it seem as though I have no advanced degree.

"Dr. Gelernter: People with advanced degrees aren't as smart as they think they are. If you'd had any brains you would have realized that there are a lot of people out there who resent bitterly the way techno-nerds like you are changing the world and you wouldn't have been dumb enough to open an unexpected package from an unknown source."

CHAPTER NINE

NEUTRALIZING INTRUSIONS FROM FBI HEADQUARTERS

(A Field Office SAC managing any major investigation had to answer to layers of Bureau supervisors at FBI Headquarters. UNABOM demanded bold, decisive and creative decision-making. The only effective solution was bypassing the established bureaucracy).

I WAS IN THE MIDDLE OF THE HALF MOON BAY GOLF COURSE taking a break from UNABOM on Saturday morning, December 10, 1994, when my pager started going off. It was from Turchie's number at the office, so I knew it was important. Maybe we caught the SOB, I thought briefly—always the optimist. We were near the clubhouse, so I signaled my partner that I had business to attend to and turned the cart toward the clubhouse. It took only a couple of minutes to get to a phone.

"Terry, what's up?"

"Jim, we've had another bombing. It's at the home of an advertising executive named Thomas Mosser in North Caldwell, New Jersey."

I interrupted. "Do we know anything about injuries? Was anyone hurt?"

"Mr. Mosser died instantly. Family members were in the

158

house, but no one else was hurt." Terry's voice was solemn as he continued. "I got a call from the SAC up there, Barry Mawn. He's on the scene now. The North Caldwell police reached out to the FBI almost as soon as they got the call about an explosion inside the house, especially after a family member told them that Mosser received a package in the mail with a return address in San Francisco. The police picked up on the possible link to UNABOM and asked Barry how the FBI wanted to handle it. I told Barry to treat this as a UNABOM crime scene, close it down, and wait for Tom Mohnal from the FBI Lab to get there. Then, I called Mohnal and he had already made plans to be on the next plane out to Newark."

Again, I interrupted, with my interest in golf quickly waning. "I've known Barry for a long time and he'll be solid in dealing with us. But, I don't know Mohnal. Let's make sure that the Lab people stick to their bomb examiner role—period."

Terry had something to say on this point. "I'm with you on that. Mohnal is our man right now. He's going to call me as soon as he gets to the scene. He'll take a quick look and come out and tell me what he thinks. We should know in a matter of hours if this is a UNABOM attack. But, it has all the indicators of one."

It wasn't a time to belabor the point, but with the crime scene a couple thousand miles away and this being the FBI's premier unsolved investigation that was about to be linked to its second fatality—I knew instinctively of the minefield of media frenzy and bureaucratic second-guessing that was coming. The next few hours would be a crucial test for the UTF.

"Terry, if this is another UNABOM killing there will be intense heat from the Washington bureaucracy and the New York media like you have never felt. You and I have to hang tough on this. There's no one in the FBI that has anywhere near the case expertise and ability to solve this case than our UTF people. Maybe Barry and his New Jersey agents will get lucky and catch the guy in the next day or two; I certainly hope so. If not and we don't take control of the situation, the case strategy will be thrown aside in a rush to gather any low hanging fruit. Then, after hitting dead-end after dead-end, they'll dump it back on our plate. No thank you! Been there, done that."

My decisions over the past nine months flooded into my thoughts: First, by stepping out on a limb by assigning Counterintelligence-trained Turchie to head this major criminal investigation, then, by centralizing everything contrary to the traditional field office hierarchy, and, by pushing back on the quality of profiling resources assigned to the case, and finally, by criticizing the FBI Laboratory. I began to imagine all manner of consequences that might be coming home to roost. I had upset fragile egos in the FBI and likely among our UTF partners.

As my thoughts sank in, I could almost hear the knives being sharpened. There were those who would use the murder of Mr. Mosser as an opportunity to blame my management style, decisions, and approach to the case.

Terry's response was sober and deliberate. "I knew the risks when I took the assignment and I understand what we have to do. The main thing now is to hear from Mohnal to confirm this was the Unabomber. We're working it and I have started to move some UTF teams into place.

"I've alerted Neil Oltman and Tony Muljat. They're booked on a flight to New Jersey and will be there tomorrow early. That will give the UTF an essential presence at the crime scene. I've been talking to FBIHQ every few minutes and I'm staying in touch every hour with Barry Mawn. As soon as I hear from Tom Mohnal or if something breaks, I'll call you."

"Okay. That works for the time being. Have you let Max know?"

"I have. Max is out on a weekend trip and will be back Monday morning, unless needed sooner. I've got the phone number to his hotel room, so he and I can stay in contact."

I agreed and we terminated the call until more information was forthcoming from New Jersey. I lost any desire to continue playing golf. In the five minutes it took to drive to my home, I struggled with wanting to drive immediately to the office in San Francisco where I could relieve my tension by barking orders. But, I knew all too well that would be counter-productive. My personal challenge was to stay sufficiently in the background to allow Turchie space for the tactical coordination of the UTF, while interacting directly with him and the leadership team in brainstorming and planning our investigative strategy. Taking over and giving orders when the going got tough would have been so much easier for someone of my temperament.

As a distraction while waiting for word from Turchie and Mohnal, I began to mentally review the bureaucrat's case that would be made against our formula for managing UNABOM. The prescribed Bureau way would have required that Terry and I communicate directly and often through mid-level supervisors at Headquarters, who would then consult with Unit Chiefs and Section Chiefs and perhaps a Deputy Assistant Director to decide a tactical issue in the field or to settle a dispute between field office commanders. Often, there would be interim consultations with lawyers in the U.S. Department of Justice to arrive at a prolonged and wordy decision. That process was functional for the majority of FBI cases; but it was downright ineffective in fast moving investigations.

I often tell the story of how I was placed in similar pressure situations in Miami, when I was directing the FBI response to an aircraft hijacking or one of several kidnapping cases. My boss, Joe Corless, was a seasoned New York agent that had been a supervisory Agent at the bank robbery, turned movie, Dog Day Afternoon. He proved to be an excellent teacher and mentor.

His advice to me when faced with a crisis situation and the inevitable call comes into your command post from the FBIHQ supervisor—Joe had said, "Get your youngest, most inexperienced rookie agent and establish him on the phone as your only communication link to Headquarters. That will keep them both out of the way and you can get on with the important business at hand."

And, from my own Agent assignments in the back alleys of Los Angeles and Long Beach Harbors and on the streets of Miami, I had learned and retained an important truth in dealing with gutter rats and bureaucrats alike. The premise is "when outgunned, your strongest ally in avoiding a fight is to display an aura of confidence and professionalism." This was particularly true in the years before SWAT teams could be called in to bail you out of trouble.

There was and is immeasurable power associated with the command, "Freeze, FBI" or any number of variants of that theme. The bad guys usually assumed that you had more manpower or firepower than they could see. I knew this was about to be tested again on the bureaucratic front—probably within the week.

I felt good that the Special Agent in Charge in Newark was Barry Mawn, a seasoned street agent before getting into management. He'd served in San Francisco as an Assistant Special Agent in Charge and we all knew each other. He would be a good ally in supporting the concepts of the UTF and it didn't hurt that Barry shared my knack for the unconventional and challenging the system. But, there was likely to be enormous pressure exerted on him from the U.S. Attorney, the Department of Justice, and HQ's Criminal Division to take over the investigation of such a high profile murder case with the compelling signature of a serial bomber.

Terry had seemed calm and deliberate in our phone call, but I could wait no longer. I placed a call into the office and had the duty agent track down Turchie, who was eating a sandwich that someone had brought in.

I picked up on our previous conversation. "Okay, one more thing. Have you let Rick Smith know what happened? For now, the UTF shouldn't be making any media statements at all, but make sure Rick is aware what's going on and to expect to begin receiving a flood of media calls if our guy really did this. Also, we will need to prepare and coordinate a public statement with Barry and the Bureau so there is a consistent message. Let Rick know to keep a lid on saying anything substantive about Mosser until we have that."

Turchie again assured me that he was on top of it and Rick was on notice and he would call as soon as he heard anything new.

I didn't want this to turn into a significant loose end that hadn't been coordinated at the outset. Rick Smith was my media coordinator in the San Francisco office and he was experienced and well known to the local media. Rick understood the delicacy and balance that's required in high profile investigations and I was confident in his ability at handling his job, so we could do ours. There would be no opportunity for a "do-over" in a national news story of this magnitude, and watch out if this latest murder is the work of the Unabomber.

I had just about convinced myself that I could make it to the office before the bomb examiner's report was called in from New Jersey. But, then my wife called out that Terry was on the phone and said it was urgent. I grabbed the phone. "What've we got?"

"Hi Jim, I got a call from Mohnal when he arrived at the Mosser residence and before he entered the house. He has linked up with Barry Mawn and met the on-scene police and fire department commanders. The new information is that the house has been sealed since the explosion and he's taking precautions on the possibility that there has been a buildup of gas inside the house. No one has gone in or out for quite awhile. The family was evacuated several hours ago and Mr. Mosser's body is still inside."

I expressed concern about Tom entering the house before the gas leak was checked out, but Terry continued. "He said that he's fine and then he left to go into the house. We'll have to wait for another callback."

Now, I was really frustrated that I hadn't left immediately for the office. "OK, but you keep an open line to me until that call comes in." While waiting, Turchie said that he had an appreciation for what Mohnal was facing inside the house. As a rookie FBI agent in Portland, Turchie had investigated two murders on an Indian reservation and the grisly crime scene had been hard to take and those horrible memories were obviously still fresh in his mind. That aside kicked off an exchange of "war stories" between Terry and I, which is what agents often do to kill time and reduce tension.

In about fifteen minutes, Mohnal called Terry, with me hearing only Terry's side of the conversation. When he hung up, Terry immediately caught my attention by launching into a description of how much Mohnal's voice had changed in the short time between calls. "His voice wavered and even over the phone, it was obvious that Mohnal was visibly shaken by what he had seen in the house."

In a nutshell Mohnal had said, "Terry, this was the Unabomber. There's absolutely no question in my mind. We'll get the full Evidence Response Team into the house as soon as we're sure it's safe, but there's no doubt in my mind that it's him."

No sooner was Terry off the phone with Mohnal, than he was back on with me. The only information that he added was that Tom was pretty sure it would take a full day on Sunday and maybe longer to fully process the crime scene.

Next, Terry shared some breaking news from FBIHQ. "The Criminal Division is scheduling a conference call with a boatload of Headquarters Supervisors on Monday. I'm planning to be in the office tomorrow with Joel, so we can hopefully have a quiet Sunday to plan out a schedule of leads for Monday and next week."

I didn't like the sound of that at all, but I wouldn't trouble Turchie with my concerns until tomorrow. "Well, alright. Let's keep talking if something new develops. Is there anything more you can think of?"

"I can't think of anything right now." Terry was stressed and tired; I could hear it in his voice, and so was I. After less than an hour of paperwork, I decided to call it a day in favor of a bright and early start.

When Terry and Joel showed up at the office early Sunday morning, I was already there with coffee in hand.

"What?" I enjoyed the incredulous look on their faces.

Sunday would be our only remaining day to think and plan without the noise that was already ramping up from Headquarters. Sunday news shows were already full of the Mosser story and speculation of another Unabomber hit was rampant. By Monday morning, Headquarters would be in high gear responding to urgent inquiries from the national media and the likes of The Attorney General's Office, Senators and Congressional staffers, the Chief of the Postal Inspection Service, and the Director of the Bureau of Alcohol, Tobacco and Firearms and Explosives, et al.

I had served two stints at FBIHQ and the drama staggered the imagination. Before all of that could get started, we made good use of the day. When Tony Muljat and Neil Oltman arrived in New Jersey, they started their interviews of Mrs. Mosser and other family members and business associates to find out as much as they could about Thomas Mosser's personal and professional histories. They called Terry and Joel throughout the day using a conference telephone and I listened in as time permitted.

"Neil, start with the package delivery and tell us how it went down," I directed Oltman.

"Mr. Mosser had been traveling and just got home the day before yesterday. His wife had left the mail addressed to her husband for him to open when he returned. He was in the kitchen with the mail and had put it down for a minute while his young daughter was running around."

"How old are his girls Neil?" Terry asked.

"Kimberly is thirteen and her sister Kelly is fifteen months," Neil answered, paused and then continued.

"The family was discussing going out to buy a Christmas tree. The girls were still in their pajamas. Susan Mosser rounded them up and off to their room to get dressed. As near as we know, Mosser grabbed a package that had his name on it and bore a San Francisco return address. It exploded violently when he began opening it."

Neil continued to report that the mailing label was largely intact with the return address being from an H.C. Wickel, Department of Economics, San Francisco State University, San Francisco, CA, 94132. The address on the package was written as Thomas J. Mosser, 15 Aspen Dr. N Caldwell, NJ, 07006-4555.

"Hi Jim and Terry," Tony Muljat suddenly interjected. "Tom Mohnal just came out of the Mosser house for a minute, so Neil went to see him and get more information. Let me fill you in on the package while we wait for him to come back. 'Priority Mail' was stamped on the outside of the white cardboard box. There were four one dollar Eugene O'Neill stamps and three twenty-five cent Flag and Cloud postage stamps used to mail the package. The Eugene O'Neill stamps were from a coil as opposed to being what we call sheet stamps. These particular coil stamps weren't made for sale after January of 1991, but post offices kept selling their supplies until they were out. The Flag and Cloud stamps were from a booklet version."

"Tony, have you been able to find out where the package was mailed from?" I was getting impatient to give our San Francisco based UTF agents something to start working on at the point of origin—which appeared to be from San Francisco.

I looked at Terry and gestured that we had to get it moving. "We need to get on these leads," I told him as Tony continued.

"Yes, I talked to Paul Wilhelmus. He and several other Postal

Inspectors are going to be contacting postal stations and substations today and tomorrow and all week until we come up with something. You know, Jim, the package bore a cancellation stamp impression and we may be able to trace it to the post office that made that mark on the package," Tony said as he wrapped up.

"Good," anything that sounded like action was what I was after. This was a serial murder case and every minute we didn't do something the Unabomber was getting further from our grasp and crawling back into his hole.

While we were talking with Tony, Turchie was pulled away to take a phone call in another room. It was Neil and he was upset at being stuck in New Jersey while the Unabomber was obviously in or around San Francisco.

When Terry returned, he said with some exasperation that Neil was visibly shaken by all that he had seen, heard and been exposed to during his short time in New Jersey. "His plea was to get back to the Bay Area, where there are important leads to be covered. He is of a mind that Mohnal and Barry Mawn have charge of the crime scene search, so he doesn't see a need to be in New Jersey."

Terry told us that he held firm in telling Neil, "You're the only FBI Agent there representing the UTF and we need you there as our point of contact. We'll revisit this after we have a conference call with the Bureau tomorrow, but not now." It seemed now that even Terry was getting impatient and on edge.

Our Sunday grew even busier as Don Davis, showed up in the office to coordinate the efforts to locate the station where the Unabomber had mailed the package to Tom Mosser.

"We're working on a mock-up of the package based on the descriptions coming from New Jersey. The sooner we can get out to these stations the fresher people's memories will be," he explained.

That sounded fine to me. I left to get caught up on some other work while we waited for a status call from Mohnal. Joel retrieved me from my office when the call came in and we rejoined Terry who was on the speaker phone in his office.

"Hi Tom," I announced to Mohnal. "Joel and I just walked in."

"Oh, hello Jim. Let me catch you up on what we've been talking about. I was telling Terry that the bomb was made to fit inside an aluminum pipe. Both ends were sealed with metal plugs and locking pins secured the plugs to the pipe. An improvised wooden switch was used just like in the Epstein and Gelernter devices. The switch was built to fit into a bracket made from aluminum with metal pins and brass screws designed to allow the switch to pivot. From the fragments of Douglas fir, redwood and particle board, it looks like the bomb was inside a wooden container and then placed in a corrugated cardboard box for mailing."

"Was FC stamped on the end plugs?" Terry interrupted.

"No, we haven't found FC on anything. But, again, there's no question from the components and the switching device in particular, that this is a UNABOM device."

"Well, it's interesting that he didn't put FC on this bomb, or it got completely blown to bits," Terry observed.

"Again, we're still processing the scene and it's one of the worst I've experienced. In addition to all the shredded wire that acted as shrapnel during the explosion, this time he added green colored paneling nails for extra shrapnel. We've found remnants everywhere—in the kitchen, in the adjoining room, in the living room, in the walls and the ceiling. One of the nails even went through an iron skillet hanging above the counter. The force of the blast did ungodly damage to Mr. Mosser's head and upper body. I've not seen anything like it."

"This Unabomber guy is getting more aggressive than ever—and downright evil. He breaks seven years of silence with Epstein, Gelernter, and now this." I let it trail off and then added, "Do you have anything else to tell us Tom?"

"Not really. We'll know a lot more when all of this evidence gets shipped to the lab and we can start examining every little piece."

"Okay, if that's it, then we'll talk again very soon—probably sometime tomorrow," I concluded the call and looked over at Terry and Joel.

Terry looked at his notes from the series of calls that had kept him busy all day and proceeded to call out a list of leads that were beginning to pile up. If our strategy was on the right track, every move we made from this time forward had to bring us closer to the Unabomber.

Terry began reeling off the next steps. "We'll assign agents to check on the significance of H.C. Wickel, the return addressee on the package. We'll identify every Wickel we can find and make sure we eliminate anything that isn't relevant. I'll coordinate with Don Davis to keep the Postal Inspectors working non-stop to find where and when this bomb was dropped into the mail stream. Whatever comes from that, we'll be on it. We also need to know whether those green paneling nails can be traced to a specific retail source, so I'll make certain that Tom knows to work that angle when he gets back to D.C. We'll get the word to the whole UTF tonight that we'll be giving a briefing tomorrow morning at 7:30 a.m. on what we know up to now about the bomb and the mailing package."

When Terry stopped talking, I got up to leave the room—but paused to urge both he and Joel to keep everything moving at hyper speed and to keep me up to speed on any important developments.

"Tomorrow is going to be nothing but pressure, especially that conference call with the Bureau. So be ready; be prepared to take on their questions and to have some answers—but don't BS your way around the tough questions. It's better to say 'We don't know; but we'll get back with the answer.' Be professional and exude confidence; that's what it takes. In fact, don't even worry about the Bureau, as the pressure they put on you will pale in comparison to what you're going to be getting from me." I smiled with the intention to lighten the tension, but from the look on their faces my comment missed the mark.

With that said, I turned to leave the room.

The westbound Sunday traffic was light, as most of the vehicles were returning over the hill following a day trip to Half Moon Bay. But, that was not the case on Monday morning as commuters alternately idled and revved their engines on the two roads to the outside world—one northward along the coast and across Devil's Slide; the other eastward over the coastal range to intersect with I-280. I had left extra early to avoid most of this, but I was not alone in that strategy. I had plenty of time to contemplate the upcoming conference call and to wonder what level of Bureau officialdom might be attracted to it.

That's exactly what played out during our conference with FBIHQ on that December morning when we discussed the wanton murder of Thomas Mosser.

Don Davis from the Postal Inspection Service and Max joined Terry and I as we placed our call to the Bureau on a conference phone. Lining up on the other end was Bill Perry, the Deputy Assistant Director of the FBI's Criminal Division who was a former colleague of mine in the Miami Office; Dennis Weaver, the temporarily assigned Bureau supervisor for UNABOM along with his boss Howie Apple, the Unit Chief over the UNABOM case, and other assorted FBI supervisors whose roles were unfamiliar to me. The questions flowed to us in a torrent, with another question thrown at us before we even finished answering the previous one.

Terry took most of the questions, as I quickly tired of justifying our decisions on one thing and then another from the outset of the call. We had important work to do, without engaging in what amounted to an educational call for a flock of Bureau officials. It was evident that they were wary of being second-guessed by the Director or the DOJ Attorneys, who would be seeking answers of their own. Most of their questions had already been answered, if they had read the stream of UTF reports.

Then, a question of a different sort came out of left field. I was particularly irked that it wasn't directed at me. I had no idea how many other people were sitting in on the other side of the conference call, but from the tone in the individual's voice, it was pretty apparent that had we all been in the same room, he would have completely ignored me and turned to Terry to say, "Terry, we've been discussing this here at the Bureau and think that you need to get out to Newark to help run the investigation over there."

This was an absurd notion that my head of the UNABOM Task Force should have to fly three thousand miles to supervise the Mosser portion of UNBOM which, as terrible as it was, constituted only a part of the continuing investigation. Here it comes, I thought; history is repeating itself—stop what you are doing and fly off to the scene of the latest bombing. Did someone back there forget or overlook that the Unabomber was actually in San Francisco when he mailed the bomb? He's not in New Jersey; probably has never been in New Jersey. I'd finally heard enough and motioned to Terry to keep quiet when he started to respond.

I answered, slowly and deliberately. "No, no, Terry stays here. I need him to run the UNABOM Task Force. We've got hundreds of leads and calls coming in from all over the country as a result of the bombing and we are keeping to our overall strategy. We already have UTF Agents on the ground in New Jersey and it would be disruptive to send Terry there." The tone and volume of my voice signaled that I was tired of being second-guessed.

"Well Jim, I understand that. But, we don't even know what kinds of leads you're talking about and we don't know...." I immediately interrupted whomever it was that was about to pose a question, or give another order.

"No," I exclaimed. "You don't understand. Louie put me in charge of this case and I'll be in charge until relieved by the Director. We'll continue to keep the Bureau informed in the normal course of business, as Terry has been doing up to this point."

Someone else offered, "Maybe what we need is to set aside three times each day where we can have these calls and then we'll have the information we need back here...."

"Are you kidding me?" I interrupted again, "We'll be spending more time getting ready for calls and feeding you information than we have to spend on the investigation."

"As a counter proposal, how about you send us a morning teletype, with a written summary of the high points from the day before to supplement your current Daily Summaries. We like reading those," it was a different voice than I'd heard up until now.

"No, I'm not...."

This time it was Bill Perry, of the FBI's Criminal Division, who stopped me. "Jim, why don't you and I talk a little later about some of this," and his tone said it was not a question.

I'd known Bill a long time and I respected his intervention before I really spun out on these people. I agreed with Bill that we'd have a follow-up call. I looked over at Terry, who could see that I was pretty hot and then another controversy flared up. Now, it was Max who was hot under the collar.

While trying to accommodate and answer an earlier question, Max was summarizing some of the prominent UNABOM leads and he had mentioned the indented writing developed by the FBI Lab on the letter from the Unabomber to the *New York Times* in 1993, "Call Nathan R, Wed 7 pm." That information had been widely disseminated through law enforcement channels and in a direct appeal to the public after the June 1993 bombings in an effort to gain the public's support. Director Freeh had gone on television and personally made the appeal.

"Hey, pal, just a minute," a voice of FBIHQ innocence interrupted Max. "Just who's this Nathan R. guy anyway?"

With that Max erupted, jumping from his chair and looking at Terry, then at me. "How are we supposed to work a case when you people don't even have a clue about the facts of the investigation? How can you not know about Nathan R?"

Max was steaming, he was so upset. And, Terry was the only one still seated in front of the telephone, trying to complete the conference call. Max flashed anger directed at the FBI supervisors on the other end of the line and stated to no one in particular that he didn't want his time wasted by people who didn't know the case.

I needed a quick solution before this went too far and I leaned down to the speaker with my finger on the disconnect button. "Look, Bill, we've been on the phone a long time and things are moving fast. I'll call you later this evening." With that comment directed at Bill Perry, I pushed the button and terminated the call.

"Gosh, Jim, that went well. I didn't even have time to say goodbye," Terry leaned back in his chair as he laughed. Max was still on fire. I left to go to my office and Terry walked off with his hand on Max's shoulder—part restraint and part calming. It was a scene between Max and Terry that would be repeated many times in the pursuit of the Unabomber.

Bill Perry and I were no strangers to fast moving investigations and we did connect by phone, as agreed. We started a useful dialogue without all of the noise associated with the conference call. Later, I received a call from Director Freeh's office arranging his trip to San Francisco with very little lead-time, which was out of the ordinary. It seemed that Louie wanted to meet with all of the management team, including officials from other agencies involved in UNABOM, and I greeted that request with optimism.

Before his arrival, a directive was put forth that after the management meeting he wanted to meet personally with the working members of the UTF. The only supervisor that he wanted with him in that meeting was Terry, which annoyed me and struck me as a bush-league management tactic. But, it also signaled to me that Louie and the entire FBI was feeling pressure to solve UNABOM. I surmised that Louie wanted to find out if everything possible was being done by the UTF. I expected a personal call to his executive in charge of UTF—but it didn't come. My perception told me that danger was approaching.

A second fatality had occurred and there remained little to no progress in identifying and arresting the person responsible. This spoke volumes to me, as I pondered the extent of Louie's lack of confidence in his own command staff that he had to personally test the waters and find out for himself. It did sting that he had not called me personally, relying instead on personal assistants to make all the arrangements.

The time for his visit came quickly and, as expected of any SAC worth his salt, I was at the airport gate to meet the Director on his arrival. Louie was cordial, but brusque in his greeting. Definitely, he was not the same person that handed me the UNABOM torch in his office a few months earlier. He had a carry-on bag and a heavy-looking leather briefcase, but he rebuffed my offer to carry one or the other bag. His demeanor was approaching rudeness and I accepted it for what it was—trouble for yours truly.

I did take great pleasure in walking alongside the mighty Director of the FBI next to his legal counsel, Howard Shapiro, and John Behnke of his security detail, as he chafed under those heavy bags. It was all the more pleasing that we were walking the full length of the longest concourse at SFO. In this job, you have to accept the little pleasures where you find them.

Back at the office, that first meeting with all the agency supervisory types seemed to go about as well as expected. The wild card that we hadn't thought about was that some of the agency heads and number two guys they brought with them to meet Director Freeh had never attended even one of our UNABOM briefings and knew almost nothing about the case.

When Terry and I had a moment to talk, he said what I was already thinking. "Where in the heck did all those people come from? Half of them, I've never seen before and some of the others only show up at UTF briefings about once a month and have no idea what we're doing to find this guy. I hope the Director sees through the charade and doesn't get the wrong idea."

Later, as I watched Terry and Louie leave for the closed door meeting with UTF members only, I knew that I personally, and the UTF had a lot riding on what happened in that room. All the work that Terry and I had done to design a new UTF would rise or fall based on the impressions that Director Freeh gained from the investigators working the case and his instincts on how they felt about their leaders. What a way to run a railroad! That was the ultimate question that Louie was here to address–whether he could trust me to continue managing what was rapidly becoming the Number One investigation in the FBI and also whether Terry was the right point man to carry it through. It was a helpless feeling and not one where I would nominate Louie as Manager of the Year.

I was excluded from the room and I did not like it one bit. Later, Terry and Max provided me with a detailed and colorful description of their first-ever interaction with a Director of the FBI:

"Director Freeh," Terry started as they began their short walk down the hallway.

"No, no, Terry, call me Louie," he had quickly corrected my young supervisor.

"Louie," Terry did as he was told, while his brain kept telling him, no, no, you don't call the FBI Director by his first name. "We're all really glad you came. I've let everyone know that they should feel comfortable talking to you however they wish to about the case. We're all pretty honest with each other and I've always encouraged them to be truthful with me, so I don't know exactly what you should expect in there. There's a lot of tension with the murder of Mr. Mosser, but we're confident we have the right strategy in place to find this guy."

As Director Freeh and Terry walked into the squad room and the doors closed behind them, the next two hours seemed the longest of my entire career. About thirty members of the San Francisco based UTF were on hand to hear what the Director had to say about UNABOM. After some introductions, Director Freeh thanked everyone for their hard work and then, during several uninterrupted minutes, he spoke to them with an amazing command of the known facts of the UNABOM investigation. He ended by telling them that we had his full support. There would have been a big "whew" on my part, but I didn't know about this for sometime later.

This is how the rest of the meeting proceeded:

"I've reviewed the UNABOM strategy that Terry and Jim have put together. It's a good plan." He cast a nod in Terry's direction, which brought him instant credibility. "These cases are rarely solved by luck—they're solved through strategic planning and the UTF has the right strategy," Louie announced.

As he finished, the squad room was completely silent. He asked for questions. Still, there was silence. Never have thirty criminal investigators representing three Federal agencies been so quiet. He asked again, but the second time he phrased his inquiry differently.

"Are you facing any obstacles in trying to do the job or is anything inhibiting your investigation that I should know about?"

When he stopped, the room went from silent to a rumble of noise that was almost sullen. Max took it as his cue to speak.

"Director Freeh, several of us here in the room have served on the UTF since its inception in June, 1993. We've put together a list of things that have been inhibiting to our investigation. I've been asked by the squad to present those things to you," Max was calm, but voiced considerable emotion as he spoke.

"First, we have a problem getting UNABOM leads covered on a timely basis. Our UTF leads sent to other FBI Divisions have deadlines of ten days. Those deadlines are being ignored."

"So," the Director stopped Max, "do you have an example?"

"Yes. An example is the coverage of our 'Nathan R' leads. As you know, 'Call Nathan R, Wed 7 pm,' was the indented writing found on the note to the *New York Times*. One of the foundations of the task force in 1993 was to identify anyone and everyone across the country with such a name. We've identified hundreds of Nathan R's and sent out leads to have them interviewed. When I called a Los Angeles supervisor to find out why they hadn't completed our Nathan R leads I was told that Los Angeles management sets priorities for their Division and they'll do our leads when they get around to it. As field agents, there isn't anything we can do to get the leads covered and we need your help."

"Okay, what else?" the Director was engaged.

"The FBI Lab doesn't conduct the examinations we request them to do in a timely manner."

"Do you have an example?" the Director cut to the chase once again.

"We asked urgently that a videotape from a San Francisco Post Office be reviewed and the still photos enhanced. When we didn't get what we had asked for after it was promised, the Explosives Unit told us the person who does that job had to catch a ride with his car pool and couldn't do the review or he would miss his ride home. The same unit has told us they are overworked and simply unable to respond to our requests promptly. The final point about the Explosives Unit is that they think they are directing this investigation, instead of responding to the priorities and leads of the UTF. It creates a constant tension."

"Yes, yes. What else?" Director Freeh cast a glance across the room to Special Agent John Behnke of his security detail and Howard Shapiro, the FBI's Chief Legal Counsel. Both men had quietly walked into the meeting as it started and posted themselves discreetly behind the group of UTF investigators. Had Louie not looked beyond the group and straight at his two most trusted assistants, they might never have been noticed.

Turchie winced and I was happy not to be there after I heard his account of the meeting. Max was relentless as he continued. "We've been very unhappy with the level of support provided to the UTF by the Behavioral Science Unit. They've failed to provide an updated profile, haven't completed a comprehensive review of the sites of UNABOM events, and have never responded to a request the task force made for them to do an analysis of the book Ice Brothers. That was the hollowed out book sent to Percy Wood by the Unabomber in 1980 along with a letter that he should read that socially significant book. We ended up having to go to the other side of the house right here in San Francisco to get someone capable of helping us get this work done."

"The other side of the house," Director Freeh repeated as a question. Kathleen Puckett and several other UTF members laughed.

"Yes. Kathy Puckett had provided behavioral assessments for terrorist and espionage subjects on behalf of the Counterintelligence Division—the other side of the house," Max answered.

"I see. Is there anything else on your list?" The Director didn't smile, but came close. He had long since gotten the picture.

Max was not to be deterred. "Well, one more thing, yes. There isn't any continuity at FBI Headquarters with the Supervisory Special Agent who is responsible for UNABOM. There have been several people in that job and we end up answering to people who don't know the case." Max finished by giving the Director some colorful insight into the conference call after the Mosser bombing.

Director Freeh thanked Max and the UTF and looked over at Turchie. "My office will coordinate with Terry and we'll get those issues addressed," and with that the two and a half hour meeting with the UTF was over.

While that meeting was still ongoing I had managed to ask one of Louie's assistants what dinner plans were needed for the evening and the surprising response was that the Director and his team wanted to have pizza brought in to eat with the UTF agents. Then, as the meeting was breaking up, the same assistant showed up in my office and said there was a change of plans. Now, Louie wanted to accompany the supervisory staff and me to dinner at a local restaurant.

"Louie is partial to small, family-owned Italian restaurants like he finds in New York and would very much like to sample San Francisco's pasta and sourdough bread."

With that change, I knew that we were in the clear and I quickly tasked Janet to find the perfect cafe for Louie. She did such a good job that we received notice in Herb Caen's renowned column that week—albeit tongue in cheek about FBI men-in-black-suits.

The next day, John Behnke and Howard Shapiro cornered Max and Joel and spent half a day discussing the investigation and delving into some of the issues raised by Max the day before. Afterwards, they visited Terry in his office and closed the door.

What Terry learned was that Behnke's relationship with Director Freeh had begun years earlier when Louie was a Federal prosecutor and John was a first office agent in Atlanta, who was designated the case agent for the murder/bombing of U. S. District Court Judge Robert Vance in Alabama on December 16, 1989. Judge Vance was assassinated when opening a mail bomb sent to him by an individual eventually identified as Walter Leroy Moody, Jr., who was seeking vengeance over a prior conviction.

And, Howard Shapiro first met Louis Freeh after graduating from Yale Law School. He eventually worked as a prosecutor with Freeh in New York on the landmark case that broke the back of the Mafia's heroin distribution enterprise in the United States and

Italy, resulting in twenty-one convictions in American courts and over three hundred convictions in Italy, effectively destroying the Mafia there. The case became known as the "Pizza Connection." Shapiro later worked on the Judge Vance bombing as well.

Over the years, Freeh, Behnke and Shapiro had formed an unbreakable trust born of hard work, long hours, and the pursuit of justice.

The meeting inside Terry's office in San Francisco between him, John Behnke and Howard Shapiro put the Director of the FBI solidly behind the UNABOM strategy Terry and I had developed and was implementing and would be the start of big changes in Terry's future in the Bureau as well. "Terry," Behnke said as they began to talk, "here are a couple of phone numbers. Hold on to them and anytime you feel you need help from our end, you call us. The Director feels real good about what he saw here and you can count on our support."

It was the beginning of a unique relationship within a highly structured organization that in effect blessed our own bypassing of that very structure. We didn't know it then, but this team at the top of the FBI organizational structure was about to provide "cloud cover" for our efforts as we broke the rules and changed the game to identify and successfully arrest the Unabomber.

In a matter of months, the Unabomber unleashed a string of communications to the public, all the while taunting the FBI and adding a significant new dimension to the chase. In one letter, he utilized the inclusive "we" in reference to F.C., which was an attempt to confuse his pursuers and also to appear larger than life to the public that he had begun to court with his writings:

"We blew up Thomas Mosser last December because he was a Burston-Marstellar executive. Among other misdeeds, Burston-Marstellar helped Exxon clean up its public image after the Exxon Valdez incident. But we attacked Burston-Marstellar less

for its specific misdeeds than on general principles. Burston-Marstellar is about the biggest organization in the public relations field. This means that its business is the development of techniques for manipulating people's attitudes. It was for this more than for its actions in specific cases that we sent a bomb to an executive of this company."

Aerial photograph taken over the Gehring Lumber Mill property showing T.K.'s cabin at the base of the mountain, mostly hidden from view by the forest.

The road above T.K.'s cabin, showing FBI SA Dave Weber and USFS agent Jerry Burns on snowmobiles, preparing to conduct a surveillance of the cabin.

FBI SA Noel at the Marysville Steak House—a favorite dining spot!

Max, Terry, and Jim Freeman in Marysville "ghost" town.

Montana Route 279 from Helena, MT to Stemple Pass and Lincoln, MT.

Lincoln Public Library where T.K. befriended the librarian Sherri Wood and worked on his Manifesto.

T.K.'s mailbox on the side of Stemple Pass Road.

Approaching T.K.'s cabin and "looking south" towards the cabin from the approaching trail.

T.K.'s cabin in the snow.

The only door to T.K.'s cabin.

Looking up at the loft of T.K.'s cabin, where holes needed to be cut to gain safe access and light for the search.

Inside T.K.'s cabin showing location of T.K.'s "bed," with his rifles hanging above.

Inside T.K.'s cabin after entering through the only door.

The mail bomb found under T.K.'s bed during the FBI's search of his cabin.

Inside T.K.'s cabin showing the loft and items contained therein.

An animal "kill" located on the grounds of T.K.'s cabin.

One of the "junked" cars found up the logging road from T.K.'s cabin and a source of some of the aluminum for his bombs.

Another one of the "junked" cars found up the logging road from T.K.'s cabin.

The Smith Corona typewriter found in the loft of T.K.'s cabin and used to type the Unabom Manifesto.

The "robot" used to remove the "live" bomb found in T.K.'s cabin.

The Sandia Lab scientists who built the customized UNABOM bomb disrupter at the FBI's request about a year before the identification of T.K., accompanied by the FBI L.A. Bomb Technician who worked with them. (FBI SA Patricia Clothier, Sandia bomb technicians Chris Cherry, Rick Owemby and L.A County Sheriff Bomb Technician Vic Poisson).

The "live" bomb preparing to be "disrupted."

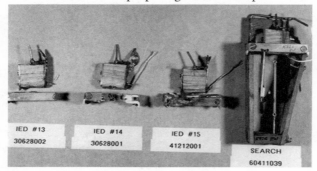

Remnants of hickory wooden "switch" mechanisms found at the scenes of UNABOM attacks in 1993 and 1994 and a complete switch found inside T.K.'s cabin.

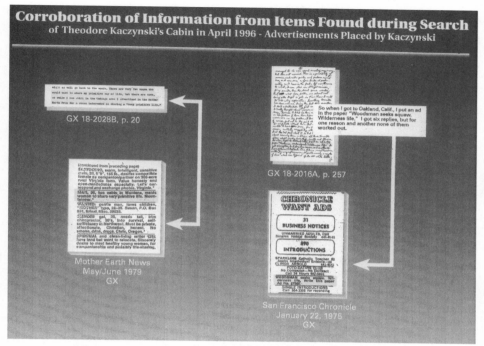

Corroboration of Information from Items Found during Search
of Theodore Kaczynski's Cabin in April 1996 - Advertisements Placed by Kaczynski

GX 18-2028B, p. 20

GX 18-2016A, p. 257

So when I got to Oakland, Calif., I put an ad in the paper "Woodsman seeks squaw. Wilderness life." I got six replies, but for one reason and another none of them worked out.

Mother Earth News
May/June 1979
GX

San Francisco Chronicle
January 22, 1975
GX

Advertisements placed by T.K. in *Mother Earth News* and the
San Francisco Chronicle looking for a "woman" or "squaw."

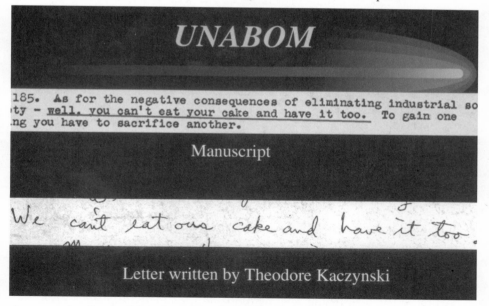

UNABOM

185. As for the negative consequences of eliminating industrial so
ty – well, you can't eat your cake and have it too. To gain one
ng you have to sacrifice another.

Manuscript

We can't eat our cake and have it too.

Letter written by Theodore Kaczynski

An example of one of the phrases in the UNABOM Manifesto that also appeared in one of the known letters of T.K. Notice that the phrase is the reverse of the normal English usage. This was one of over 100 similarities between the UNABOM Manifesto and the known writing samples of T.K.

The New York Times
229 WEST 43 STREET
NEW YORK, N.Y. 10036

ARTHUR O. SULZBERGER, JR.
Publisher

To The Staff,

Tomorrow morning, The New York Times and The Washington Post will jointly publish the manuscript sent to both papers by the Unabomber. I say "jointly publish" because while the full text of the manuscript will appear only in The Post – because of its daily printing and inserting capabilities – both papers will share the costs and the responsibilities for this action.

The decision whether or not to publish the Unabomber's document has been a difficult one, with powerful arguments on both sides. Last week, Attorney General Janet Reno and F.B.I. Director Louis Freeh requested that we publish the manuscript for public safety reasons. Both Don Graham, the publisher of The Washington Post, and I agree that, in this singular case, the potential of saving lives should be the paramount consideration.

Nevertheless, our decision to publish raises some legitimate concerns. It will be argued that we're giving in to the demands of a terrorist and that the only certain result will be similar demands from others threatening violence. Any journalist knows that newsrooms regularly receive messages from people threatening dire actions unless their demands are met. Our traditional response will continue to serve us well -- we notify law enforcement officials, when appropriate, and print nothing.

This case differs in the most obvious way. Here we are dealing with an individual with a 17-year record of violent actions. Hard experience proves that his threat to send another bomb to an unspecified destination must be taken absolutely seriously.

A copy of a note to the staff of the *New York Times* written by
Arthur Sulzberger, Jr. and advising of the decision by the *Post* and the *Times*
to publish the UNABOM Manifesto.

The Unabomber's demands pose no First Amendment issue. For us, the issue really centers on our newspaper's role as part of a community, with concerns about the safety of that community and its members. It's difficult to put complete faith in the words of someone with the record of violence that the Unabomber has. But the best advice available, from the F.B.I. and others, is that the Unabomber may well not bomb again if his material is published.

The Unabomber has professed to be tired of killing and promised to desist forever if we print his manuscript in either The Times or The Post. At the same time, however, he has threatened to continue non-lethal sabotage. Finally, he also has demanded that he be allowed to have further communications published once a year for the next three years.

I remain deeply troubled both by his threat of continued non-lethal bombing and by his demand for further publication of his ideas. We do not draw the same distinction as does the Unabomber between bombs meant to kill people and those which, by their placement, merely threaten to kill people. Whether or not we print further communications from the Unabomber will be guided, in part, by the Unabomber's continued abstention from all bombings - not just those targeting people.

A.O.S., Jr.

September 18, 1995

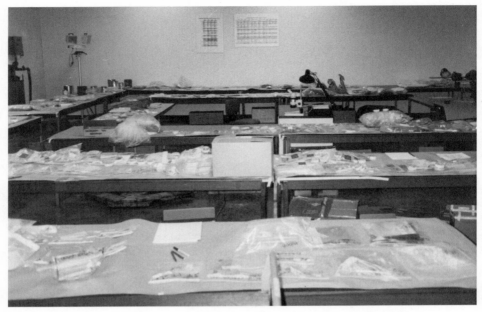

Evidence taken from T.K.s cabin organized at FBI Headquarters in Washington, D.C. by the FBI Lab.

One of the only photos capturing the entire "management" staff of the UTF. This was taken by a photographer from *Fortune* magazine and appeared in an article titled, "Unabomber: The High-Tech Chase," in the *Fortune* issue of August 21, 1995. (Jim Freeman, FBI; Don Davis, USPS; Mark Logan, BATF; Terry Turchie, FBI; and Dennis Hagberg, USPS).

Photograph taken on the night of T.K.s arrest showing him with Max Noel and Tom McDaniel, both of the FBI.

CHAPTER TEN

TAKING ON FBI FIEFDOMS
AS BOMBS EXPLODED

*(The FBI valued an entrenched tradition of program integrity since the
J. Edgar Hoover days. Line item budgets held more sway than real time
crime trends and field office fiefdoms grew and were protected by immovable Federal judiciary boundaries. Bureaucrats in every agency thrived
in protecting the status quo. Our UNABOM brand began to challenge
every one of these artificial restraints, moving forcibly through them if
necessary to solve the case).*

TERRY AND I HAD DOZENS OF ONE-ON-ONE MEETINGS AS WE
managed the daily activities of the UTF. We met in my office, his
office, or even in the middle of an airport lounge. We discussed
everything from explosives to explosive personalities. We had long
since promised each other that during our meetings we would
come up with solutions to the issues that continuously confronted
us, but the meetings also became therapy that gave one or the
other or both of us an opportunity to vent, de-stress and talk in
great detail about the things that were on our minds. Terry walked
into my office one day, slouched in the chair across from my desk
and vividly described a meeting he had just come from. I had
become an expert at imagining I was there, as Terry laid out the
following story on that particular day:

Terry was inside his office on a conference call with FBI Headquarters when the closed door swung open and Max appeared, reading glasses on and waving an official looking communication up and down in the air.

"I'm not going to this meeting. I'm not wasting my time when we have important work to do. I've never seen a meeting of the 'Misters' where anything gets done and I am not going to this meeting." Max had made his point.

Motioning for him to quiet down by putting his finger up to his lip, Terry was listening to Max and at the same time trying to stay with the phone call. It wasn't working, so he told the group of FBI supervisors on the line that he would have to go because something had come up.

"Max, we've got a new supervisor assigned to UNABOM at FBI Headquarters. And, how's this for different? He actually said that he'd be there until the case is solved. His name is Tom Nunnemaker and he seemed like a decent guy." Terry hoped to cheer Max up with the good news, but it wasn't working.

"So Max, what's wrong?" Terry stood up to emphasize that Max now had his full attention.

"Have you even seen this? Headquarters wants to have a UNABOM conference in Washington and they want all of these people speaking at it. These people don't have anything to do with the investigation—and look, look at this." Max pointed to the document that listed an expanded agenda of speaking topics and introduced one "expert" speaker after another; always listed as a "Mr. Whoever." Max's face was tight and a little red. "I've never seen a meeting of Misters amount to anything!"

"I haven't seen this yet," Terry studied the document that Max had shoved his way. "I didn't know anything about the meeting. But you know what—you and I and Neil are going to this thing. We'll make flight reservations before we go home tonight."

"Come on, Terry. This is going to be a huge waste of time. All these people want is to be seen and heard. For crying out loud, they can't be too interested because they don't even read most of what we send them as it is," Max protested.

"It'll be good for them Max. Here's what we'll do—Neil can speak about forensics from the perspective of the UTF projects we are working on. I'll speak about our computer strategies and how we are implementing a different approach to the case. Then, you can fill in the details of what we're getting out of that strategy so far. It'll be fine." Terry stopped, but then added before Max could counter again. "Besides, Max, I need you there with me."

I smiled when Terry finished his story. He had learned how to push the right buttons with Max. It had taken some getting used to for both Terry and I, with Max having a short temper and a propensity for saying what was on his mind; but after spending time together you could see his kindness and decency showing through the veneer. On the professional side, Max clearly had an insatiable desire to go after the bad guys and you knew that he would never be dissuaded by armies of defense lawyers, union racketeering thugs or any number of Washington bureaucrats.

Max was needed in the dynamics of this case to bring his opposite personality type with Terry into a counter-balancing form of "good cop, bad cop" routine that I had seen work extremely well in the UTF environment. And, I was intrigued as to how the duo would play the "big stage" at Headquarters. For that reason alone, I was almost sorry that I had other pressing matters keeping me away from the meeting. Although, I did agree with Max that nothing productive came from meetings like this.

I heard all about it from the three of them when they returned. Traveling to the "meeting of the Misters" turned out to be a big step in testing their approach. Walking through the double wooden doors into the Charles Bonaparte Auditorium at FBI Headquarters, Neil, Max and Terry were surprised to see dozens of officials milling about or taking their seats. There was a low murmur from sidebars throughout the room and the eye was treated to an ocean of dark suits, floating above a splash of white and blue shirts with pinstriped ties.

It was hard to imagine that much "thinking outside the box" would occur in such an atmosphere. I surmised that a good percentage of the people in the room had invested several years of their career in working inside the Washington Beltway and then digging in to protect their investment. Thankfully, there were exceptional individuals at Headquarters that waged their own battle against the forces of inertia; and these stalwarts were sought out and cultivated by those of us of another mind set. When needed, they would respond to keep the wheels turning in the right direction.

Max, Terry and Neil found seats among the last rows of the auditorium, a long walk from the stage and podium that had been set up for the multitude of speakers. U.S. Postal Inspectors and ATF officials from their respective headquarters were seated toward the front. And, DOJ attorneys from what many referred to as "Main Justice" had walked across the street to join the meeting. Scattered among the crowd were a number of local prosecutors and Assistant United States Attorneys from around the country representing jurisdictions plagued by a UNABOM crime. It was a very august group amid the Misters from FBIHQ, as Max irreverently called them.

The FBI's Assistant Director in Charge of Media and Public Affairs called the meeting to order. An affable and professional speaker, he began by thanking everyone for taking the time to attend the meeting and for the tireless efforts they contributed to try and solve the UNABOM case. Terry anticipated what Max was already thinking—that the majority of people in the room didn't know much of anything about UNABOM; or had familiarity only with the bombing events or investigative leads in their specific area. One by one, the identified speakers introduced themselves, and preened to the Headquarters audience—taking advantage of the personal exposure to higher-ups that might someday give a helping hand to a career. Then, Neil was invited to come forward and speak from his viewpoint as case agent for UNABOM.

Neil showed discomfort in speaking before this large and intimidating group, but went on to outline in some detail the UNABOM events that had occurred between 1978 and 1994. He discussed the premise that the Unabomber might be working in or familiar with the aviation industry. This focus was because some bombings were suggestive of anger towards aviation, and also due to the unique way the bombs were crafted and put together.

Of particular interest to the UTF had been the independent observation of the National Transportation Safety Board that several elements of the bombs and their packaging materials resembled aircraft construction techniques in miniature. This made for some lively discussion of possible motives and appeared as a bright spot in a meeting that had begun to drag on.

When Neil concluded, Terry spoke at some length about the strategy we had embarked upon back in April. He emphasized why it was important for San Francisco's UTF members to travel personally to other jurisdictions to gather and review the extensive case files and evidence reports; and either to coordinate or actively engage in the reinvestigation of each of the UNABOM crimes. Despite the Director's explicit authorization of this activity, there was defensiveness expressed at the meeting from various quarters.

I wasn't surprised when I was apprised of this, because the FBI had a firmly entrenched tradition and culture of program integrity since the Hoover days that was more closely aligned to Congressional line-item budgets than to real-time crime trends. Upon debating this point, it was seldom necessary to go beyond an historical description of the budgetary mandate from Congress that for decades had placed an emphasis on interstate car theft instead of providing the FBI with investigative freedom to look into the thinly veiled backrooms of Mafia operations across the country. And, then there are the field office fiefdoms that had grown since the Thirties with immovable judicial boundaries that effectively restrained cooperative relations among neighboring fiefdoms. And, our UNABOM strategy was moving diametrically in the opposite direction.

There was a positive response from some prosecutors in the room as Terry described the new team of analytical investigators with unique specialties on the series of UNABOM crimes with an ability to discern how the pieces tied together and an ability to document a trail of known facts that would ultimately tie back to the single responsible individual. But, there were mutterings that lingered among the Misters.

In the same vein, Terry alluded to efforts by the UTF to seek opinions from outside forensic experts in private industry. This was seen by Max and Terry and I as a reasonable request with potential to broaden the expertise on the immense problem that we faced in solving UNABOM. But, while this approach might possibly develop something new, the unspoken truth from the 800 pound gorilla in the room was fear of the unknown—that evidence may have been missed over time in the original forensic examinations. Terry was intimately aware of this sensitivity and chose to save that fight with the FBI Laboratory for another day.

Terry then introduced Max as a speaker, and returned to his seat next to Neil.

Max eyed the dignitaries sitting in the room as he spoke from the heart. "We shouldn't be sitting around patting ourselves on the back saying what a good job we've been doing." He had gained their singular attention. "I don't think we have anything to be proud of. I would wager if we talked to the widow of Thomas Mosser about our performance during the past sixteen years that she wouldn't think we'd been doing so good." The silence between words was pervasive.

Neil penned a note on the paper in front of him and moved it discreetly to let Terry read it. There was a stricken look on Neil's face.

"Can't you stop him?" he had written. Neil was watching the audience. Tobin from the Lab was sitting in the row in front of him with a wide smile on his face as Max talked. Everyone else seemed to be looking at the person sitting next to their right or left, to see how they should react. Terry commented later that the auditorium was hushed to the point of evoking and perhaps defining an image of "sounds of silence" that was conjured up in the Simon and Garfunkel song from the '60s.

"No. It'll be fine" Terry turned to Neil and scribbled an answer to the note.

Max concluded his remarks. "It's simply about time we pull ourselves up by the bootstraps, get serious, do our jobs, and solve this case."

Several others in the room got up and left the auditorium as Max sat down. Minutes later, the double doors to the side of the room creaked open and several bodies could be seen silhouetted against the dark of the hallway outside. A finger crept through the opening and summoned Terry to leave the meeting and join them in the hallway.

It was a silent march to the office of Section Chief Howie Apple. By the time Apple and the others were ready to address Terry about the meeting, Max and Neil showed up at their door and came into the office.

"A bridge builder you aren't, Noel." Apple poked Max in the stomach as he spoke.

"The Bureau's not paying me to build bridges, but to solve a previously unsolvable crime," Max retorted without surrendering a step to Apple.

Neil quickly disappeared to discuss forensics with Tom Mohnal while Max took his leave to make the acquaintance of Nunnemaker, the new Headquarters supervisor that Terry had met over the telephone and seemed to like. Howie Apple walked Terry into his office and gave him a handwritten note. Tom Thurman, the Explosives Unit Chief of the FBI Lab wanted to have dinner that evening with Terry in Old Town Alexandria. The name of the restaurant and a time were written down. Terry readily accepted and told Howie to let Thurman know that he would be there.

Turchie looked at the night out as a pleasant break from the pressures of the day and dinner with Tom Thurman would give him a chance to get to know him and explain in much greater detail why our present day UTF had embarked upon a dramatically different approach to UNABOM.

Upon their arrival that evening, Terry's first order of business was to impress upon Thurman why we felt it so important to have the FBI Lab coordinate the evaluation of some of the forensic evidence gathered at crime scenes with "other experts." Wood fragments, wire, batteries, nails, aluminum flakes, and specks of paint were just a few of the items, where outside experts might be able to add to the conclusions already made by the FBI, Postal or ATF Laboratories. Terry used the example of the NTSB report as helping the UTF assess the possible significance of the aviation industry in some types of evidence left behind in the wake of the Unabomber and his bombs.

Thurman had years of experience with bombings and explosives and had assisted Director Freeh and John Behnke years earlier in the Judge Vance bombing, so he was no stranger to their line of originality. It also became obvious during the discussion that he had been made aware of the UTF meeting in San Francisco with Director Freeh long before he and Terry met for dinner.

Thurman told Terry he didn't have any problems in helping the UTF pursue this line of reinvestigation. Since Terry believed he was making progress with Thurman, he continued by pursuing another unresolved issue with the Lab. Fifteen UNABOM crimes up to that point had left literally thousands of fragments of forensic evidence and the UTF needed faster turnaround from the Lab examiners and their help in maintaining track of all of the various exam requests and responses during the reinvestigation phase.

Again, Terry scored a win—the result being Thurman's commitment to assign an FBI lab supervisor, Tom Jourdan, to the San Francisco FBI office to serve as the Lab's direct liaison with the UTF. Later, Terry told us of feeling excited about the dinner and the issues he thought he was resolving with Thurman—to the point that he jumped at the chance to order coffee and dessert. And, that's when everything changed. Thurman's down to earth charm disappeared, his gaze became more intense, and he suddenly assumed the role of interrogator more than colleague.

"Terry, it was embarrassing in there for a lot of people today when Max was talking," he stopped to let the sentence sink in. It was obvious that on this point Thurman was the chosen voice to speak what certain others had wanted to say.

"You and Jim Freeman are going to need to move him off the task force," Thurman kept sipping his coffee as if such a topic was everyday fare.

"Tom, it may have been uncomfortable in there today. But, those things had to be said. We won't be moving Max anywhere. Max, Jim and I are in this until the end. In a few short months, we've been through hell and high water together. There's going to be much more said about things that won't exactly make people feel good. I'm sorry, but everyone is just going to need to learn that this is the way it's going to be."

Terry was just hitting his stride, as he continued to lecture. "I realize you want to solve the case too and I know you must be under stress, but all of you back here need to get used to this—it's just the way it is. People are dying, while we debate who should be assigned to the case. If Max leaves, then all of us in San Francisco will find something else to do. After all, it's UNABOM and I'm not aware that people are crying out to work eighteen hour days and asking to be constantly soaked in the pressure cooker like this."

Terry's crescendo effectively ended the discussion and the two headed for the door, parting as two professionals from a routine business dinner. Arriving back in his hotel room for the night, Terry found his phone ringing. It was Neil.

"That was awful today, Terry, just awful. I need to be transferred from UNABOM." Neil's pain came through loud and clear over the phone.

"Neil, it's all good. You're not going anywhere. There's no need to. This is tough stuff and we'll all get through it. Tomorrow, you and I and Max will go over to DuPont Circle and get a steak and close the week out relaxing a little." Neil got off the phone after promising Terry he would stop reliving the day's events.

The next time the phone rang it was Max on the line.

"Terry, I want to be transferred from the UTF. I've been thinking about this and it's time I left." Max was no longer asking to get off the task force to make his own life easier. Now, he thought he would be making things easier for Terry and me to deal with the consequences that were inevitable after the meeting with the Misters.

"C'mon Max, you're not going anywhere," and Terry proceeded to outline his own experiences at dinner while omitting the demand that Max be summarily removed from the UTF. Terry made it clear to Max that the battle lines were drawn and the UNABOM Task Force was marching forward with our strategy intact.

As Terry was bidding goodnight, he said, "So I'll meet you

tomorrow morning and we'll get some coffee before we go over and meet Tom Mohnal to talk about forensics."

The next day, the two met up as planned and headed over to Headquarters to see Mohnal. As they were making their way toward Mohnal's elevator bank in the underground basement of the J. Edgar Hoover Building, Terry ran into someone he knew and the two started talking. Max continued on to see Mohnal and by the time Terry opened the door to Mohnal's office about ten minutes later, the sparks had already erupted into fire.

Mohnal had immediately challenged Max about the assertions he made to Director Freeh during the UTF meeting in San Francisco. Specifically, he was very upset that Max had used the story of the employee who had to catch his car pool as an example of the Lab not doing its work. When Mohnal told Max he didn't like his attitude, Max led with a four letter response and soon others flooded the room from both sides.

As Terry walked in, it didn't take long to figure out what happened. Most of the dialogue going back and forth centered on the letters "F.U.," so Terry just sat down and gave it a minute before jumping into the fray.

"Max, sit down; and Tom, you both need to stop. Max isn't going anywhere and I need you guys to get along with each other. You both have a big role to play in this case," he looked back and forth at each of them as he spoke.

Max and Tom looked at each other without a word and just as suddenly, it was over. The "discussion" was therapeutic; they got down to business that day and the air remained clear between Max and Mohnal from that day forward.

Upon returning to San Francisco, Terry came to my office to fill in the gaps of the phone advisories that he had given me during the trip. We both had a good laugh about the scene when Terry arrived as Max and Tom Mohnal were tossing F-bombs back and forth.

I was pleased and concerned at the same time. Max's business etiquette was a weapon to be used sparingly and a cause for concern if displayed at the wrong time. With Max, I had learned how intense he could be and Terry had figured out how to blend their personalities for maximum impact, when necessary. I had recruited Terry and then we worked to retain Max to fulfill a distinctly different role on the task force and neither had disappointed.

One quality they both had in equal amounts was a look on their face if they were holding back information or needed to tell me something that I didn't want to hear.

As he sat in front of me, it was obvious Terry was having one of those moments. There was something on his mind that day and he needed to tell it.

"So what else are you thinking about?" I asked after we had talked about the progress of various UTF projects.

"Well, I haven't thought it through yet, but are you receptive to some ideas for a further enhancement of the UTF?"

"You mean more agents?" I asked with a critical gaze.

"Yeah, I'm prioritizing investigative projects, but the leads are mushrooming every day. A few more agents would allow us to move those along faster. There is a pay-off even when we eliminate a blind alley, because we filter out or accept new pieces of information all the time. It all contributes to the mosaic we're constructing about what is myth versus rock-solid facts about the Unabomber."

"Get your data together and we'll talk it through. I'm not opposed to more agents, but in light of the recent negativity in Headquarters we have to be careful about what we ask for and how we justify the need."

Terry nodded in agreement, got up and walked towards my office door, reaching to open it. I didn't feel like he had discussed everything on his mind.

"Terry," I raised my voice and he turned around. "Why

haven't you applied for the position as my Assistant Special Agent in Charge of the Counterintelligence Division?" The job had opened up since Ed Appel was being transferred to Headquarters and I was looking for a replacement that would be compatible with my management team and would interface well with all of the employees in the office.

"That's funny," Terry laughed and then added that he had his hands full with UNABOM and didn't believe he should even think about getting off the UTF. I was aware that he had promised everyone that he was in it for the long haul and wanted each UTF member to feel the same way. Even so, I was surprised that he had not asked to be considered for the promotion.

"Besides," he added, "the word is out in the office that you have a good choice that you've settled on."

"Well, today's the last day to apply," I told him. When that failed to solicit the proper response, I changed my tone, "Apply for the damned job!"

Terry nodded and left my office. A few weeks later, Terry was named the Counterintelligence ASAC with my blessing and with approval from FBI Headquarters. I named Joel Moss as the interim UNABOM squad supervisor, reporting to Terry, but the overall alignment of the reporting relationship of the UTF to me and ultimately to the Criminal Division at FBIHQ remained as before.

Then, on the morning of April 19, it all changed anyway. It seemed like hundreds of phones throughout the office erupted on cue that morning. In one instance we were all going about our business, and in another we all recalled exactly what we were doing when the phones let loose. A horrendous explosion had just destroyed the Alfred E. Murrah Federal Building in Oklahoma City. Immediately, the networks were running stories that the bombing was the work of Arab terrorists. Hundreds of innocent civilians, including dozens of young children in a day care facility inside the building, had been killed or injured during an explosion that ripped the building in half, dropping much of it onto the ground in a heap of metal, wire, toxic fumes and jagged concrete.

I called Terry as soon as I received word about it and asked that he divert UTF personnel and activate our office command post. We had no idea if this was the work of the Unabomber, but it didn't feel like it. I asked him to get a "psych" opinion from Kathy Puckett as to the chances the Oklahoma City bombing was the work of the Unabomber. We both anticipated a torrent of calls from FBIHQ and the media asking the same question and we needed a reasonable basis for our answer.

San Francisco joined fifty-five other FBI field offices that morning with instructions being coordinated by the Strategic Information Operations Center (SIOC) at FBIHQ, where personal appearances by Director Freeh and Attorney General Janet Reno were not infrequent. Almost at once, leads were emanating from Oklahoma City and FBI agents all over the world were fanning out to put the pieces together even as the fires still smoldered and burned at the scene. Terry named Joel Moss to cover our command post and assigned FBI analysts Alexandra Jacobson and Maggie Stringer to assist him.

Terry received a call back from Kathy Puckett just in time before the call arrived from Headquarters.

"Kathy, it's ridiculously short notice, but from a behavioral perspective is the Unabomber likely to be responsible for Oklahoma City? You know that question is going to be asked. In fact, Jim is already thinking about how to address it and there is little time to chat."

Kathy delivered without hesitation, because she had anticipated the same possibility from the time she heard the news report. "The Unabomber is a lone, serial killer who has used only mail bombs for his last three bombings. Since the early years, he has become increasingly surgical and deliberate with nothing that leads me to believe he is a mass murderer. The Oklahoma City bomber was an indiscriminate mass murderer who used a truck bomb. I don't believe the two are related." Kathy was deliberate and confident in her assessment–exactly as needed.

"Okay, thanks Kathy. Look, the phones are ringing off the hook. Bob Conforti and Tom Nunnemaker at HQ are holding for me on another line. Would you go to Jim's office, fill him in on what you just told me, and get it down on paper as soon as possible so we are consistent in our message. Tell him I'll be there as soon as I get off the phone with them." As Terry hung up the phone, Kathy was already moving toward my office. When Terry showed up twenty minutes later, Kathy had already left.

"Jim, sorry I was delayed. Just as you predicted, Bob Conforti and Tom Nunnemaker at HQ called with the question of the hour—asking if we thought the Unabomber was responsible for the Oklahoma City bombing. So, I filled them in on my conversation with Kathy and one answer led to another of their questions. You know the drill. They seemed convinced of her rationale, but things are hopping back in D.C. and people are throwing out all sorts of theories."

"That doesn't surprise me. And, what Kathy said makes great sense. Hopefully, that will give us some breathing room. Conforti and Nunnemaker seem to have common sense. Have you put the UTF team jersey on 'em?" I kidded.

"I think they're solidly in our court, but time will tell," Terry responded.

"So, you started to tell me the other day about needing to add agents to the UTF. What are your thoughts today, knowing that the Oklahoma City bombing will be burning up FBI resources that are even more competitive now?" I asked.

"I've got at least fifteen investigative projects on hold now, because we don't have enough people to do them justice. We're still working out from under a backlog of leads being generated by your increasing level of media exposure. It's keeping the public alert and aware of the Unabomber threat, but the workload is going through the roof. And, there's an even bigger resource issue on the horizon, as we are close to generating our own suspect targets based on our computer data runs. We don't have enough analysts to deal with that new work stream right now."

Terry finished and a rush of questions immediately came to mind. The computer records project was at the top of my priority list and we had to get sufficient manpower to get it moving. It was becoming a question of what projects to stop or scale back in order to get to new opportunities. What I needed at this moment is, "where does it stand and what is needed to make it happen"?

Terry read my face and responded. "Fred Dexter from FBIHQ and Casey Henderson, the private contractor that has been working on UNABOM data management for months, have finished measuring and going through the millions of computer records collected over fifteen years of bombings. They repaired bad and defective tapes, put all of the records in a consistent format, and have identified duplicates, missing records, and other issues to correct all of the known issues. Now we can start doing computer runs of UNABOM historical data with reasonable assurance of consistent results.

"Here's one of the top requests on my list. Give us a set of names of everyone who was at Northwestern University in 1978 and 1979; then showed up in Utah in 1981 with a driver's license, property record, or university affiliation; and later had affiliation in or around the University of California in Berkeley in the 1980's."

No kidding, I thought. The Unabomber might actually appear in that bucket of names. But, how are we to recognize him from all the rest? "We have already found and eliminated some names common to all the places and at all of the times you just gave in your example, but now being capable of instantly adding new factors to the search parameters—that's a major advancement of our strategy." It represented a big start, a very big start of something new and different for UNABOM.

"Yes, in the first computer test we came back with dozens of names," Terry pointed out, adding, "it's a pro-active way of isolating a list of potential suspects who were in all the locations of UNABOM bombings, including university affiliations, and at the same approximate timing. The limiting factor is the approximate age range of the subject, but we'll start with the likeliest possibilities and eventually work through them all."

I was stoked with the enormous potential. "That's exactly what this investigation needs—a proactive initiative with potential to blow the lid off this case. Put it on paper with an urgent request to FBIHQ for additional manpower and make a call to Conforti and Nunnemaker to give them a chance to support and run with the request. Just to be sure, I'll call Esposito when our paper is ready to send. Give them the courtesy of knowing that I'll be kicking the request up the line to the Deputy Director and to Louie, if necessary."

Bill Esposito was the FBI's Deputy Director, the number two FBI official after Director Freeh, and a friend from the past who had years of experience in working organized crime and informants and complex cases. He was operationally oriented and knew how to sift through the bullshit of routine requests from field office managers asking for more manpower. He would give our request due consideration even without my phone call, but with the competition for resources from the Oklahoma City bombing—it would be a touch and go proposition.

"Terry, I also called SAC Dick Ross in Sacramento. I want the two of you to meet and get comfortable with UNABOM work passing across our field office boundaries without interference or professional jealousy. He and I go back a long way in the Bureau. Brief him on all the issues; such as any UTF leads that are past due and whatever else is needed to clear the air. I'm making a standing invitation for him to send some agents here to work UNABOM with us."

"That's sounds good. I'll be back if I hear anything else today about Oklahoma City," Terry turned and left the room, off to a busy start as the newest Assistant Special Agent in Charge.

I was tied up, but Terry drove to Vacaville the next day to meet Dick Ross for lunch. A serious, bespectacled veteran of the FBI, Ross was a thinker whose calm demeanor hid his intensity. He seemed eager to solidify his support of the new UTF methodology. With the Unabomber passing into and out of both Sacramento and San Francisco to mail his package bombs, it was difficult to see how the case could be solved if both offices weren't joined at the hip.

It was an easy sell to Ross, but there was a history of animosity between the two offices dating back long before UNABOM. From my perspective, the Sacramento agents had a stepchild complex when it came to their counterpart in San Francisco. In fact, Sacramento was at one time a subordinate Resident Agency assigned to the larger San Francisco FBI Division. Three to four times Sacramento's size, the San Francisco Division got the lion's share of attention from back East and that translated to even more manpower and budget.

Ross was intimately aware of some experiences and stories his agents had related about their dealings with San Francisco agents. He understood the history of the two offices and was also a student of human behavior. Later, Terry told me how much he had enjoyed the meeting with Ross. The two had agreed on a coffee shop located off of Interstate 80 about mid-way between San Francisco and Sacramento. They found a table in an isolated corner of the room from other diners and were able to have a good and discrete conversation that Terry described for me, as he told me about their meeting:

Ross set a positive tone from his side of the table almost immediately after sitting down to eat, telling Terry, "I know there have been issues and hurt feelings in the past. But, I don't have time to relive all that. Jim Freeman and I have worked well previously and it's important for us to be together now on UNABOM,"

"Jim and I are both extending an offer to have Sacramento agents working alongside us in San Francisco. Any time you want them to be there, the offer stands." Terry emphasized to Ross in return. "This is a topic that is very important to both Jim and I."

"Thank you. I'll follow-up with my agents and we'll find a way to take advantage of your offer," Ross responded in appreciation.

Terry gave an operational briefing to Ross and focused on the key aspects of our strategy. Ross acknowledged the different style and substance we were applying to UNABOM, and then shared with Terry some observations on a recent trip he had made to FBI Headquarters in Washington, D.C., telling Terry, "I was in Washington last week and had a chance to talk to Louie. He alluded to some developments and discoveries you've made in the case—which is pretty amazing after so many years of having some of that information right in front of us!" This was good feedback that we were continuing to get high-level cover where we needed it.

The time Terry spent with Dick Ross was time well spent. It was good news for UNABOM, and there was more to come that day. An alert Oklahoma state trooper had stopped a car on the highway a few miles from the bombing scene in Oklahoma City. It had no rear license plate. He became suspicious of the driver and his behavior.

Within minutes the trooper's suspicions translated into the arrest of Timothy McVeigh. In time, the association was linked to the Oklahoma City bombing. The news was breaking and FBIHQ was confirming it internally to FBI field offices. McVeigh it seemed was a good bet for being the horrendous mass murderer.

With McVeigh's arrest, the pressure was off any need to prove to a certainty that there was no connection between the

Unabomber and the Oklahoma City bombing of the Federal Building. Kathy Puckett had gained credibility with her timely behavioral assessment of the Unabomber. Still, the country was nervous and the FBI now had the stress of a mass murder on its hands in Oklahoma to go with the string of unsolved UNABOM bombings.

Just five days after the Oklahoma City bombing, early on the afternoon of April 24, 1995, Terry was preparing for a meeting when he was paged on the office intercom for a phone call. It was Dick Ross in Sacramento. Ross' voice was controlled, but shaken.

"Terry, we've had a bombing up here. Everything about it looks like UNABOM. I've closed down the scene. I need help as soon as you and Jim can get it to me."

The earlier meeting paid off, as Terry and Dick didn't need to have a prolonged discussion to get up to speed. Terry and I felt comfortable with Dick's knowledge of the case and Dick had a newfound confidence in his neighboring office. Terry promised that help was on the way and got off the phone, while asking his secretary to find Pat Webb and me. Webb was a San Francisco Division squad supervisor and trained bomb expert. When Webb called in, Terry was in the midst of briefing me and we put Webb on the speakerphone to tell him what had happened.

"Pat, there's been a bombing in Sacramento at the California Forestry Association. I just got off the phone with Dick Ross and he's closed down the crime scene. The President of the CFA was killed with a mail bomb. We need you to go up there and link up with Ross at the crime scene. You'll be the UTF senior representative for cooperation and coordination with the Sacramento team. Survey the scene, figure out what's needed, and call us right away."

Pat didn't waste words. "Thanks Terry, I'm on it. I'll call when I get there and get my bearings." Pat had worked on last year's bombing of Epstein in Tiburon and hundreds of other crime scenes. He was the right man for the job.

Pat grabbed his brand new Bureau car that had just arrived and found that the siren hadn't yet been installed, but its emergency lights were intact. With lights flashing, he crossed the Bay Bridge and sped off towards Sacramento on Interstate 80.

Pat arrived in Sacramento in record time and met Dick Ross and his Sacramento agents outside the California Forestry Association offices. He found that they had done a good job in coordinating with the Sacramento Police Department and closing the site for evidentiary examination. Pat made an initial assessment there and then assembled all of the investigators at the nearby Fire Department Command Post, where he briefed them thoroughly on the particulars of past UNABOM crime scenes. Due to the massive bombing and forensic examinations that were ongoing in Oklahoma City, Pat knew that help from the FBI Laboratory would be delayed.

At about 5:30 pm, Pat Webb along with Sacramento FBI's senior bomb investigator, a Sacramento Police detective, and a member of the San Francisco Evidence Response Team entered the CFA office for an initial walk-thru evaluation. They observed the effects of a bomb blast that appeared to be the most powerful of the UNABOM series. Numerous items had been blown over sixty feet from the site of the blast. Although the walls remained intact, there were pieces of broken furniture, splinters of wood, and bomb fragments scattered over a wide radius.

Mr. Murray's body was still at the crime scene, as were remnants of the package that he had opened. The package had not been addressed to him, but to his predecessor at the CFA, William Dennison. Mr. Murray suffered massive trauma as the benign-appearing package exploded while he held it.

As Pat looked through the debris, he picked up on the telltale signs of the Unabomber. Pieces of brown wrapping paper were glued to the remnants of a wooden box. Batteries were wrapped in filament tape with the outside wrappers removed, which was a classic tradecraft of the Unabomber. When Pat eyed a cross-pinned, metal end plug among the debris, he had seen enough and he left the scene immediately to make his call to Terry at the UTF Command Post in San Francisco.

"Terry, I'm sitting outside on the curb in front of the California Forestry Association building with Dick Ross. He said to say thank you. Terry, this is a UNABOM event. There's absolutely no doubt in my mind." Pat rattled off some of the observations he had made inside the crime scene.

"Okay, Pat. Keep complete control of the crime scene and do what's necessary to keep it locked down until the rest of the San Francisco ERT arrives." Terry didn't need convincing that it was the Unabomber.

Pat returned to Dick Ross and the group of investigators who were assembling for another briefing and confirmed to them that the bomb was UNABOM Event Number 16. Shortly, the main party of the San Francisco Evidence Response Team arrived and began the exhaustive process of slowly searching every inch of the crime scene. At about 10:00 pm, the Sacramento County Coroner arrived and by 11:00 pm had removed Mr. Murray's body. The job of collecting the evidence of the latest UNABOM attack was completed at a little after 1:00 am.

Mohnal called Terry from the scene of the Oklahoma City massacre and said he would be flying to California on a Bureau aircraft. He wanted to retrieve the evidence from the latest UNABOM bomb in Sacramento and get it back to the Lab immediately so they could start working on it. It occurred to me that maybe some things were changing after all.

Within days the Unabomber unleashed four handwritten letters—one was again sent to Warren Hogue of the *New York Times*. In the letter to the *Times*, "FC" offered to "desist from terrorism," if the paper agreed within a certain timeframe to publish a manifesto that the terrorist group was in the process of completing.

These letters were a new beginning for a task force accustomed to no solid leads to the identity of the Unabomber and his motivations. Although the cost in lives and injuries had been completely unacceptable, I took some solace and more than a little pleasure in recognizing that this strong urge to communicate was the beginning of the end for the Unabomber. The more you write, the more we learn!

"This is a message from FC, 553-25-4394... We have no regret about the fact that our bomb blew up the 'wrong' man, Gilbert Murray, instead of William N. Dennison, to whom it was addressed... It was reported that the bomb that killed Gilbert Murray was a pipe bomb. It was not a pipe bomb but was set off by a homemade detonating cap."

"This is a message from the terrorist group FC... In a letter that we sent to the New York Times at the time of our bombing at the California Forestry Association, we offered to desist from terrorism if a manuscript we were preparing were published in accord with certain stated conditions."

CHAPTER ELEVEN

WHAT'S SO SPECIAL ABOUT THE AGENT IN CHARGE?

(Special Agents in Charge of FBI Field Divisions normally run the office and leave operational decisions on individual cases to Assistant Special Agents in Charge and their teams of squad supervisors. UNABOM demanded more and I had to figure out how to increase my involvement without alienating the agents assigned to the case).

W E WERE BUSY BEFORE MR. MURRAY WAS MURDERED IN Sacramento, but the workload and tension increased a thousand fold afterwards.

I organized the Unabomber's letters on one side of my desk, beginning and ending my days in the office reading and re-reading the rants of an ego gone wild. His most recent letter to the *New York Times* captured my attention:

"The people we are out to get are the scientists and engineers, especially in critical fields like computers and genetics. As for the bomb planted in the Business School at the University of Utah, that was a botched operation. We won't say how or why it was botched because we don't want to give the FBI any clues. No one was hurt by that bomb."

"...The FBI has tried to portray these bombings as the work of an isolated nut. We won't waste our time arguing about whether we are nuts, but we certainly are not isolated..."

"...Clearly we are in a position to do a great deal of damage. And it doesn't appear that the FBI is going to catch us any time soon. The FBI is a joke."

The bomber was on a power trip. After the murder of Gilbert Murray, he sent letters to three more people besides the *New York Times*—they were timed to arrive on the day following the explosion. Each one was postmarked at Oakland, CA; right under the nose of the UTF. Two of the letters contained personal threats and were sent to recent Nobel Prize winners in scientific fields—Richard J. Roberts and Phillip Sharp. The other letter taunted a previous victim, Dr. David Gelernter. It also highlighted the Unabomber's newly found theme of taking shots at the FBI. The return address on the Gelernter letter was Ninth St. and Pennsylvania Ave., N.W., Washington, D.C. 20535; the location of the J. Edgar Hoover FBI Building. I re-read the Gelernter letter:

"People with advanced degrees aren't as smart as they think they are. If you'd had any brains you would have realized that there are a lot of people out there who resent bitterly the way techno-nerds like you are changing the world and you wouldn't have been dumb enough to open an unexpected package from an unknown source."

When Janet came in for a delivery of mail to my inbox, she feigned a back injury from its weight. I casually thumbed through the stacks of summaries of teletypes from our Sacramento office, from the FBI Lab, from Newark FBI, from the Criminal Division at HQ, and dozens of other places. Easily, 80% of the material that found its way to my desk these days carried UNABOM on its title page. I realized that the sheer volume of paper was a threat— it could marginalize my effectiveness with UNABOM and my other responsibilities, if I let it.

"Janet, I'm going to need more time with Turchie. Let's over-haul my calendar. Push out anything that's not nailed down and make room for additional one-on-one meetings with him every day until further notice. I can't let this mound of paper dictate my life."

This burst of directions elicited only an "uh huh" look from Janet, and then she was gone.

As the days progressed and the work pressure increased, Terry and I saw a lot more of each other than before. We reached many decisions during these sidebars, held both before and after our daily UTF leadership meetings.

Terry didn't seem to mind, but I sensed that my hands-on approach was not welcome by everyone. It just wasn't the way the Bureau normally ran investigations.

Terry and I had long since concluded that UNABOM was not the normal FBI-led task force investigation and we were deter-mined to alter, modify, and invent whatever structures and strate-gies were necessary to work the case effectively. We were build-ing a management style on the fly without consideration beyond identifying, arresting and convicting the Unabomber. Perhaps we were influenced by the fluid and open corporate structures that were springing up in the Silicon Valley to the south of our field office, where there was a fine line between the chief executive and the inventors of the new technologies that put these companies on the map. Our success or failure was very much in line with these tech start-ups, and Terry's role was becoming more and more like that of a company's Chief Operating Officer.

On one occasion, I managed to test Terry's limit for patience and endurance. I had finished reading a memo from Agent Neil

Oltman on a very viable suspect and I wanted to know more–immediately. I wanted to know why I was just now hearing of it. I set off for Terry's office to get more information. He wasn't there, so I walked into the UNABOM squad area where a number of UTF personnel were busy at their desks.

"Maggie, have you seen Terry?" I wandered over to Maggie Stringer's cube, where she quickly told me she hadn't seen her supervisor for about an hour. But, since I was in the neighborhood, she asked me to look at an analytical project she was wrapping up on the Chicago neighborhood environment where the Unabomber had roamed in the late 1970's and contrasted it to the similarity of a neighborhood here in the Oakland area that the bomber had used as a return address on a package bomb.

"Really interesting Maggie and I'd like to have a follow-up discussion about that, but right now I need to find Terry."

Other UTF members were sure Terry was on the floor, but didn't know where—or they chose not to tell if they did know. Then it hit me—Terry must have found a quiet place where he could avoid disruptions, phones and yours truly. I knew that feeling and I also knew my way around my own office space. I stepped into the hall and walked to an area of two small rooms and a large storage closet leading into a separate squad area. I popped open the door to the storage closet and the look on Terry's face was priceless. He was momentarily quiet, closed his eyes and rubbed his forehead and then opened them in the hope that I had been a mirage and would no longer be in the room. But I was still there, with an even bigger gaze meeting his steely and frustrated look.

"Trying to hide from me, huh?" I couldn't help but gloat. "Think I can't find you in my own field office?"

Terry wheeled around from the desk that was stored inside the closet. From the looks of the neatly stacked papers on the desk and an orderly arrangement of filing cabinets taking up the rest of the small windowless room, it was apparent that Terry used this hideaway often.

"How in the heck did you think to look for me in here?" he asked incredulously.

"If there is a place to grab some privacy in this office, I should be the one to stake a claim to it." Our face-off inside a closet had its moment and a good laugh, but then I nodded for him to follow me back to the front office.

Once there, we filled our coffee cups and settled into a sitting area next to my conference table.

"I know what you want to talk about—its Neil's suspect. Before you get too worked up over it, let me give you some background and tell you what we're doing and what I already told Neil."

Terry launched into the story. A caller to the 1-800-Hotline reported knowing someone that fit the information released by the FBI right down to the drawing that he saw on TV. Neil got the referral from a hotline employee, saw that the tip had real potential, and claimed it for his own. As he looked further, it got real interesting.

The suspect was from Illinois and had attended college at Chicago Circle Campus, where the Unabomber had left his first bomb in the parking lot of the Science and Technical Building. He eventually moved to the Bay Area and earned a graduate degree in science at the University of California at Berkeley. While there he played a joke on another student by placing a fake bomb in the student's gym locker. He taught at a local college. By the time Terry finished telling me these particulars, I was ready to call out the cavalry. But, there was more.

"Jim, there are things that look really interesting about this guy, but there are other things that just won't ever fit. We've already started a timeline comparison and no matter what we do, this guy and the Unabomber are ever so slightly separated in time and space when you get into the details."

Terry hesitated in outlining the specific steps being taken to eliminate the suspect and I took his reluctance as a polite way of asking me to back off so that he and the agents could run down the remaining loose ends. But, it just isn't in my nature and especially not with UNABOM. I reminded him of the need to be absolutely certain every time we made an important tactical or strategic move, because each step was under microscopic scrutiny on several fronts.

I wasn't pleased to have been kept in the dark. And, it wasn't like Neil had developed this suspect of his own accord—it was a hotline tip from the public, a product of our well-documented strategy. Not a time to get territorial, I thought.

"Have you instituted surveillances of this guy?" I snapped.

"No, I think we should hold off for now. We're making plans to conduct a trash cover to try for DNA or fingerprints. I'll be bringing you the memo, as it still requires SAC approval," he responded.

"It's approved. Just get it to me ASAP! And let's get the Special Operations Group out into this guy's neighborhood to keep a discreet eye on him." The SOG was the office's full-time surveillance team that was deployed on assignment to follow persons of interest from mobsters to members of drug gangs. If it later proved that this guy is the Unabomber, we had to know where he was at all times while we were trying to gather evidence and put together the facts. Of great concern to me was that he might drop another bomb into the mail while we were trying to sort out his suspect status.

"Jim, if we decide to conduct a surveillance of the guy, I believe at the very most we should use the SSG." Terry clearly wanted to move slower on this suspect case than I did and his counterintelligence roots were showing.

I became concerned that his preference for the Special Surveillance Group, or SSG as the Counterintelligence team is called, might be perceived by the predominately "criminal" agents of the UTF as a lack of faith in our primary surveillance group. Agents with extensive criminal investigative experience staffed the SOG, but the SSG was made up of non-agent support personnel that received highly specialized training in counterintelligence surveillance techniques.

It was a big red flag and I was not about to go down that road and start a controversy of unknown magnitude. In fact, there was a better than an even chance that some of the UTF agents in San Francisco had already passed this nugget of information to their contacts in the Criminal Division at FBIHQ. I don't think Terry had that possibility on his radar scope.

"Terry, I want the SOG placed on this case, now, and as soon as we get any results from the trash cover, let me know. I'm placing a call to the Bureau on this suspect and you need to speak with Tom Mohnal at the Lab about processing the results of the trash cover for fingerprints, DNA, and whatever else they can turn up for us."

Terry half-smiled and took a deep breath. "Neil was right," he said, as he started to turn and leave the room.

"What do you mean, 'Neil was right?'" I asked.

"He was worried we would tell the Bureau about this suspect so he made a direct plea to me to let him work the guy without opening a suspect case at this point." Terry responded, and then waved me off with his hand in the air.

Then, he continued. "Don't worry; I wouldn't have approved that. But, I have to tell you I think there's no way this is the Unabomber, even though there are some interesting aspects to the guy's background. I'll notify Mohnal, get the trash cover going and brief the SOG myself. I'll come back this afternoon and we can talk about everything that's going on in the investigation."

This was the closest thing to a real confrontation between Terry and me up to this point. But, I left unsaid what I was feeling—"So, this is how it works? Our strategy produces a viable suspect and I'm the last to know because I'm the damn SAC?" I knew that deep down Terry understood. But, he was caught between being a street agent and being their manager—the proverbial rock and a hard place.

I was ultimately responsible for every investigation in the office and I was certainly not going to take any chances with UNABOM. Terry's instincts on the guy's lack of viability as a suspect may have been right on, but that wasn't good enough for UNABOM. The suspect clicked on exactly the criteria we were looking for and if this actually wasn't our guy, we had to have solid evidence to eliminate him.

We worked well together because I had a short memory and Terry reacted to all of my personal forays into the case with his usual calmness. Then again, even that calmness caused me to worry from time to time. I went back to work, trying to concentrate on the broader aspects of running the San Francisco Office, but I was being drawn ever deeper into this compelling and mysterious case that we called UNABOM.

Terry cranked up the suspect investigation to a speed that was more to my liking. And, he calmed Neil down even as he confirmed Neil's worst fears that the Bureau and I were riding shotgun on his suspect case!

* * *

Turchie and the UTF had turned a major corner with the FBI Laboratory since the Director's visit to San Francisco after the Mosser bombing. The toxic meeting between Tom Mohnal and Max Noel back in Washington had blown over and our relationship had become productive in those weeks. I had dispatched Terry on a couple of trips to the Lab with the sole intent of patching up things with Tom Mohnal and Tom Thurman. It had worked and the results were impressive.

Bill Tobin, the FBI Lab's primary metallurgist saw fit to travel to San Francisco to meet with Terry, Max and Neil and he had plenty to say about the Unabomber's use of aluminum and lead in his devices. It was Tobin's belief that the Unabomber's use of aluminum was sufficiently unique that it might provide an avenue for linking the bomber to his tradecraft.

The top brass at the Lab even changed their position against allowing the UTF to consult with outside forensic experts and scientists. Foremost among them was the Lawrence Livermore National Lab (LLNL) in Livermore, CA, about an hour east of the San Francisco FBI office. Their scientists pointed to the bomber's use of aluminum end plugs in his pipe bombs and said that he likely had melted down scraps of aluminum himself in some sort of melting pot. Some aluminum samples appeared to have originated from pieces of screen doors and auto parts. The explosive powders used were simple pyrotechnic mixtures, although the bomber apparently experimented with gasoline as an accelerant to achieve the larger explosive force that he desired. Eventually, the bomber settled on and stayed with mixtures of ammonium nitrate, aluminum powder, and potassium chlorate to achieve an explosion that could be initiated by a hot wire.

Terry and Max walked into my office one afternoon with news from the SOG team that was working Neil's suspect. They had pulled a piece of wood from the suspect's trash, as well as hair from dryer lint. The FBI Lab examined the wood and hair and the results were startling.

"Jim, the piece of redwood we found in the trash bears similarities to a piece of redwood used in the Gelernter device. The Lab will need to do additional tests on it, but both pieces had beveled edges, probably from a jigsaw. The preliminary DNA test found some similarities between the suspect's hair and hair found at the scene of the Mosser bombing. The Lab has given us the option of further, more conclusive tests—but the downside is that they would have to use up all of the existing specimen hair, leaving none of it for further examination in the future."

A similar piece of redwood and some similarities in the hair samples, but none of it was conclusive. "Have you guys talked this over? What do you think?"

"Jim read this before you make any decision," Terry handed me a memo. "Max wrote a very good assessment of this suspect. We both believe he is not the Unabomber. I'll let you read his analysis on your own, but here is what really stands out. Tammy Fluehe the eye witness in 1987 saw the bomber standing up, bending down, moving around and walking away. She never mentioned anything about the bomber limping or having a hard time walking. But this suspect had a terrible accident many years ago and has an extremely difficult time walking and getting around. He has a noticeable limp. This can't be our bomber."

I wasn't going to debate the merits of physical versus eyewitness evidence, but we couldn't afford to leave this stone unturned. "I hear what you guys are saying, but the physical evidence is giving us a different message. Let's get Doug Diedrich on the phone."

Doug Diedrich was a deliberate talking FBI Lab expert who had been in the same New Agent's Training Class with Terry. Apparently they hadn't spoken or seen each other for years, as it took a few minutes for them to catch up on the phone. Diedrich had a reputation for excellence in his examinations of hair and fiber and had testified in the criminal trial of O. J. Simpson about the impressions left at the scene of the murders by someone wearing Bruno Magli shoes.

"Keep in mind that our hair analysis is limited because we don't have any known hairs from the Unabomber," Diedrich began his explanation of the procedures. But we can sequence pubic and head hair from the dryer lint and compare it with the final three inches of hair from the Mosser crime scene. We've already used an inch of that hair for the first test. The test normally takes a few weeks, but we'll expedite this as much as possible."

"Let's do it, Doug. Get back to us as soon as you can." With our phone call concluded, we parted ways and I could see the disappointment that Max and Terry were wearing on their faces when they left my office. But, I had no choice.

We had plenty to keep us occupied. After all the venting about the need for more immediate and continuous behavioral support, Jim Wright, our contact at the National Center for Analysis of Violent Crime (NCAVC) came to San Francisco with a new profiler in tow. They finally seemed ready to make amends in providing a new kind of behavioral support. Terry, Max, Kathy and Joel all came to my office for introductions all around to Jim Fitzgerald. He was a Philadelphia police officer before becoming an FBI agent and was newly assigned to the NCAVC. Fitzgerald's boyish appearance and soft-spoken manner concealed a gruff and seasoned street cop interior.

Terry liked him because he was quiet and soft-spoken. Max was pleased to find a street cop—turned behavioral analyst. Kathy liked him because as she said later, "He's easy to look at." And, I liked him because his competence and street smarts showed the minute he started talking.

"I'm here to support the UTF and be a team player," was his lead off remark. It's all we needed to hear.

Fitzgerald went to work immediately to prove his value to the UTF. The combination of Kathy's instincts in clinical psychology and his unique sense of street smarts invigorated the behavioral side of UNABOM. At the same time, Terry was maintaining contact with John Behnke in the Director's office, which provided personal and discreet access to the top of the FBI's food chain; while my communications with Louie were formal and at arm's length. It was a delicate balance and Terry had to be cautious in playing the hand, but it was a great hand to have!

On his trips to Washington, Terry always called on John as both a courtesy and because the two had become friends. John provided insight to Terry on the only other bombing case the FBI had worked that had been remotely similar to UNABOM. It was titled VANPAC and was the case where John became acquainted with the young prosecutor, Louis Freeh.

As Terry related Behnke's account of the murder of U.S. District Judge Robert Vance, it was astounding to hear of the similarities in the VANPAC and UNABOM attacks. The bomber had sent four explosive devices to various targets and one had hit Judge Vance in his home—leading investigators to believe he was of special interest to the killer. The FBI Lab said that the homemade bombs were simple and easy to construct. The bomber wrote letters claiming responsibility, including a letter to Atlanta newscaster Brenda Wood in 1989. He had also provided a secret code so that he could be properly identified in any future correspondence. He hand-painted the inside of the boxes that contained his bombs and used finishing nails as shrapnel.

All sounded eerily familiar and it caused me to wonder if the Unabomber had studied the progress of that other investigation.

John introduced Terry to Bill Hagmire, the NCAVC profiler that had worked alongside him on the VANPAC investigation, and Hagmire picked up the discussion at the point leading to the arrest of Walter LeRoy Moody for the murder of Judge Vance. In August of 1989, Moody sent a letter to radio stations that he was declaring war on the 11th Circuit Court. Moody had an ego, little regard for investigators, two years of law school under his belt, and he was an active litigant. As the VANPAC killer, he selected the New York Times, Time Magazine and Newsweek as "cut outs" to talk to law enforcement. He relished the spotlight and the real target of his anger had been Judge Vance all along. The other bombings were created as a diversion and to complicate things for investigators.

"Bill, has the Bureau conducted any behavioral assessments of serial bombers that might help us now?" Terry figured that any analysis of even a select few serial bombers might shed light on our own prey.

"Terry, you can count our collective experience thus far on one hand. There's VANPAC and then a case we called ICANBOM in the late 1970s; the infamous George Meteskey, the 'Mad Bomber of New York,' who called himself 'FP'; James Genrich, who murdered people in Grand Junction, Colorado with four anti-personnel devices; and Dean Harvey Hicks, an aerospace engineer in southern California who was angry at the IRS. Hicks used thirteen pipe bombs in an attempt to kill IRS employees in 1991. It's not a broad enough sample for a definitive study of behavioral characteristics.

Terry's interest in behavioral studies on serial bombers prompted Jim Fitzgerald to schedule a meeting in Quantico with the elusive ATF agent Joe Chisholm. At least he was elusive as far as the UTF was concerned, as he was attached to the NCAVC specifically to travel to all of the sites of UNABOM attacks to take photographs and look for additional aspects of the case through the light of his "profile." It was especially irritating to Terry, because Chisholm had never shared his findings or his photos with the San Francisco based UTF.

"Joe, we've got to have your assessments and photos. While you're at it, throw in your analysis of the other serial bombers like Meteskey, ICANBOM, Genrich and Hicks," Terry said firmly, having long since lost his patience in waiting on what he considered an important product needed in timely fashion. Puckett, Fitzgerald, and Joel Moss, who accompanied Terry to the meeting, surrounded Chisholm as they all talked.

"I can tell you a great deal about Meteskey, we've done profiles on Genrich and assessments on ICANBOM, but we never did much follow up on Hicks. And, you're right. I owe you and the UTF the write up on my around the country trip to the scenes of UNABOM crimes. I'll finish it up and come out to San Francisco and walk you through every photograph I took." And, in due time, Chisholm was true to his word and imparted his knowledge of the case to the UTF agents.

While Terry was momentarily preoccupied with the history of serial bombers, I took to the airwaves to paint a picture for the public of who I thought we were looking for—integrating all that we knew or thought we knew about the Unabomber. It amounted to a marriage of our investigative results, some behavioral analysis, and a deep-seated feeling within the gut.

In my first conference with the media to launch our more aggressive media strategy, I discussed in some detail the UTF's beliefs about the Unabomber's profile. It would be a topic I returned to frequently. "We have a great concern the bomber will strike again. I believe someone knows or suspects the identity of the Unabomber. The only known sighting of the bomber was in Salt Lake City in 1987. He is a white male with a ruddy complexion and blond to red hair. He was wearing a hooded sweatshirt. We're releasing an enhanced sketch done by the artist, Jeanne Boylan, whose sketch of the suspect was used in the Polly Klaas kidnapping case and aided us in solving that crime.

"The FBI's National Center for the Analysis of Violent Crime believes the bomber is in his late 30's or 40's; he is probably a loner, has a high school education with exposure to and familiarity with college, and has a degree of familiarity with the areas where the bombs have been mailed from or placed. Based on our investigation and the westward progression of his activities, we believe that the Unabomber lived in and around the Chicago area in the mid- to late 1970's and likely relocated at some point to Utah and possibly into Northern California. If this information matches or is similar to someone that you know, you are requested to notify the FBI or call the UNABOM hotline...."

I would repeat the message numerous times in the succeeding months, hoping it would bring the break we all needed. But, breaks in the UNABOM case had been non-existent since the lone eyewitness report way back in '87. Following my latest UNABOM press conference, a call was waiting for me. Doug Diedrich had completed his DNA test of the hair found in the trash of Neil's suspect. They were not identical. I asked Janet to page Terry, who was with Max at an agent's retirement luncheon.

Terry called me back from a pay phone and through the background noise I heard him relay to Max, "You were right on. The hairs don't match."

"I'll close this suspect case when I get back to the office this afternoon," Terry advised me in a straightforward manner.

"Okay, I'll see you when you get back. We'll move on." I was satisfied, even though the experience had left a bitter taste and frustration for some. I accepted it as the price for being the Agent-in-Charge.

* * *

At the next management meeting in my office, a report from Don Davis dominated our discussions. Postal Inspectors had fanned out to the mail processing facilities in San Francisco, Sacramento, Oakland and San Jose during the previous week. They distributed photos of mock-ups of the Unabomber's mailed devices and provided awareness training to postal employees by encouraging them to be pro-active in reporting suspicious circumstances.

Briefings were given to over one hundred and fifty postmasters and supervisors and they had prepared a training video for employee viewing at every post office. Davis felt strongly that they could identify one or more Bay Area postal processing locations where UNABOM devices had been mailed.

"Interesting proposition," Terry's eyes lit up. "Jim, what if we could put twenty-four hour camera surveillance at those locations? Maybe we could catch the Unabomber in action."

Davis responded quickly before I could answer. "I checked with the Postal Lab to see whether we could do that, but we don't have the capability, money or equipment to make it happen." And, now he was waiting for what I had to offer.

"I'll call the Deputy Director, Bill Esposito, and see if the

Bureau will spring for the research and development of 24 hour camera surveillance at key postal facilities in the Bay Area. Terry, you call Tom Nunnemaker and tell him what we're up to out here. Max, you talk to Tom Mohnal at the Lab. If we work it from all three levels, we might get some traction." I jumped on the idea, as I liked being pro-active in our thinking.

Almost as one, we jumped from the camera idea to the operational dilemma we would face if we were lucky enough to intercept a live UNABOM explosive device. If we found a bomb, we needed to have the capability to safely dismantle and preserve it for detailed forensic examination. It was futile and counter-productive to "render it safe" in the usual manner—by blowing it up.

"Max, when you talk with Mohnal, ask him about the possibilities of getting with the right people to design and build a bomb robot that can handle and disable the Unabomber's unique devices. And, tell him to consider all the possibilities—without consideration of cost."

I had added that last comment in the spirit of excitement with the possibility of intercepting a live bomb in the mail stream. Perhaps we were becoming delirious with the hours we were putting in, but it was better to just go with the flow. To revel in the possibility that this could take us to the serial killer that we so wanted to find.

Our afternoon calls brought outstanding news. Esposito said the FBI would find the money for the camera surveillances, as well as putting people to work finding or inventing the right kind of robot to handle a live bomb. Tom Nunnemaker reassured Terry he would get started writing the reams of paper necessary to make our dreams a reality. And, Tom Mohnal had the best news of all. He told Max of a scientist friend at Sandia National Laboratory in New Mexico, who thought he could put together a small team to design and build a first-of-its-kind "bomb disrupter." All he needed to get started was the green light from FBI Headquarters to Sandia Lab's front office.

Good news never lasted long in UNABOM. Within days, I took a call from the San Francisco Chronicle during the late afternoon. As soon as I got off the phone, I called the switchboard and asked them to find Terry. He was heading home on the Bay Bridge when he was summoned by the radio dispatcher to return to the office to meet with the SAC.

I met him in the garage and opened the passenger door. "Terry, the San Francisco Chronicle called. They've received a letter from FC. I said we would be right over to meet with their editors."

"Do we know what the letter says?"

It didn't take long for us to find out. Upon our arrival, we were quickly escorted from the lobby of the *Chronicle* to its administrative offices, where we met the managing editor of the paper. He turned over a letter that bore a return address of Fredrick Benjamin Isaac Wood, 549 Wood Street, Woodlake, CA 93286. Woodlake, California was located in Tulare County, but the address on the envelope was fictitious. Neither Terry nor I overlooked the bomber's crude attempt at humor, contained in his creative return address—"FBI" Wood. It wasn't funny, but the letter inside was even less so. It gave us the clearest message to date of the Unabomber's next objective:

"…The terrorist group FC is planning to blow up an airliner out of Los Angeles International Airport some time during the next six days."

The race against time and the Unabomber was on.

CHAPTER TWELVE

PUBLISH OR PERISH

(The FBI doesn't negotiate with terrorists; it is anathema to all in law enforcement. The Unabomber demanded that his Manifesto be published and his demands were universally scorned as the rants of a madman. But we were convinced his Manifesto represented the bomber's lifelong philosophy, surely recognizable by someone who heard the bomber express his ideas or turn a unique phrase at sometime in the past. In order to find that person and stop the bomber from killing again, would it be necessary to recommend its publication with all its attendant risks?)

IT WAS ALREADY AFTER FIVE AS TERRY AND I DROVE THE SHORT distance from the San Francisco Chronicle back to the FBI office. And, time wasn't on our side.

"Terry, I'll call Bill Esposito and make sure he and Louie are briefed on the threat to airplanes out of LAX. Call Tom Nunnemaker so he hears what is developing and gives notification to the FAA at the national level. Get our remaining ASAC(s) and Supervisors who are still in the office and line up the troops to staff our command center."

There were a hundred things to do at the same time, but I needed to start with FBIHQ and Terry could get our office and the UTF organized for a crisis management drill—except this was no drill.

After I briefed Deputy Director Esposito on the situation, I was on the phone to Charlie Parsons, the FBI's Agent in Charge for the greater Los Angeles area. Charlie was a friend and colleague who could act quickly and decisively when all hell was breaking loose. We had been expecting to receive the Unabomber's manifesto any day. None of us expected another bomb, especially on an airplane.

Parsons quickly set up a Crisis Management Center inside the FBI office and at Los Angeles International Airport. While Parsons briefed several Federal and State officials based in Los Angeles, I reached out by telephone at the Director's request to get word to California's Governor in Sacramento. I didn't have the phone number of the Governor's residence at my fingertips, so I decided it would be more expedient to work through Dan Lungren, the Attorney General of California and head of the California Bureau of Investigation. I had recently met Dan and his team at a law enforcement conference where of all things— there was discussion of UNABOM.

"Hello, Dan, this is Jim Freeman at the FBI. Sorry to call you at home, but the Unabomber just threatened to take out a plane leaving LAX."

He was immediately all business and took down the details of how to get in touch with Parsons in Los Angeles. And, he was quite happy to pass the word on to the Governor. Next, I was on the phone with Dick Ross, Sacramento's SAC, to give him details of the bomber's threats and of my call to Lungren. Ross volunteered to follow up with the State Bureau of Investigation and enlist the cooperation of the California Highway Patrol and other statewide offices.

When Parsons had a moment the next day, he described the initial bedlam at the Crisis Center and the line-up of officials who showed up at the airport—Federico Pena, the U.S. Secretary of Transportation; Los Angeles Mayor Richard Riordan; California's

Lieutenant Governor Gray Davis and Los Angeles Police Chief Willie Williams. Then there were the local representatives of the Federal Aviation Administration (FAA), the Postal Inspection Service, ATF, U.S. Secret Service, the Airport Police, the LA County Sheriff, LAPD and LA Fire Department; all of whom contributed manpower to the 24-hour staffing of the Crisis Center.

Over the next few days, Terry camped out overnight on the leather couch in his office. It was also hard to get Joel to leave the UTF Command Post and we got used to seeing him there day and night. Kathy Puckett and Jim Fitzgerald isolated themselves with every known word the Unabomber had written in various letters over the years with the goal of piecing together any credible thread that might lead to his identification. Terry and I were on the phone constantly with FBI Headquarters, the FBI in L.A., other field divisions and each other. In between the phone calls, it was one meeting after another.

We were constantly busy, but at the same time—watching and waiting for the other shoe to drop. This blatant threat reached into everyone's consciousness. The Unabomber held the attention and fears of the entire country and it fell upon us to stop him from blowing an airplane full of passengers from the sky. He had already put a bomb on a plane in 1979, so we knew he had the will and capability to do it. Despite our best efforts, the bomber was still holding the cards.

At LAX, highly skilled bomb technicians from the FBI, LAPD, and LA Sheriff's Office were in the command post and ready to launch in any direction on a moment's notice. FBI teams inspected close to two hundred tractor trailer loads of mail being loaded onto outbound planes. Passengers boarding flights waited for hours to get through the newly implemented screening procedures. The FAA issued requirements that each passenger must be asked individually about who had packed their bags and whether they had left their baggage unattended at any time. Awareness alerts were issued throughout the day and night.

In San Francisco, Kathy Puckett and Jim Fitzgerald requested an audience with Terry, Joel, Max and me; and then tried to make sense of the words and thoughts appearing in the Unabomber's latest letters.

"In the letter to the *New York Times* he spelled the word installment with one 'l' and Burson-Marsteller as 'Burston.' There were strikeovers in the letter and we felt that the letter was prepared in a more hurried manner than previous correspondence." Fitzgerald had obviously read every line and then between every line.

Kathy picked up a copy of the Unabomber's letter. "The bomber repeats several times that he will desist from terrorism if his manifesto is published. I don't believe that he can actually do this, even if he wants to. It's just not possible for him to stop the bombings." Kathy read a passage from the letter:

"...By terrorism we mean actions motivated by a desire to influence the development of a society and intended to cause injury or death to human beings. By sabotage we mean similarly motivated actions intended to destroy property without injuring human beings. The promise we offer is to desist from terrorism...."

"Then, what's the bottom line Kathy?" I asked. "The question I think about is what happens when he mails out this manifesto to the *New York Times*, or similar media outlet. Will the media publish on their own? Will they ask for the FBI's recommendation? And, if placed in a position of deciding whether to advocate for or against its publication, what's our position on that?" It was a rhetorical question and I glanced toward Terry as a reminder that he and I would ultimately be responsible for the answer, if it came to that.

Kathy's conclusions were sobering. "He's a bomber and will continue to bomb. He can't help it. Bombs don't have boundaries. And sabotage is potentially as deadly as terrorism, even using the Unabomber's definitions."

Even as we discussed our dilemma, the Unabomber was implementing the next phase of his plan. We didn't have to wait long for it to unfold.

On June 29, the *New York Times* heard from the Unabomber again. This time, he sent a letter attached to a copy of his long-awaited manifesto. In the letter, the Unabomber tried to display a sense of humor and again no one was amused:

"Since the public has a short memory, we decided to play one last prank to remind them who we are. But—no, we haven't tried to plant a bomb on an airline (recently)."

That bastard...! That's all that came to mind.

Before the week was over, four more copies of the manifesto with accompanying letters arrived at their destinations—the *Washington Post* and *Scientific American* each received copies. Another was directed personally to Bob Guccione at *Penthouse*, which was a strange twist. And a letter and copy of the manifesto was mailed to Professor Tom Tyler, a social psychologist at the University of California at Berkeley. Each was potentially a treasure trove of hidden clues.

Kathy and Terry quickly headed for Berkeley to meet in person with Tyler and to see if there had been any previous contacts with the Unabomber. It turned out that during the past year Tyler had been interviewed for an article that appeared in the *San Francisco Chronicle* about social malaise. If the Unabomber's personal letter to Tyler was prompted by that newspaper interview, this put the bomber somewhere within the distribution network of the *San Francisco Chronicle*.

Professor Tyler was responsive to their questions. "I'm very pleased the Unabomber wants discussion of these issues. Ultimately, discussion is better than violence." Tyler eventually gave similar statements to the media, and we hoped his comments would elicit a written dialogue with the Unabomber. But, it didn't happen.

* * *

The bomber had changed the game again. First, it was years of silence—letting his bombs do the talking and only an occasional introductory letter to some of his victims as an enticement to open an exploding package. Then, he cracked the door open a little with the first letter to the editor of the *New York Times*—the one with the mysterious "Nathan R" indented writing on the paper. Following a progression of more lethal and deadly bombs, there was a small flurry of letters. Some letters taunted injured victims and others made fun of the FBI.

Now, the Unabomber had unleashed a torrent of words in a manifesto that was dozens of pages in length. Maybe it would be a game-changer; this time in our favor. It must have meaning to someone.

Janet brought me back to earth, signaling that I had a phone call and mouthing that it was the Deputy Director.

"Jim, its Bill Esposito. The Director wants me to come out there for a visit. We need to know your plan for moving forward and want your recommendation on what to do with this damn manifesto. I'll see you on July 12. That should give you enough time to decide on a strategy in view of the recent developments."

I was surprised, but managed to respond light-heartedly, "Come on out, Bill. We'll put on a fitting reception for someone of your esteemed stature."

Bill was a valued confidant and a kindred spirit who had served just down the road as SAC of the San Diego Division before getting bumped up in rank to the Bureau. In truth, he had retained his street smarts even after being promoted to senior executive positions at FBI Headquarters in Washington, D.C.

Our UNABOM leadership meeting the next day was more

somber than most. Everyone appeared with their copy of the new "best-seller" in law enforcement circles—the Unabomber's manifesto. I found it a tough read for the most part. Terry told them of the Headquarters' contingent coming our way in July and that served as a springboard to start our discussion.

I began the meeting on a high note. "Tony, we heard from the Bureau today. It looks like our letters and phone calls worked out. I was informed that your retirement from the Postal Inspection Service is held in abeyance at the special request of Louis Freeh to allow additional time for you to work on UNABOM."

Terry and I had gone to bat over Tony Muljat's mandatory retirement from the Postal Inspection Service and even Director Freeh ran interference to make sure Tony could stay on UNABOM with a one- year extension. He was, after all, one of the longest running investigators to work the case. Besides, Tony worked hard and we all liked him.

"Thank you Jim and Terry," Tony decided to give us his feel for the recent developments in UNABOM. "I think all of you know I want to pull out all the stops with the examination of the bomber's written words. The work I was doing on the History of Science, the letters with the pseudonyms Enoch Fischer and Ralph C. Kloppenburg, and the general idea of associating the bomber's connection to universities has now become even more important with this manifesto and what's contained in it."

Terry took it from there. "Kathy and 'Fitz' are jumping into every word of this manifesto, looking for anything and everything of value. I've already given Tony the green light to pursue his linguistic related projects and Joel will help him with some of the on-campus interviews. And, I'm taking Neil Oltman with me to meet a renowned professor at Berkeley who will be reviewing some specific samples from the manifesto to see what he thinks about the bomber's academic affiliations."

"Terry, we need to remind Jim that we're also going to drive over to Fresno to interview Dr. Eric Hickey, a criminal justice professor and psychologist who has some ideas on the loner aspect of our bomber," Tony added.

Max had been unusually quiet, so I turned to him in particular. "What are your thoughts, Max?"

"I think we have to be careful to stick with the facts. We have forensics, we have solid information that we've developed from our reinvestigations, and we have specific leads that need our attention. I think that's where and how we're going to find the Unabomber. I'm a little concerned that by completely turning off in the direction of this manifesto, we might be separating ourselves from the sound strategy that we've patiently developed and stayed focused on. That's what has made us different."

Max was deliberate and chose his words carefully, as he realized that his opinion was in the minority among the attendees. And, he wasn't finished. "When I talked to some other agents yesterday and gave them a feel for my thinking, they expressed similar views. In fact, several believe the manifesto is a red herring— a purposeful false lead set by the Unabomber to mislead the FBI."

Terry leaned toward Max as he finished. "I know we need to be careful, but we have several who can pursue this new line of investigation without diluting what we are doing elsewhere."

"That's right. And, some of them have approached me. These are seasoned investigators. We should keep their opinions in mind." Max had made his point and I accepted it as a new reality for our UTF.

As one day bled into the next, ongoing developments in the case only postponed the decision that Freeh and Esposito had asked for about the manifesto. But, there was a lack of conviction as to which direction to take.

Terry and Joel and other members of my UNABOM leadership team were routinely out hustling leads and conducting interviews themselves, which illustrated how dramatically we had altered our original approach. Still, our approach was yielding positive results—inch by inch.

Joel and Max continued to attempt to identify the red 1976 Spider Fiat seen leaving the Caams Computer Store parking lot after the bomb explosion in February of 1987. Max had identified this unresolved lead in one of his earlier trips to Salt Lake City in January 1994. He and ATF Agent Tom Atteberry had returned to Salt Lake City several times, visiting auto body shops and crawling through auto wrecking yards, along with Utah DMV Investigator Jim Erickson. Their efforts had not identified the elusive Spider Fiat's owner. Joel finally got a break and identified a contractor who had driven to Caams on the day of the bombing, delivering some wooden cabinet pieces. He confirmed to Joel that he owned a red Spider Fiat, which he used to make the delivery to Caams the day of the bombing. That put an end to the long-standing lead to find the red Fiat.

Joel then researched the possible origins of the Unabomber's secret code (nine digits) that was provided in his most recent letter to the *New York Times* with an instruction to use the code for authentication purposes. Surprisingly, it turned out to match the actual Social Security Number (SSN) of an inmate who had never held a job and had been incarcerated most of his life in the California prison system.

When Joel related that tidbit to us, I steeled myself for another of the weird coincidences of UNABOM. The inmate was arrested in 1985 in a theater parking lot in Sacramento. Upon questioning by Agent John Conway, the arrestee believed that he lost his SSN card at the scene of his arrest. The theater was long since defunct, but on a visit to the location Joel said that he looked across the parking lot and in the distance he saw the back door and parking lot of the former RenTech Computer Store. Hugh Scrutton's life was brutally cut short at that precise location on a December day in 1985. "Could the Unabomber have found the lost SSN card in the area and saved it for future use?" It raised interesting possibilities, but none that led us any closer to identifying the Unabomber.

Professor Eric Hickey at Fresno State College was not shy in asserting his conclusion that we were dealing with a lone bomber, likely having a blue-collar background, and who was doing all the right things to make sure we didn't identify him.

A professor from University of California, Berkeley also offered some advice. "You might well look at assistants to university professors or anyone operating at less than a professor level in this kind of environment," he explained. "The goal at any university is to reach that esteemed level, and the vast majority of these people have huge egos and pretty narcissistic attitudes of themselves. They can be very petty and hold long and deep grudges. Your bomber could well have fit into that kind of category and may have worked at a place like this."

This was the diversity of advice and public comment that Terry and the UTF had been working through on a daily basis for more than a year and whenever I was exposed to the daily traffic of Hotline messages and interview results, I appreciated their task and dedication all the more. I had appointed Terry to coordinate the UTF and then we promoted him to the broader role as the ASAC of San Francisco's Counterintelligence Division. But, UNABOM was all consuming work and he had done little else. The murder of Gilbert Murray and the more recent flood of correspondence from the Unabomber had quickly overwhelmed our organizational planning and threatened to supplant our original strategy. A fork in the road and a potential change in strategy loomed ahead of us.

* * *

Bill Esposito arrived in San Francisco with a small contingent from Headquarters. The word quickly spread among UTF members when they became aware that he was the FBI agent who had overseen the investigation of countless organized crime cases, including the disappearance of Jimmy Hoffa. Terry and I met Bill in the office reception area and guided him and the accompanying entourage to the conference room across the hallway.

To the relief of Terry and others, the Deputy Director invited a level of comfort by removing his suit coat, rolling up his sleeves and asking for coffee before everyone had settled at the table. Tom Nunnemaker, the young Bureau Supervisor, wore a serious expression as he reached for his pen and yellow legal pad. Section Chief Bob Conforti sat quietly with an aura of self-confidence.

"Good to see you again, young man," Dennis Weaver, the Violent Crimes Unit Chief at FBIHQ extended his hand to Terry with a big smile. Weaver had an easy going manner that made him hard not to like, but his habit of worrying over every minute detail of an issue made everyone crazy.

"That's my job," I mused to myself.

I opened the meeting with an overview of the UTF organizational structure and our pressing needs for additional manpower. Next, Terry reported on current UTF projects and then turned to our most recent development.

"As we began reviewing the UNABOM manifesto, we quickly realized the writer referenced four books by name in his 35,000 word thesis. One of the books was 'The Ancient Engineers,' by L. Sprague de Camp. We have set out a lead to have Mr. de Camp interviewed and tasked agents to go to every university associated with a UNABOM event to see whether the book had ever been used as reference material in any of their classes."

Terry continued, "FBI Agents in Chicago found a professor at Northwestern University who taught a class in the late 1970's and early 1980's called the History of Engineering. About seventy students attended the class and they used 'The Ancient Engineers' as a textbook. Coincidentally, their classroom was just a floor above the location of the second UNABOM event in May of 1979. We plan on finding and interviewing every one of those students; four of which live in California."

"Were any members of the Dungeons and Dragons among them?" Esposito quipped with a smile. It was an acknowledgement that he had more than a casual knowledge of the years-old UNABOM investigation.

Esposito was here for a purpose, which included a real-life assessment of our personnel and equipment needs. Terry and I faced a balance between asking for what we needed versus asking for the moon, until we realized there was little difference between the two. The Deputy Director of the FBI had not traveled across country to San Francisco just to say no to our needs; as he could have done that on the phone. There was an unprecedented opportunity here.

Following our staff meeting, Esposito and I walked to my office where he placed a call to Director Freeh. Several minutes of conversation ensued with questions and answers regarding our discussions and Louie was particularly interested in identifying what was needed to take advantage of the recent Unabomber communications. His answer exceeded my expectations. I listened as Esposito related the Director's pronouncement to Terry.

"Here's what the Director has approved," Esposito began. "We're moving to create a separate UNABOM Office within the San Francisco Division. The organizational structure is unique. Jim will be the SAC of both entities and you, Terry, will be the Assistant Special Agent in Charge directly accountable to UNABOM. We are adding two additional squad supervisors to bring the number of dedicated UNABOM squads to three. You can devote one squad to investigating suspects, one to special projects, and one for logistics and the Hotline.

He had even more to say. "We're transferring thirty analysts to San Francisco for sixty days, so you can run with 24-hour analytical support. We're sending fourteen agents from other offices on a rotating sixty day basis to manage information coming from the Hotline; and we have committed to Jim that for the long-term we will increase the agent complement in San Francisco by thirty-eight agents and thirty-four support employees for the duration."

Terry gave me the look and smile that said—this almost triples the size of the SF team working on UNABOM. Esposito continued, "We'll also make sure you get all the computers, cars and any other equipment you need." This was a field executive's dream and the knowledge of that was not lost on Esposito; it was evident in his mannerisms and big smile.

Esposito was enjoying this to the fullest extent, but then he punctuated his message with an admonition—"Now, solve this damn case will you. It may become necessary to face the Director and the Attorney General with a tough decision on whether to sponsor the publishing of the UNABOM manifesto. The media moguls are saying they won't do it without our public endorsement."

Prior to departing for the airport, Esposito and I stepped into my office for a wrap-up on the visit and to discuss the ramifications of acceding to the Unabomber's demands that the manifesto must be published. I framed the viewpoint of some SF agents that the manifesto was likely a red herring, but added that Terry and I and others of my leadership team felt that it was vital to get the public focused on the actual words and ideas expressed by the Unabomber. Bill stated his understanding of our situation. He told me that many others were saying the same thing inside the Washington Beltway.

My commitment to him was to bring the UTF to a consensus on the manifesto. Although it was unspoken, it was clear that Louie needed to know who had his back on this decision. And, given my free-range with the media on UNABOM matters, it was understandable to affirm that my position and that of the UTF would be supportive of the final decision to publish or not publish.

Later, while Terry and I were in my office digesting the logistics of absorbing the promised new arrivals into our organization, the UTF leadership team filtered into my office without announcement or interception by Janet. She had recognized the priority of the moment when approached by Joel, Tony, Max, Kathy, Don Davis, Jim Fitzgerald, and Mark Logan, the newest ATF ASAC assigned to the UTF.

At first, there was a reticence among those present to speak up. Their mood bordered on silence. Even Tony, never the wallflower, glanced out of the corner of his eye waiting for others to speak.

"Well," I began, "Louie Freeh and his Deputy Director have asked us for a recommendation on the manifesto. It's a very tough call and the UTF needs to be firmly behind the decision."

"It's no wonder." Jim Fitzgerald broke the quiet. "If we advocate publication and he bombs again, we're screwed."

"Is that the behavioral term?" Terry tried to lighten the mood.

"Yep, that's directly from Quantico," Jim dug at Terry's penchant to hate all things behavioral from Quantico.

"If we don't publish and he bombs again, the result is the same; we're screwed either way." Joel opined.

"A perfect Catch-22," someone offered. I mused that it was probably from Tony, as he and I were of the generation most likely to be familiar with the classic novel where a situation is presented with only two possible choices and both will result in a negative outcome. It did seem to fit.

Kathy hoped to avoid any possible misunderstanding. "I'll repeat that if we overlook everything else, we can't afford to overlook a major psychological component; even though he says he will desist from terrorism, he can't. Even if he wants to, he won't be able to avoid sending more bombs. That's why he gives himself an out in his ultimatum. No terrorism, but reserving the right to commit sabotage. We just can't forget that."

Terry took to the high road. "This comes down to how confident we are in the investigation we've conducted. I tell people all the time that we feel we're close. And, don't forget what Joe Chisholm said to us a few weeks back," Terry grinned before he finished. "You've already solved the case. You just don't have the bomber's name yet."

Max again was the voice of caution. "We've put journeyman agents on this case. We need to listen to them. They want to follow the facts and the good leads based on the facts, just as you guys have emphasized from day one. We can't afford to get completely away from that strategy."

There it was again. Max had tossed a cautionary glance at Terry and it was apparent to all that there was tension on the UTF. It wasn't just about publishing or not publishing; it was about wasting too much time on the manifesto in the first place. Some UTF members didn't agree with it and they were looking to Max as their spokesman.

I looked around the room and then settled my gaze in Max's direction. "Some people say publishing is giving in to terrorists. But when we have a kidnap-for-ransom case, don't we sometimes offer to exchange the ransom as a tactic to identify the kidnapper and to lead us to where the hostage is being held? Isn't there a difference between a tactical maneuver and giving into terrorists?"

"Oh, Jim, I like that." Tony Muljat emphasized the like.

We debated, argued, and tried to reach the "right" decision on publication of the UNABOM manifesto. We all agreed that the bomber would continue killing people if the *New York Times* and *Washington Post* refused to publish his manuscript or didn't comply with his demands to publish correspondence from him on an annual basis. He'd given a deadline of September 24 to either publish or make a public announcement committing to publishing the manifesto, and if neither happened, his bombings would continue.

There was agreement among us that someone might recognize the writings and call the UTF to identify the author. On the other hand, there was an overriding concern against creating a precedent where the FBI was giving in to a terrorist.

The UTF leadership team vacillated constantly back and forth on the recommendation we would make to FBI Headquarters. In the end, there was one solid choice that prevailed.

I moved to restate the agreement, so there would be no misunderstanding in the message that the UTF would send to the Director. "Okay, then, to make it clear, we have all agreed to recommend against promoting the publication of the manifesto and giving in to the demands of a terrorist. Further, the UTF believes that our broad-based, but discreet investigation will accomplish the same goals as publication without creating an unwanted precedent for the future." I felt confident in saying the words, but there was a hesitation in the back of my mind; although that feeling was quickly dismissed amid the sight of heads nodding in agreement.

"Great. Terry will work with you in preparing a formal position paper. Esposito wants the UTF position in writing." When I looked at Terry, I sensed some discomfort in his expression; but he said nothing as he turned to leave.

What later ensued was a complete surprise to me. During a subsequent one-on-one meeting with Terry, I asked him what had gone on behind the closed doors of his office when we were deliberating on whether to publish the Unabomber's manifesto. As he became expert in doing, Terry answered with colorful detail. This is how he described to me one of the watershed moments of UNABOM:

With the door to his office closed, Terry stood behind his desk and was met by puzzled faces, all stamped with the same expression.

"What?" Obviously something was very wrong.

"We made the wrong decision over there." Jim Fitzgerald and Kathy echoed in unison.

Terry fell back in his chair, "I know. I feel it too."

Another two hours of discussion followed, with many of the same points hashed and rehashed. But, one difference emerged.

Finally, Terry called a halt to the unending discussion. "I think we've figured it out. We were so hung up on the traditional position—'don't give in to the demands of a terrorist,' that we forgot the overriding principle that we've instilled in the UTF since day one—just do the right thing." Terry knew they all felt the same way. "So now what?" he asked.

Max piped up. "One of us has to go tell Jim Freeman and that'd be you."

"That's why you get paid the big bucks and have the nice office," Fitzgerald added. There was laughter by all–the kind that comes after a heavy burden is lifted. Even Max appeared happy with the twist of position.

When Terry returned alone to my office that day, I thought it was to deliver the position paper. Instead, it was a reversal in the previous agreement. "Okay, let's hear it," I sighed.

"Actually Jim, I have good news and bad news,"

I cut him off from the game he wanted to play. "Sit." I motioned at the hot seat directly in front of my desk.

"We think we made the wrong decision this morning. Everyone is unanimous. We think we should recommend publication of the manifesto."

"Whoa, everyone was unanimous earlier. Now, you are unanimous again? What persuaded you?"

As Terry recounted his last two hours of continued discussion, it became apparent that everyone had been uncomfortable with that initial decision. But, we still needed a formal, written statement of the UTF recommendation and it had to read better than Terry's attribution—"just do the right thing."

As Terry recounted additional details of that discussion, I finally grasped the point. The question of whether or not the publication of the Unabomber's manifesto was an act of giving in to the demands of a terrorist—that's a national policy decision. The UTF was operational in every sense and our recommendation on the matter should be solely in the interest of advancing our long-standing investigative strategy. And, we firmly believed that publishing the manifesto would help us identify and capture the Unabomber. That would be the gist of our message to Headquarters.

Terry and I had reached an agreement and he nailed it in his summation. "Jim, I'm confident in the investigation that we've conducted and in our strategy. We have collected many of the missing pieces. We think the manifesto is the guy's real thoughts and philosophy. And, he's so passionate about it, he has surely told someone over the years about how strongly he feels. We need to find that person. Publishing his manifesto will help us do that."

Our position paper was sent off to FBI Headquarters that night; and Director Freeh and Bill Esposito had it the next day. We made our feelings clear from the outset.

"It is the position of the UTF that the manuscript submitted by the UNABOM subject...should be made public."

Our ultimate decision to recommend publication of the UNABOM Manifesto to advance operational interests, was in concert with Kathy Puckett's advice that the bomber couldn't stop bombing even if he wanted to. In the eventual search of Kaczynski's cabin, we found, in his own words, confirmation that the bombings would never stop until he was found.

"Because I no longer cared about death, I no longer cared about consequences, and I suddenly felt that I really could break out of my rut in life and do things that were daring, 'irresponsible,' or criminal."

CHAPTER THIRTEEN

IN PURSUIT OF WORDS

(The FBI was just as uncomfortable forging an alliance with two of the most powerful media organizations in the country as it was acceding to the demands of a terrorist. If the FBI Director agreed to publish the UNABOM Manifesto that is exactly the ground we would be walking).

TERRY, KATHY, AND I TRAVELED TO WASHINGTON, D.C. TO MEET with Director Freeh at the J. Edgar Hoover FBI Building to discuss our recommendations on publication of the Unabomber's Manifesto. The Hoover Building, as FBI employees refer to it, is located on Pennsylvania Avenue, mid-way between the United States Capitol and the White House and directly across the street from the Department of Justice. Although it reports to the Department of Justice, the Hoover Building is just tall enough to look down on the Justice Department Building, causing one to wonder if it was designed that way from the beginning to send a message to any politicians or Attorneys General who think they are in charge of the FBI. We made our way to the Director's Office and waited in his outer reception room, sandwiched among a couple dozen FBI officials from Headquarters and a scattering of SAC(s) from regions that had experienced UNABOM events. The mood in the room was both somber and engaging as colleagues who hadn't seen each other for awhile caught up with one another, and then were brought back to earth by the reason we were all summoned to see the Director—the FBI couldn't solve UNABOM. It was wearing on us all. Terry didn't know many of the FBI officials in the room, but all were my contemporaries and peer group. Some were personal friends. We had grown up in the FBI at the same time and now found ourselves poised to advise the Director on a significant and potentially momentous decision.

"You're not really going to tell the Director we should publish this manifesto, are you Freeman?" was passed along to me in a brush contact.

"Publishing this would be nuts," was a common theme of whispered conversations.

Terry was silently studying the faces crammed into the room, obviously repeating in his head the points he wanted to make in front of the boss.

"Wow, my colleagues don't seem too keen on our recommendation, Terry. You think we missed the mark?"

"Why are all these people here anyway? I don't recognize many as being involved in the investigation." It was reminiscent of the "Meeting of the Misters." Terry had no time to finish his point, as the doors facing the inner corridor swung open and we were summoned into the Director's massive conference room.

"Jim, Terry, and Kathy, come up here and sit in these chairs," Louie motioned for us to take the three chairs to the left of his seat at the conference table. Little time was wasted as the doors closed and the Director began the meeting. He jumped right to the point, thanking the assembly for all the work that was being done to solve UNABOM and then introducing me to discuss recent developments.

I quickly summarized our evolving UTF strategy and structure for dealing with UNABOM and alluded to the investigative opportunities presented by the recent spate of communications from the Unabomber.   After advising the Director and others that the UTF had reached a difficult decision to recommend publication of the Unabomber's manifesto, I turned to Terry to lay the background of how and why this was a justifiable and desirable course of action with the potential to move this investigation to completion.

Terry began by summarizing key developments in the reinvestigation that have immediate relevance to the writings of the Unabomber. Among the events that he chose to emphasize was the 1985 bomb mailed to Professor James McConnell that was accompanied by a letter referring to the "history of science." Terry opined that the bomber likely had studied the relatively obscure history of science somewhere along the way. We also believe there is relevance in the Unabomber's mention of another text, *The History of Engineering*, in the body of his manifesto.

"Professor Tom Tyler of UC Berkeley was singled out to receive a copy of his manifesto, which appeared to tie back to an interview and article written by the *San Francisco Chronicle* containing Tyler's comments on the malaise of society. These separate studies and theories appear to have struck a chord with the Unabomber," he explained.

No one in the room, except the Director, expected that we had anywhere near this level of detailed analysis. And, Terry was just getting warmed up.

There wasn't a sound in the room as Terry continued. "Finally, our review of the manifesto leads us to believe that it represents the Unabomber's long-held philosophy and viewpoint that he has likely represented to others. Our proposal for publishing the manifesto is to take advantage of the massive media attention that it will attract and with the expectation, or hope, that someone will recognize the writer's unique thoughts and will report his identity. It's an operational opportunity not to be missed."

Terry paused before finishing. "The investigation we've put

together thus far has a lot of pieces. One more piece and we may have the case solved. I think Kathy has something important to say that we all have to keep in mind."

Terry turned and nodded to Kathy, "They need to hear your opinion about whether the subject would really stop his bombings if we publish his manuscript."

Kathy's message as the clinical psychologist assigned to the UTF was short and to the point. "Whether we decide to publish the manifesto or not, the bomber can't stop bombing. It's not in his make-up to do so. Our recommendation to publish is based upon what Terry said. Someone will hopefully identify his writings and we will arrest him before he kills again."

At this point, Jim Wright of the Behavioral Science Unit at Quantico interrupted, "The BSU views this a little differently. We believe the bomber has put a lot on the line with the public and wouldn't want his perceived credibility hurt by another bombing. Our opinion is that he will cease the bombs if his manifesto is published."

Kathy fired back politely, but gave no ground. "And while I would agree that he really does want to stop bombing, I simply don't think he can stop. That's the reason he left himself the option of committing sabotage, but not terrorism by his definition. It still allows him to bomb if he must."

Kathy paused and then finished with the Unabomber's own words. She put her glasses on slowly, looking even more like the clinical psychologist she was, picked up the letter from the Unabomber that discussed his offer and read a portion of it to the group, occasionally looking up at everyone for emphasis:

"The article will not explicitly advocate violence. There will be an unavoidable implication that we favor violence to the extent that it may be necessary, since we advocate eliminating industrial society and we ourselves have been using violence to

that end... How do you know that we will keep our promise to desist from terrorism if our conditions are met? It will be to our advantage to keep our promise. We want to win acceptance for certain ideas...

"Our offer to desist from terrorism is subject to three qualifications. First: Our promise to desist will not take effect until all parts of our article or book have appeared in print. Second: If the authorities should succeed in tracking us down and an attempt is made to arrest any of us, or even to question us in connection with the bombings, we reserve the right to use violence..."

Kathy continued to emphasize her point: "As we've already discussed, the Unabomber distinguishes terrorism from sabotage and reserves the right to commit the latter. But even before getting to his final caveat, he allows himself to commit further bombings if his article doesn't appear in print in its entirety, or if the authorities even try to question him or the other so-called members of 'FC.' He's given himself ample room to commit more bombings and then blame us for them because we didn't adhere to his conditions. He did all that because he knows he can't stop bombing, even if he wants to."

There was complete silence in the room and I knew that Terry and Kathy had finished their briefing. "Louie, we will answer any questions you or the group wants to ask of us," I concluded.

"Kathy, thank you. Terry, Jim, excellent summary," Louie looked around the room, seemingly pleased and offering no hint of how he felt about the behavioral disagreement that played out in front of him. "Any other opinions?" he asked, making contact with the group of eyes in front of him.

No one in the room spoke. I couldn't tell if they were so pleased with what we had to say that they had nothing to add or whether UNABOM was becoming such a tiring topic that they just wanted to get up and attend to things they could control- or solve!

"Very well, then. Jim, Terry, Kathy, meet me after lunch and we'll go over and give a briefing to the Attorney General," **Louie said to us as he got up and out of his chair and quickly headed back to his inner office.** The room quickly emptied with a far more lighthearted attitude in evidence than when we started.

As we exited the Hoover Building in search of lunch, Terry glanced at me and took a deep breath.

"I assume you plan on briefing the AG?" he asked.

"Are you kidding? You're on a roll and Louie will be looking for you to brief the AG, but I'll give you a great introduction." We both laughed and knew we were blazing a new trail for UNABOM.

Just two steps away from her reception room, the AG's outer office is guarded by double wooden doors. A large conference table separated an ornate desk piled with neatly managed stacks of paper from the personnel manning the reception area.

Exactly on time for her meeting with us, Attorney General Janet Reno appeared from somewhere beyond her outer office and greeted each of us with a smile and an outstretched hand. Tall, and somewhat regal and humble at the same time, she immediately relieved some of the tension that I knew Terry and Kathy were feeling.

"Follow me on up here," she motioned to chairs on either side of the table, clearly indicating she wanted us sitting on opposite sides of the table from each other and close to her seat at the front of the table. The AG was doing all the right things to make us feel warm and invited.

Director Freeh took a seat midway on the same side of the table as me. The Deputy Attorney General, Jamie Gorelick, happened to show up about fifteen minutes after the meeting started. The minute Gorelick sat down she barked a question at Terry, disrupting the eye to eye connection he and the AG had established during his briefing. As Terry paused and started to address her question, one of the more memorable moments of the meeting occurred.

"He already covered that," Ms. Reno shot back at Gorelick. "If you'd been here when we started, you'd know the answer!" The AG then looked back at Terry.

"Go on and continue where you left off," she folded her hands together on the table in front of her, reminiscent of a school principal hearing out the kids while the parents were in the room. Our meeting continued as Terry led the AG through our strategy, structure, old myths, and new revelations about the Unabomber. He concluded by describing our rationale for publishing the manifesto and the AG immediately indicated her agreement and support. There was no deference to her Deputy for a second opinion.

"Louie, can you stay behind for a minute," AG Reno glanced at the Director as the rest of us headed for the door. She saw us out the reception room doors with an even bigger smile than when we arrived. I nodded my approval at Terry, but he and I knew better than to take anything for granted. As we climbed aboard an empty elevator, Louie caught up with us and kept his face pointed down at the floor until the elevator doors were securely shut and the elevator moved.

"Did you see how the AG slapped down the Deputy," Louie exclaimed with a grin on his face. We shared a big laugh together, but had reassumed our solemn demeanor by the time our elevator doors opened on the first floor of Main Justice.

"She wanted to see me afterwards to tell me that was the best briefing she's ever had on UNABOM. In fact, she said that's one of the best briefings she's ever had on anything." Louie was beaming as we walked across Pennsylvania Avenue to the J.E. Hoover Building.

"She wants us to set up the briefing and lunch for the people from the *Washington Post* and *New York Times* tomorrow in our lunchroom. We'll recommend publication of the manuscript then."

Important people made time on their calendars and that meeting was put together the next day as planned. "We need to get together like this more often," Director Freeh broke the ice and had everyone at the table laughing, as we started one of the more unique and potentially historic meetings in terms of FBI media relations.

Attorney General Janet Reno and Deputy AG Jamie Gorelick sat together next to Freeh, while Terry, Kathy and I sat on the opposite side of the conference table. Looking at each other across the table, almost as opposing forces, were the editors and staff of the *New York Times* and *Washington Post*. I've never before or since seen so many media heavyweights in the same room— Donald E. Graham, the publisher of the *Washington Post*, came to the meeting with Leonard Downie, Jr., the paper's executive editor. *New York Times* publisher Arthur O. Sulzberger, Jr., brought along his executive editor, Joseph Lelyveld.

Director Freeh briefed the distinguished group on the FBI's strategy in the investigation of UNABOM. They hung on every word, eager to hear details of the investigation that had not previously been made public, but also aware that all participants had pledged to keep the specifics of this particular meeting confidential.

It was staggering, I thought to myself, that the top executives of the U.S. Department of Justice were sitting down with the top newspaper moguls in the country to discuss and decide whether to publish or ignore the Unabomber's manifesto. Then, my thought process was interrupted as the Director turned to introduce us.

I leaned forward and introduced our proposal. "Our purpose in coming here today isn't just to recommend that you publish the manifesto, but to tell you how our task force plans to take advantage of the publication. We feel strongly that the content of the manifesto is recognizable to someone and that it represents deep-seated theories and a social philosophy that the Unabomber has shared with others. If enough people read it, then our chances are greatly improved that someone out there will recognize the writings and hopefully will call us with his name. If you agree to publish, then we have additional recommendations on the how and wherefore that may give us an advantage in meeting our law enforcement goal—to identify and arrest this guy."

I gave Terry the look that signaled for him to pick up where I left off.

"As Jim said, we think someone out there will recognize the Unabomber's manifesto and call us. We know the specifics so well at this point that when the right call comes in we'll know it and can exploit it. We've thought about various ways to take advantage of the actual publication day." Terry's pause was interrupted by one of the editors.

"Take advantage of publication day?" he asked seeking clarification.

"Yes. Our behavioral specialists believe there is an excellent chance that the Unabomber will purchase a copy of the paper as a memento. Further, the Unabomber's recent activities when mailing package bombs has shown a migration to the San Francisco Bay Area. What makes this very interesting for us is that in the San Francisco Bay Area, we've determined the locations where same-day copies of the *Post* and *Times* are sold and the number of newspapers sold each day at each location. For our purposes, it would be preferable for the *Washington Post* to publish the manifesto because of the more limited circulation at San Francisco news kiosks."

I interjected a thought. "We would dearly love to grab the Unabomber while purchasing a souvenir copy of his manifesto."

My interruption allowed for Terry to be stopped by another question. "You actually know how many copies of our newspapers are sold every day?" the editor asked.

"Yes, down to the specific locations," Terry smiled and then stopped abruptly, as he realized there might be proprietary information at stake between these two competitors.

"Well, we'd like to know how many papers we sell out there. I don't think we've ever been sure of the exact number," someone added, as laughter erupted.

"Go ahead and tell them," Director Freeh responded in good humor.

"Well, on a good day, the *Washington Post* sells a handful of papers at only four newspaper outlets in San Francisco and none in the surrounding Bay Area. That is, except for home subscriptions. The *Times*, on the other hand, sells a relatively large number of daily papers at many outlets." Terry appeared a little sheepish in delivering the news.

"That confirms what all of us have thought for years," Director Freeh grinned. "We're the only ones who care what happens day in and day out—and then only if it happens in New York or in Washington."

"This meeting has been far more worthwhile than we could have ever thought," joked the *New York Times* editor, with laughter breaking out among his peers.

After a pause, Terry picked up on his delivery. "In San Francisco, we plan on setting up surveillances at the two locations where the *Washington Post* is sold on the day of publication until such time as the copies are sold out."

I added, "That's why we recommend that the Post be the first to print the manifesto—it comes down to our operational control and logistics. It's not practical for us to watch all the places where copies of the *Times* are sold. But, we can do it for the *Post*. The challenge is in making sure the Unabomber knows that the Post will be publishing it as an exclusive and in knowing that soon enough to be in a position to purchase his copy on publication day."

We had received forewarning that the publishers and editorial staff would balk at anything perceived as receiving or accepting direction from the Government. Our proposal was based on the proposition that this was in furtherance of a law enforcement purpose with the potential of saving lives. There was anticipation that we could pull it off, else they wouldn't have agreed to the meeting.

"We might agree to publish, and I'm thinking of perhaps a partnership where one paper shares the cost with the other, but then what happens if he bombs again?" The conference turned deadly serious as executives from both newspapers turned to Louie Freeh and Janet Reno for the answer.

The Attorney General rose to the occasion. "You can say that I asked you to publish the UNABOM manifesto."

"The AG and I feel the same," Director Freeh continued. "The FBI and the Justice Department support the law enforcement rationale for publication of the manifesto and accept responsibility for that decision."

I thought there was an audible sigh of relief in the room. Regardless, the publishers and editors of the *Washington Post* and the *New York Times* convened a brief sidebar to discuss their own operational complexities of agreeing to our publication strategy. Ultimately, they decided that the *Washington Post* had the stronger capability to produce a news insert on short notice and could publish the manifesto in one edition and in its entirety. The *New York Times* would share the cost.

"So what's out next step?" they asked.

That was the response we wanted and I moved to outline some additional requests. "Between now and the actual publication date, we will be circulating the manifesto among college and university professors and an assortment of other people in the hope we might be able to identify and arrest the bomber before you have to publish. At the same time, Terry and I will do media interviews in New York, Chicago, Washington and San Francisco to set the stage in requesting the public's help in carefully evaluating all of the Unabomber's written words—including the positions expressed in his manifesto. It'd be helpful if your newspapers would interview us sometime prior to publishing."

The looks on their faces signaled that would not be a problem.

"Also, we want to give consideration to breaking the publication into multiple segments, such as a weekly serial format, to enhance our surveillance opportunities. But, we still have work to do in terms of assessing how the Unabomber might react to this deviation in his publishing plan. We'll get back to you on that point."

Our return flight to San Francisco gave me time to reflect on the progress we had made in just fifteen months. Although sad and disheartened by the recent killings of Tom Mosser and Gilbert Murray, I felt increasing confidence that we were on the right track and that more and more people in the FBI were seeing things our way. Director Freeh and Attorney General Reno boosted our credibility and the morale of the UTF with their decision to go forward with our recommendation to publish the manifesto based on an operational scenario. Of course, all of those good feelings would instantly evaporate with the explosion of another bomb signaling that nothing positive had happened as a result of publishing the manifesto. But, that was a worry for another day.

Time flew by as Terry and I moved quickly to restructure the task force, absorbing the expanded manpower and other resources the Director had approved for the investigation. We formed an investigative support squad and I approved Terry's request to place another counterintelligence supervisor, Penny Harper, in charge of it. She had a long history of solid accomplishments, but without substantial criminal work in her background. I felt positive about her personally, but I was becoming apprehensive about the appearances within my office of over-weighting the supervisory roles to members of the counterintelligence program.

"Terry, what if we miss something coming from the public outreach? Is Penny the one to hold everyone accountable?"

"She'll be fine Jim. There'll never be a time when I'm not

talking with her about the hot line, the suspects that are surfaced, and everything else about UNABOM. Besides, Joel, Max and I will all be working closely with Penny."

That allowed me to feel a little better, but no way would I stop dwelling on the topic and I was certain to be looking for additional criminal investigative expertise in the UTF supervisory ranks at the next opportunity.

By the time we completed our organizational transition, Penny's support squad had thirteen permanent agents, thirty-five temporary duty agents on thirty to sixty day rotations, and twenty-five analysts. The squad performed a variety of vital functions—managing the UNABOM budget; providing computer equipment and support; managing subpoena service and returns; assigning surveillance teams; manning the UNABOM 800 hotline, which received over 53,000 calls and analyzing those phone tips and incoming mail; coordinating forensic exams with the FBI Lab; training new arrivals to the UTF; and providing summary communications to Headquarters and other FBI offices to keep them constantly updated on our investigation.

Within two weeks, I became a very big fan of Penny. As she joined our morning meetings, I watched Penny manage all those responsibilities by yellow post-it notes (or FLYNs as they were not so politely called—for F...ing Little Yellow Notes). She was always equipped with yellow post-its. Her office was wallpapered with yellow post-its. On more than one occasion, I would give Terry my "are you sure about her" look, only to elicit his reassuring "yes I'm positive" look. Post-its or not, she was on top of her game and kept a lot of important UTF functions in motion.

We assigned Joel to lead the suspect evaluation squad. He managed sixteen FBI and ATF agents, as well as three analysts, and they all worked closely with the around-the-clock analytical group that Esposito had helped to create. They developed UNABOM suspects from analyzing the vast collection of data that

Fred Dexter's computer support team at Headquarters had pieced together from the multi-years worth of UNABOM information.

Key to that team's effectiveness was the creation of a suspect protocol and an analytical worksheet. Suspect cases involved a three-tier system of evaluation, with techniques becoming more progressive as the inquiry moved on from Tier I through Tier III.

A Tier I inquiry involved a detailed search of FBI records and reviews of public records; such as the collection of Department of Motor Vehicle records, photos, and vehicle registrations across fifty states. A review for criminal histories and NCIC wanted person data, completed the Tier I process before a final evaluation and movement of the suspect to Tier II, if certain criteria was present.

Tier II suspects met the full investigation criteria, which allowed for subpoenas of birth records, evaluation of financial history, education, employment and local criminal records as a means of comparison with the movements and whereabouts of the Unabomber on certain dates when bombs were known to have been placed or mailed. Military records, telephone records and examinations of utilities might also be queried to round out the Tier II examinations. Most of the suspect cases washed out in the earlier examinations and only a very small number possessed significant similarities and characteristics to be classified for additional investigation.

In Tier III investigations, legal access might be requested for tax records and for the use of special techniques such as mail covers to record the return addresses of incoming letters, pen registers to list outbound telephone numbers dialed, or physical surveillance to record daily movements; and then only as warranted by individual circumstances. In the end, only a handful of suspects approached this level of investigative effort and the supervisory oversight in the field office and by FBIHQ was appropriately rigorous to protect individual liberties.

For the third UTF squad, Terry asked Max to put his name in the ring for supervisor of the Investigations Squad to focus on past and any future bombings. For this position, I was strongly aligned with the need for a highly experienced criminal investigator. Although Max initially balked at walking the fine line between a street agent and taking a risk on becoming known as a bureaucratic "mister," Terry assured him that his responsibilities as a Supervisor would be no different than they had been up to this point. Max sought counsel from his former squad supervisors, Skip George and Tom Carlon, two individuals Max regarded highly. They convinced Max to go for it, as much for the pension benefits as anything.

In this job, Max supervised eighteen FBI and ATF agents and Postal Inspectors, plus one analyst. At one time, Max and his team conducted fifty different investigative projects. Don Davis played a major role in keeping track of these investigative projects, as his organizational skills proved to be of great assistance.

Terry held dozens of weekly meetings, large and small, to keep track of all the details arising from the three squads and then more sidebars with me and periodic briefings to keep key FBIHQ constituents in the loop. Then, just a couple of weeks before the manifesto was scheduled for publication, Terry received a frantic call from Tom Nunnemaker at FBIHQ. The AG was leaving on vacation and wanted a fresh update on our progress.

I was of a mind that there was sufficient rapport between Terry and Janet Reno that she would understand if Terry provided a telephone update, but this was clearly not the approach being taken by Bureau officials. Nunnemaker told Terry that he was to travel to FBIHQ for the briefing. They had already orchestrated a defined agenda that involved a general introduction by the Assistant Director of the Criminal Division, who would provide a summary of the resources approved and devoted to the case, and then he would introduce Terry to give some updates on case specifics. It seemed like a case of professional jealousy, but I couldn't run to Louie every time one of his top assistants made a decision that was unpopular with us. I informed Terry to pack his bags for Washington—and to get on the first available return flight!

Upon his arrival at Headquarters, it started. "Terry, can I have a copy of your briefing paper so we can coordinate our comments?" Dennis Weaver sat down at his computer to prepare his briefs for the Bureau officials.

"I don't have any briefing paper. I just brought these talking points," Terry handed Dennis a single sheet of paper listing a few topics and bullet points. "The AG is already familiar with the case from my previous briefing and she can use this paper to follow along while we talk. I expect that she will ask questions and I'll just go with the flow in answering them."

Apparently, Weaver almost had a coronary while Nunnemaker stood nearby with only a blank stare. Terry took great delight in describing it to me upon his return from this odyssey.

"Oh, no, no, we can't be doing that. We have to sit down here and write up an official briefing paper—at the very least so the rest of us aren't repeating the same things over there."

And, the bad news didn't end there. Terry had to spend most of the morning and early afternoon while a briefing note was created. Then, to Terry's chagrin, he had to participate in several rehearsals before the afternoon meeting with the AG.

None of it mattered anyway. The plan changed abruptly when Attorney General Reno met the group of Bureau officials in her outer office, told everyone to wait there, and she took Terry aside and through a maze of small work spaces to a parlor-like room covered with briefcases, legal papers and materials. She arranged two armchairs face-to-face and motioned for Terry to sit down. She listened intently to a thirty minute update on UNABOM, while asking detailed and relevant questions; all the while smiling and engaged.

"Can I keep this copy of the talking points? The UTF is doing a great job," she said while holding out her hand and guiding Terry back to the waiting FBI delegation. "Thank you," she offered and the meeting was adjourned.

* * *

Terry returned to his primary task of keeping up with the massive investigation unfolding around us. He and I worked jointly to keep our work focused and our strategy on track. UNABOM had a way of being unforgiving to mistakes and we knew we couldn't afford any setbacks.

I began a series of interviews with local and national media outlets; always stressing the talking points that we wanted the American public to hear and think about. I told them to think first of the Unabomber in Chicago, then moving westward to Salt Lake City, continuing through Sacramento, and finally on to San Francisco and the Greater Bay Area. I called attention to his writings and to the newly updated drawing of the Unabomber as both representing a means of "recognizing" the bomber. I took our case to *Fortune*, *Time*, *Newsweek*, and *Forbes*; while Terry interviewed with the *New York Times*, *Washington Post*, and *Chicago Tribune*. I worked with *National Geographic* in contributing video footage while describing the extensive history of UNABOM. Terry and I both mentioned the Unabomber's interest in academic topics, such as the history of science, and we made sure the public stayed aware of his penchant for frequenting universities and college campuses. All the while, anticipation was building toward the publication of the bomber's manifesto.

When the day came, I was called upon by Director Freeh to make the public announcement on the official FBI position to publish the Unabomber's manifesto.

"...Concern for public safety ultimately led the Attorney General and FBI Director to recommend that the manuscript be published. The UNABOM Task Force continues to encourage the cooperation of the American public in providing any information that may be helpful."

Joel implemented our surveillance strategy, timed with the publication of the UNABOM manifesto on September 20, 1995. Through the office command post (CP), he coordinated the radio communications to and from approximately fifty agents, who had started their day at 5:00 a.m. They dressed discreetly for the neighborhood and watched the two newsstands in San Francisco that offered copies of the *Washington Post* for sale.

"We're 10-8 at Harold's news stand," one of the surveillance units reported to the CP, echoed by several more unmarked cars arriving at their locations.

"10-8 at Nick and Mel's," and others began to report their arrival in the vicinity of that location.

Large crowds were congregated at both newsstands starting well before their opening at 7:00 am. Each outlet had fifty-five copies of the *Washington Post*. By ten minutes after opening, both locations had sold all their papers and our CP suddenly was trying to coordinate radio reports of multiple moving "targets" under surveillance.

One team followed a car with Illinois license plates to a transient hotel. The driver had tried to buy a copy of the paper, but left empty handed and was openly angry upon learning that they'd all been sold. They tracked him to a local bar, engaged him in casual conversation, and later reported that they were able to eliminate him as a UNABOM suspect. The same pattern repeated itself throughout the morning and into the afternoon. One by one, we were able to identify and then eliminate buyers of the paper as not being relevant suspects. By late afternoon, only one of our surveillances still continued.

Harold's was located just west of Union Square. Agents working nearby told Special Agent Stu Daly and his partner that a white male in his sixties, carrying an old leather briefcase had purchased a copy of the manifesto. He bore a resemblance to the UNABOM composite drawing. The man exited Harold's and walked to Powell Street, turned south and continued toward Market Street. The intersection of Market and Powell was crowded with tourists waiting at the cable car turn-around. Panhandlers cluttered the sidewalks, obstructing views and getting in the way. The man doggedly made his way through the congestion and disappeared down the stairs into the Powell Street BART Station.

With Daly and his partner in hasty pursuit, the man boarded a train bound for Daly City. Both agents boarded the BART train, concealing themselves in the next car, and keeping their eyes peeled on their target. As the train made its way to Daly City, the agents had trouble communicating with the CP on their hand held radios. Undeterred, they observed the man get off the train at the Daly City Station and then wait at a nearby bus stop. There were only a few people standing at the bus stop and the agents grew apprehensive that the man might notice them.

Finally, the man climbed on a bus bound for Pacifica, taking a seat four rows from the rear. There were only six other people on the bus. Daly and his partner walked past the man, taking seats in the last row. During the thirty- minute ride to Pacifica, the bus made several stops, and soon only Daly, his partner and the man they were following, remained on the bus. The man exited the bus at an area facing California Highway 1. There weren't any buildings, people or traffic nearby.

Daly and his partner waited for the man to move some distance away before disembarking. Their delaying tactics clearly irritated the bus driver. Following the man from two blocks back, they watched him enter an apartment building near the Pacific Ocean and a fishing pier. He walked up the stairs to the building's second floor. Daly read the names on the apartment mailboxes, trying to identify the man's residence. Without a working radio, they found a phone booth for a call into the office. He provided the names and addresses on the mailboxes and—bingo. There was a match with a man that had come to the FBI's attention many years previously when he had associated with some radical fringe group.

After several hours of watching the man's apartment, we gave the green light for Daly and his partner to interview the man. Identifying themselves as FBI Agents, they said they had observed him purchase the *Washington Post* newspaper at Harold's Newsstand and had followed him back to Pacifica.

The man was astounded. All of his life he had personally believed that he was being followed by the FBI. Now here they were, confirming his worst fears! The man told them that he, like the Unabomber, was anti-technology, a Luddite, and an author of anti-technology articles. He eventually settled into a discussion with the agents and let them know he had an old manual typewriter behind a closed door in the next room, but he wouldn't allow them access to the room to look at it. After an hour and a half of trying to convince the man to change his mind, the two agents decided to leave. But, while driving home that evening, Daly had nagging doubts about not actually seeing the typewriter. Checking in with the CP, Daly turned around and drove an hour back to Pacifica, knocking on the man's door at about 10 pm.

Daly told the man he wasn't convinced that he was not the Unabomber; and that he had to see the typewriter. The man finally relented, retrieving the typewriter and allowing Daly to get a typing exemplar. Daly left the apartment a second time, satisfied but annoyed; and proof that persistence pays off.

The man was positively not the Unabomber, but these were the types of situations that required quick response and perseverance on the part of the many agents and analysts working on UNABOM in the hectic days following publication of the manifesto. Regardless of their agency, position or rank, the work ethic and energy of the expanding UTF organization were sources of inspiration. And, sometimes there were the unintentionally comical moments, such as occurred when Attorney General Reno voiced an unexpected question during an afternoon conference call between our management group in San Francisco and various Washington officials.

"With thousands of moving parts, hundreds of suspects, and so much to keep track of, how will we ever know when we have identified the right person?"

I looked around and then at Terry. He had come to know her best, so I gave him the nod.

"Well, we just feel so confident that we know this case so well at this point, that we'll know him when we see him," Terry replied confidently, if not eloquently. I was hoping for something far more convincing, but couldn't have done any better.

"Great, I agree!" the AG exclaimed, while we all took a deep breath and rolled our eyes.

These were cherished moments when we could laugh together and relax the tension before again being immersed in the torrent of information, leads, and possible suspects. And, the receipt of the manifesto had definitely accelerated our learning curve in UNABOM. For all of the little grains of fact that were developed during our eighteen months of re-investigation of UNABOM events, our study of the Unabomber's own words uncovered gold nugget sized bits of knowledge that doubled our understanding of him within a couple of months. I think Terry, Joel, Kathy, and Jim Fitzgerald read the manifesto to fall asleep at night.

Surely, the bomber's mention of certain books in the manifesto was because they held special meaning for him. Would his references to "Violence in America," "True Believer," "Chinese Political Thought," and "The Ancient Engineers" be the key in leading others to recognize the author of this manifesto?

If we were to believe the words and themes outlined in the

Unabomber's Manifesto, we needed to find a highly educated guy who seemed to long for the days when people lived off the wild. It was a tall order, until we walked down the pathway to Kaczynski's remote, wilderness cabin on April 3, 1996. One of the handwritten notes we took from his cabin was confirmation that he had turned his dreams into a distorted reality:

"...I suddenly realized that what I wanted was not just to read another book on cave men—I wanted to really live like a cave man...to run around in a wild landscape hunting mammoths with a spear."

CHAPTER FOURTEEN

SUCCESS HAS MANY FATHERS BUT FAILURE IS AN ORPHAN

The FBI had waited years for the one break in a million, but when it finally appeared the fear of failure and the thirst for success were equally strong emotions.

THE DAYS WE SPENT WORKING UNABOM MOVED QUICKLY AND were never the same. But frequently they started in the San Francisco FBI Office between 6:00 and 7:00 am. I was an early riser and gained strength by getting to work early, and with UNABOM there was always a constant excitement that maybe today was the day. That's the way it was one day in mid-February, 1996. I was in my office reading some of the memos Terry had prepared for me summarizing the status of UNABOM investigative projects, the assignment of additional agents to the UTF, and identifying agents who were in a travel status to another field office. Max was in Terry's office briefing him on problems we were having with the camera system we were installing in Bay Area post offices in an effort to catch a picture of the bomber mailing one of his packages. Joel was in his office closing suspects that had washed out, opening new suspect investigations based on the criteria we had established, and sifting through the mound of mail always staring at him, representing the work of dozens of agents.

As Joel sat behind his desk reviewing the reports of suspect investigations, a voice on the office intercom barked, "Will someone from the UNABOM Task Force please call the switchboard?"

And then, a second and a third request for assistance came in quick succession from the office switchboard. I would like to make note here that the switchboard plays an important role in connecting the public with the FBI. There may be only one opportunity to receive a call from a wavering member of the public wanting to report the location of a wanted fugitive or offer information that helps solve a terrible crime. Missing or mishandling that single call had always been Terry's constant worry when it came to UNABOM. One of Terry's motivations for wanting Joel as the supervisor of the suspect squad was to minimize that possibility. Feeling mild irritation that a UTF agent in his bullpen had not responded after three announcements, Joel quietly responded to the switchboard operator.

"Hi, this is Joel," and he was put through to Special Agent Molly Flynn, assigned to the UNABOM case in the FBI's Washington Metropolitan Field Office (WMFO).

As Flynn began her story, Joel quickly lost interest in the stack of suspect cases in front of him. She spoke with conviction about information she had received from a Washington D. C. attorney named Anthony Bisceglie. Former WMFO agent Mike Harrison had referred Bisceglie to Molly. Harrison and Bisceglie were professionally acquainted. As an FBI agent in the WMFO, Harrison had met Bisceglie while working on another investigation. Although they had been on opposite sides of that case, they developed a solid relationship based upon a mutual respect for each other's work. Bisceglie had recently turned to Harrison for advice when a client told of being worried that his brother might be the Unabomber. The words were captivating right from the start— "his brother might be the Unabomber."

Bisceglie's client had given him a twenty-three page typed

essay written by his brother back in 1971. His concern was that the content of the essay was eerily similar to the ideas and writings of the Unabomber. Bisceglie wanted the essay to be evaluated by the FBI to determine if the client's suspicion had merit. His role was to shield the identity of the client and his brother until the FBI made its determination. He declined to provide his client's identity and said that he didn't know the name or location of the suspected Unabomber.

For her part, Flynn had sent the essay to the FBI Laboratory for a documents examination and comparison with the typewriting contained on known UNABOM correspondence, such as the Unabomber's letters to the New York Times and the manifesto. But the typewriting didn't match. She acknowledged to Joel that the story was a stretch, but she didn't want to let go. After reviewing both documents, she was very concerned. Molly told Joel that the 1971 essay contained ideas and concepts very similar to those contained in the UNABOM manifesto; so much so that she understood why Bisceglie's client was so interested in an FBI review.

Agent Flynn continued to unwind her story about the attorney and his client. She was emphatic that the essay not be overlooked. Her story began to sound to Joel just like one more far-fetched suspect tip. But still, there was something about the passion in her voice that made Joel more than a little curious as she told the story.

Joel told Molly to fax the document to him immediately so he could take a look at it. He waited for the document at the fax machine and carefully removed and gave a quick read to each page.

As he began to study the essay, Joel's interest increased page by page. With all twenty-three pages in hand, Joel picked up the phone and dialed Turchie, who had wrapped up his meeting with Max, gone into another briefing on the status of UNABOM subpoenas, and was then having lunch with yours truly.

"How would you like to walk over to Max' Opera Café for

lunch Terry?" Joel asked Terry without revealing the mystery he held in his hands.

"I can't Joel. Jim asked me to go to lunch today, so I'm already committed," Terry responded.

Joel didn't push the issue on the phone, instead he showed up at Terry's office only minutes later with Kathy Puckett at his side.

"Here, take a look at this," he handed Terry a copy of the twenty-three page essay, and as Terry scanned quickly through the pages, he sat straight up in his chair.

"This is why you wanted to have lunch today, right?" he asked as Kathy and Joel nodded—the sooner the better. Terry called me to cancel lunch, casually mentioning that a conflict had arisen. Next, he called Max to ask that he join them at the Café.

During lunch, they handed a copy of the essay to Max. He scanned it with interest, but quickly laid it aside knowing that its content would be discussed in due time. When Terry finished with the highlights, Max struck a familiar chord with his comment.

"Well, listen, I've said it before and I'll say it again. We've spent an awful lot of time with the manifesto and now you want to spend a lot of time with this letter and we don't even know how relevant it is to the case. Right now, it's just a big unknown. We have to be really careful and not go off on another tangent. We developed a carefully thought out investigative strategy and we need to stay with the facts. At the least, we need more information and have to talk with this attorney and also speak directly with his client before we get too carried away."

Also keeping in character, Terry responded with a positive take on the potential relevance of the essay and this suspect.

"It's very interesting on its face. This essay sure looks like it could have been written by whoever wrote the UNABOM manifesto."

Joel voiced a premonition, "When the boss reads this essay, we'll be launched into warp speed again. And, it comes at the worst possible time when everyone is already exhausted from working that other look-alike suspect. It took weeks of intense investigation to finally put that one to rest and now this pops up. I admit to being intrigued with this story; it's just that the weekend is almost here and the boss is not about to let this suspect linger without a full court press."

While Max's head nodded in agreement, Terry jerked upright with his eyes focused on the door. To their surprise and in an especially awkward moment for Terry, I walked into Max' Opera Café with another of my senior ASACs to have lunch.

"So, this is your conflict and the reason I got stood up for lunch," I was gaining expertise in finding Terry when he didn't want to be found.

"Sort of," he offered sheepishly, "but I wouldn't call it stood up."

"So what's so interesting?" I continued, seeing each of them holding a document in their hands.

"It's nothing really," as they deferred to Terry to answer. Before he could do so, I moved on to find a table.

"Oh man, I didn't think he ever came in here," Terry watched me walk to the other side of the café before finishing that thought.

"I certainly can't keep this from Jim, but I can delay it and buy some time for everyone to take a break and recover over the weekend. In the meantime, we can set some document reviews into motion and will have more to go on when we get back to work on Monday. Janet told me that Jim isn't returning to his office after lunch, so I'll go back and put a copy of the essay on his desk with a note that we should all talk about the possible significance on Monday morning," Terry ended with a sigh, feeling just a little uncomfortable with his plan.

Max responded immediately, "I'll tell you one thing for sure, when he sees this, it'll become an immediate priority for all of us —weekend or not."

Terry nodded in agreement, while directing Joel to find out as much as we could about attorney Tony Bisceglie, his client and the client's brother before Monday morning.

Their meeting was adjourned and Terry implemented his plan. The only hitch was that I did return to my office, because I was curious about what was going on. I saw Terry's note, read the essay, and was immediately looking for him again.

"I thought you were out of here," Terry half grinned as he approached my desk. I looked up through my reading glasses and spoke with more than a little irritation showing in my voice.

"Where the hell did this come from? This looks like our guy! Who wrote it and where is he now?" My reaction was as they predicted. "We've got to pull out all the stops this weekend."

To Terry's credit, his calm response and news of the additional data searches that were already underway went a long way in settling me down. I had to agree that we should initiate some preliminary work before opening this up as a full investigation, as that would trigger notification to FBIHQ and all of the ramifications that would inevitably follow.

"Okay, we'll do it your way. But you, Max, Kathy and Joel will be coming in here this weekend to work on this—with me!"

* * *

We'd hardly sat down at the conference table the next morning before Terry was excitedly recounting his discovery from the night before.

"This is incredible," he started. "In this 1971 essay, the author makes a telling comment about Perry London's book, *Behavior Control*, where it reads: 'I simply find the sphere of freedom that he favors too narrow for me to accept.' Now, compare that to the manifesto where the Unabomber says:

'We are going to argue that industrial-technological society cannot be reformed in such a way as to prevent it from narrowing the sphere of human freedom.'"

Kathy and Joel both laughed, with Kathy looking at me and

saying, "He called late last night to read that to us." Then, Kathy added, "And, don't forget that one of our academic experts commented after studying the manifesto that it appeared the Unabomber had been exposed to London's book, *Behavior Control*."

Max did not seem to be sharing in the excitement, as he'd been through this with many suspects.

"Were you about to say something, Max?" I asked him.

"You know how I feel. These are nothing but words and we need facts. I haven't seen any yet. We developed an investigative strategy and I believe we should stick with it." Max spoke with his arms crossed.

"I'm with you Max, and you do have valid points. But, I'm a risk taker and we're going full speed ahead on a side-by-side comparison of the content in the essay and the manifesto. It's only a small commitment of UTF manpower initially, but if there's a high correlation of words and phrases between the two documents—look out. Then, we would have to fundamentally reevaluate our current strategy."

Turning to Kathy, I said, "Let's call Jim Fitzgerald and have him come back out to coordinate this linguistics study!" Kathy was delighted. Fitzgerald had returned to Quantico during the late summer, but this was a potential turning point for UNABOM and we needed his passion for words.

Early on that Saturday morning, we spoke on the telephone with Molly Flynn and Mike Harrison and confirmed to them that we were highly impressed with the similarity between the 1971 essay and the 1995 manifesto. In a short time, I found myself on a conference call to the attorney, Anthony Bisceglie, with Max, Joel, Kathy, and Terry in my office. We provided him with a similar assessment of the two documents—although not yet a proven fact, it was more than enough to want to investigate the possible connection of his client's brother to the UNABOM crimes.

Surprisingly, this official endorsement seemed to open the door for Bisceglie to cooperate further. He explained that his client's primary interest was in helping his brother and if it appeared that his brother might actually be the Unabomber—then he said his brother needed to be stopped.

Bisceglie proceeded to tell an amazing story, while continuing to identify his client only as "Dave" and his brother as "Ted." Dave and Ted were born and raised in the suburbs of Chicago. Ted was a genius who went off to Harvard at age sixteen and graduated from there in the early sixties. He continued his studies at the University of Michigan, where he earned a PhD in mathematics in 1967.

Ted journeyed to Berkeley after receiving his PhD from the University of Michigan and taught mathematics at the University of California during 1968 and 1969, before returning to Chicago to live with his parent's. He worked at various jobs, had a relationship with a woman that didn't work out, and then his anger grew into a significant distraction. He eventually left Chicago, moving to Salt Lake City, where he worked for about six months in a construction job. In 1971 he purchased property and built a cabin in rural Montana.

"It's been years since Dave saw his brother during a visit to the cabin, which has no running water, gas or electricity. But Dave knows that Ted has an old manual typewriter in the cabin, and a bicycle he uses to get to the nearby town. Dave also feels that Ted resembles the rough drawing of the Unabomber."

Bisceglie stopped abruptly before finishing. "My client wants his identification kept confidential and won't provide any more information until he can get assurances from the FBI that if his brother Ted turns out to be the Unabomber, he will not get the death penalty."

That took me back a bit—an attorney negotiating to avoid the death penalty before a suspect is even identified. That spoke volumes to me about the gravity and potential validity of David's suspicion that Ted might actually be the Unabomber.

"Come on Tony. You know we can't do that," I interrupted. "Besides, we need more information anyway, before we can make any further judgments; like what is Ted's full name, date of birth, his address or location of that cabin in Montana, and things like that."

Bisceglie laughed mildly and we found ourselves in the unlikely negotiation for the identification of a suspect responsible for three murders and multiple bombings with egregious injuries. If things didn't work out, I was acutely aware that this scenario would not play well in the halls of the Hoover Building or at Main Justice.

It was a case of acting now while the opportunity presented itself and asking for forgiveness later. I agreed to provide Bisceglie a letter pledging to take into consideration everything that Dave was giving us and to let the prosecutors know how helpful he had been and how he didn't want his brother to get the death penalty, if it ever came to that.

While Bisceglie worked out our agreement with his client and waited for my letter, Joel opened suspect investigation number 2416 and assigned it to a veteran agent, Lee Stark, with Kathy Puckett named as co-case agent. I had readily agreed with Terry's recommendation that Kathy's knowledge of the UNABOM documents investigation and the analysis done on the manifesto would be a great complement to Stark's years of experience in criminal investigations.

Using the information already received from Bisceglie, searches of our UNABOM databases and of Department of Motor Vehicle records were initiated and the results were dramatic. The name of a former UC Berkeley math professor, Theodore John Kaczynski, was among that data. He was born in Chicago, Illinois on May 22, 1942. His parents were Wanda and Theodore, but his dad had died in 1990. Kaczynski had a post office box in his name in Lincoln, Montana, but there were no vehicle registrations on file.

Joel read from an analyst's report: "Lincoln is a small mining and timber town about an hour west of Helena, Montana, in the mountains near the Continental Divide. The Lewis and Clark County Sheriff's Office, headed by Sheriff Chuck Riley, an FBI National Academy graduate is responsible for policing in Lincoln. Four FBI agents from the Helena Resident Agency, a sub-office of the Salt Lake City Office, are responsible for securing the Bureau's interest there. The FBI's senior agent in Helena is Tom McDaniel."

I expressed my satisfaction to the group, only to be interrupted by a phone call from Bisceglie.

"Okay, Jim, I discussed everything with my client. Pending receipt of your letter, he and his wife can meet with your agents this coming weekend in Washington, D.C. He has agreed to provide whatever help he can so that you can eliminate his brother as the Unabomber."

The pace was unbelievable only a few minutes earlier, but now it was crazy and even exciting. This was the fun part of the job—when it feels like things are finally falling into place. I cast a big smile at the team in front of me and gave them a thumbs up. I didn't smile much, so they immediately got the message that we had a green light with Bisceglie's client. Terry, Joel and Max started planning even before I finished my short call with Bisceglie.

"Kathy, you should plan on traveling to Washington D.C," Terry told Kathy.

"Lee, I will meet you in my office in a few minutes but I want you to get ready to travel with Kathy back to Washington tomorrow. I'll fill you in on the details in a few minutes," Joel relayed to Lee Stark over a phone in my office, as Terry finished up his instructions to Kathy.

"I think they need a third person just in case something unexpected comes up," Max joined in. "I'd send Jim Willson along because he works well with Lee."

"Fine, let's do it." I sent the group on their way, knowing there was so much to do. "Terry, you stay here. We need to talk."

After refilling our coffee from the pot in the back room, we pushed back in the chairs at the conference table in a rare relaxed moment since we began working together.

"OK, do you really think it's him?" I asked and we both laughed at this request for cheap reassurance.

Terry gave a simple response, "Yes, I do think we're closing in."

"Let's savor this for a moment, but then talk about how much we want to tell Headquarters and when. The good thing is that we've been down this road so many times in the past few months with suspects that didn't pan out in the end, so they don't get too excited anymore. I'll tell Esposito and ask him to low key it with everyone there for a while. I'm confident he will understand the difference between knowing that someone is probably the Unabomber versus proving it in a courtroom. We cannot afford to lose control of the investigation until we are absolutely sure of what we have."

"That sounds good to me." Terry was obviously relieved.

"Do you think Max is up for this?" I asked Terry, having long counted on Max and his tactical skills, should we need to implement an arrest plan, but I could tell he was not overly impressed by mere linguistic comparisons of the two documents and he didn't seem as enthused about our Montana loner as the rest of us.

"Look, I agree that Max isn't enthusiastic about this suspect. But, he's a pro and will do what we ask him to do. As he tells me all the time—we should just do the investigation and follow where the facts take us. He and I will play off each other on this just like we have on all the suspects before. Besides, he has asked me for a week off so that he and his wife Kit can travel back to Nebraska to visit his aging parents. Kit and Max have been through a lot with her health issues and they need time to rest. I approved his request, but Max knows if this investigation breaks quickly we may be calling him to get back here or go directly to Montana in a hurry. He'll be fine," Terry once again echoed a comforting response.

Max headed for Nebraska as Kathy, Lee Stark, and Jim Willson boarded a flight to Washington, D.C. for a face-to-face meeting with David Kaczynski and his wife, Linda. They arrived in the middle of one of the worst snow storms of the season. Traffic was at a standstill, taxis were impossible to flag down, and even foot traffic was treacherous. Somehow, all parties made it to the hotel room that Kathy had arranged for the interview. Tony Bisceglie joined his client there as well.

Kathy had a genteel manner and knew how to make David and Linda comfortable under the circumstances. In several meetings over three days, they all stayed warm and dry with in-room dining while learning details about the life and characteristics of David's brother, Ted. When Bisceglie, David and Linda first showed up, David was cautious and careful in volunteering information. Although Bisceglie adopted a quiet and confident hands-off demeanor, it was clear that Kathy, Jim Willson and Lee Stark would need to prove themselves if they were to make the most of their interview.

This is where Kathy's own personality and many years of counterintelligence training came into focus. She had thought of all the little things that added up to make people feel good about settling in and opening up to the FBI. She'd rented a separate hotel room to hold the meeting, arranged for ample quantities of food and refreshments, and was aware of the importance of taking breaks and chatting about anything and everything that might help reduce the tension. And she was a constant example of compassion. By the end of the first day of talks, David and Linda had found a solid connection with Kathy and her team.

Before flying back to San Francisco, and pursuant to the plan Terry and I developed with them, Kathy and Lee got on the phone to brief us on the details of her three days of interviews with David and Linda Kaczynski. Terry liked to say that Kathy was the dream weaver, connecting the fabric of our UNABOM investigation to Theodore John Kaczynski. That description was lost on me, but during the phone call with us Kathy did an excellent job of describing how David and his wife had followed media reports on UNABOM and grew increasingly concerned that they could connect Ted to all of the locations associated with the Unabomber's activities—notably Chicago, Salt Lake City, and the San Francisco area.

Ted had quit his teaching job at U.C. Berkeley in 1969, met David in Wyoming and then they drove to British Columbia because Ted was interested in homesteading some land in Canada. He returned to his parent's home in Lombard, Illinois and waited for his homestead application to be approved, but found out in 1970 that it was rejected. Ted remained at home becoming more withdrawn and anti-social.

David was living in Great Falls, Montana when Ted showed up at his door one day and asked if David wanted to become fifty/fifty partners in a land purchase. Ted had found a parcel of land about 1.4 acres, near Lincoln, Montana being offered for sale by its owner. Ted and David each contributed $1,050 toward its purchase.

Ted built his tiny 10 foot by 12 foot cabin from the ground up and lived in it until late 1972 or 1973, when he went on to Salt Lake City and took a job as an unskilled carpenter's helper for about six months. He returned to the cabin in June of 1973. David last visited Ted at his cabin in 1986. While coordinating that visit, David received a letter from Ted, who said he could come between the dates of September 27 and October 4, but not outside those dates. Eventually, Ted became angry with David and said that he didn't want to see him anymore. But, during November and December of 1994, he wrote and asked David for loans, respectively of $1000 and $2000. Ted's December letter to David was prophetic:

"I need another $2,000…if and when I get over present difficulties sufficiently…There won't be any further requests for loans…if another $2,000 won't do it, then I guess nothing will, so I may as well give up."

David's wife, Linda, had never met Ted and only knew about him from the letters he wrote to her husband over the years. Even so, in September of 1995, Linda made a point of reading the Unabomber's manifesto and told David that it sounded a lot like Ted's radical ideas that were expressed at length in his letters. Following Linda's urging, David finally read the manifesto and was struck by a phrase in it that his brother Ted had used repeatedly—"cool headed logician." The phrase was related to Ted's philosophy of "rationality" being a guiding principle. Ted believed that if ideas were rationale, then any action in support of them was justifiable. David was worried that his brother might have used this philosophy to justify killing people.

"This is the best part, you guys," Kathy relished. "Over the years, Ted has written dozens of letters to David and he kept every one of those letters complete with the envelopes…"

Terry's eyes lit up. "So, that gives us dozens of postmarks and puts Ted in certain locations on specific dates. That's going to be an interesting comparison with our timeline of Unabomber activities."

"Exactly, but there's more than that," Kathy continued. "In these letters, Ted talks about primitive living in the wilderness and partial destruction of the ozone layer just like the Unabomber talks about in his manifesto.

"Finally, his letters also reference some of the same books as cited in the Manifesto: *The Ancient Engineers, Violence in America, and Scientific American.* There's an amazing correlation between the writings of Ted and the Unabomber."

Kathy was finished for the day. "We're getting ready to have some dinner. One more thing—David said Ted was also seeing a cardiologist in Montana for stress, so there you go!"

"I'd be stressed too if I were mailing bombs to people and taunting the FBI." With those words, I thanked Kathy and we ended the call.

* * *

The Monday morning meeting with UTF managers began promptly in my office at 8 am. Jim Fitzgerald had arrived late Sunday on a flight from Washington. Steve Freccero, the some-times acerbic, Assistant U.S. Attorney assigned to UTF matters in San Francisco, also joined us. Kathy was returning from her meeting in Washington, D.C. with David, et al, and Max was on leave in Nebraska.

"It's a fascinating development, but we're going to need more than what we've discussed to establish probable cause for any kind of a warrant," Steve Freccero remarked after hearing a summary of our investigation on Theodore Kaczynski.

"Just tell them I said there was probable cause and this is the guy and I've been working this case my whole life," Tony Muljat offered.

"Well that's great. I'll give that bit of information to the Department of Justice along with ten bucks so they can get coffee with my money and your opinion," Freccero countered, not real-izing that Tony had been dead serious. We all wanted to laugh, but stopped ourselves.

Jim Fitzgerald read to Steve from the notes he had prepared from reading the known and unknown writings. "Kaczynski's

1971 essay talks about control of emotions through electrodes inserted into the brain. The manifesto talks about electrodes inserted into people's heads. Kaczynski's essay describes the misery suffered by people as a result of Victorian repressions and the manifesto talks about people repressing their sexual feelings during the Victorian period. It goes on and on like this."

The objective of introducing Freccero to the new suspect case had been achieved and I didn't want this to turn into a debate where our resident prosecutor might harden his views at this preliminary stage.

"Steve, give us time to round out our investigation and complete the comparison of Ted's letters with the content in the manifesto. I just wanted to prepare you and the management team for a major change of direction in the case." It was not the first time that Freccero and I were not in synch on the merits of our investigation and it surely wouldn't be the last.

After the meeting was adjourned, I asked Terry to stay behind. "So what are you thinking?" I asked. "Is it too early to start focusing exclusively on Ted?"

"Jim, I think you and I are on the same page. I would like for us to go into the conference room and tell the UTF staff that we are shutting everything else down and turning the UNABOM ship toward one guy—Theodore Kaczynski."

It surprised me that Terry was just as ready to go all in, as that was my initial reaction too. But, my counsel was to pull it back a notch or two—that turning a battleship around takes time.

"I'd like nothing better, but in your briefing I want you to announce the very positive developments and the opening of a new suspect case which will be afforded the highest priority. But, present this as an adjustment in scope at this time. The UNABOM media posture remains the same; our hotline will continue to receive tips and they will be addressed as before. And, Terry—above all, make sure everyone understands that the cone of silence must be maintained over this shift toward a primary suspect. There must not be a premature disclosure by the media for the obvious reasons that evidence could be destroyed, the suspect goes on the run, and all the other bad things that could happen."

Terry nodded in agreement. As he stood up and turned to leave my office, I added that I was staying to make an important call of my own. "Okay, I'll make a call to Esposito to let him know and then I'll talk with Louie. My message will be essentially the same—we have a key suspect, but are continuing to cover all the bases."

We had maintained such compartmentalization in the initial stages of the Kaczynski suspect investigation that most of the UTF was dumbfounded by Terry's announcement. Emotions ranged from guarded elation to extreme worry that we were changing directions too fast. A common refrain that Terry heard and brought to my attention was, "If we were wrong, the decision had the potential to destroy our credibility and the existence of the UTF."

Terry had his hands full in conveying to the assembled UTF staff that a growing body of circumstantial evidence was pointing to this one man as being the elusive serial bomber that we had sought for so long. And, my calls to Esposito and to the Director were also received with a dose of healthy skepticism. Louie told me in no uncertain terms to be absolutely sure of my facts, and I believe "iron-clad" may have been mentioned. After all, the road of UNABOM was littered with many discredited and discarded suspects. It was hard for anyone to suddenly come to terms and accept the possibility that the end might be just around the corner.

The AG's question rang in my ears, "How will we ever know when we have identified the right person?" On this point, Max was right—it would take more than words to back up a case of this magnitude in a courtroom fight. We had undisputed similarities in the writing samples; and we were documenting timelines of all

Unabomber mailings of package bombs and letters, which dovetailed nicely with what we were learning about Ted's whereabouts. But, we also needed solid, old fashioned, evidence such as the old Smith Corona typewriter with pica style type and 2.54 mm spacing to be found in or around Ted's mountain cabin in Montana. That cabin might even be the "bomb factory."

I came to realize than an early arrest warrant based solely on linguistics analysis and timeline comparisons wasn't going to happen in the short term. But, I could see these elements as strong probable cause in support of a search warrant for that Montana cabin, which might give us the physical evidence of explosive materials or bomb-making tools to support an arrest and conviction. A search warrant would name the specific type and style of typewriters that the Unabomber had used in preparing mailing labels of package bombs, his letters, and his manifesto. Hopefully, we would find one of them in Kaczynski's cabin.

Kathy had a few surprises of her own when she came into the office the next day and gave us a full run down on her travel to D.C. "And here's the great thing. David has his own cabin in the middle of the Big Bend Wilderness area in the Texas Badlands. And, he's got dozens more letters from Ted stored there with the envelopes they came in. He's very busy at work, but said he could meet us there this weekend."

"You're good to go then, "I told her, looking at Lee. I felt that we needed as many data points as possible on our timeline comparisons and more letter content meant more potential points of reference in our linguistics study. In addition, we hoped that Ted directly mentioned one or more of the bombing victims in a letter to David. Given his propensity for expressing anger, this was a distinct possibility and must be ascertained at the earliest opportunity.

Lee answered my look by expressing an opinion. "I think we should take this a bit slower," he commented.

Terry responded, knowing immediately that this conversation

wasn't going in the right direction. "Isn't Jim Willson going with you guys? Because if he isn't going and you're not enthusiastic about going, Lee, then I guess it'll be me or Joel that goes to Texas with Kathy."

"No, I'll go," came Lee's solemn response.

"Kathy, what's going on with Stark and Willson?" Terry caught up with Kathy as she was leaving the room.

"There's just a lot of dissent right now about the steps we're taking to focus more exclusively on Ted and I guess worry over whether we're right or wrong about him," she explained. "Don't worry. We're doing the right thing and Lee will be fine on the trip."

* * *

The Big Bend Wilderness area is the size of the state of Rhode Island, with over 800,000 acres of rugged terrain and 250 miles of international boundary with Mexico. A week after their first meetings together, David Kaczynski, Lee Stark, and Kathy coordinated a rendezvous in El Paso and departed the desert border city at daybreak in a Chevy Suburban driven by a young FBI agent named Tony. More exciting than the prospect of UNABOM was cruising at speeds of up to 100 miles an hour while an FBI airplane droned protectively above the Suburban as it made its way down the highway.

"There are lots of drug gangs out here—lots of threats against citizens and law enforcement. We can't be too careful." Tony narrated as Lee hung on to his front seatbelt and David wondered how he had ever made repeated trips to the same area completely alone and always feeling safer than he did now, bumping along at warp speed with a Trekkie pilot at the wheel.

After hours on the desolate Texas road, David motioned for Tony to turn into the desert. The sand kicked up off the ground as the FBI's Suburban became enshrouded in the desert fog—a dizzying combination of dust, dirt, and swirling sand. David paid little attention to the ride at this point as he had made it many times before. Kathy was excited at the prospect of nearing another mother lode of information that might help nail David's brother Ted as the Unabomber. Lee was looking from side to side as if expecting an old west style stagecoach ambush. Tony was holding on to the wheel gunning the vehicle across the sand, with the desire to drive faster and generate more dust. Why else would any young man want to get into the FBI?

The Suburban slowed to just a few miles an hour as it crawled through a steep and rocky area of the desert until finally stopping within sight of a lone cabin visible on the horizon.

"We have to walk from here," David told the group, as they disembarked from the safety of their car and spread out across the desert landscape, walking towards a small cabin with the eaves painted a bright pink.

Once inside, Kathy took note of colorful rag rugs on a clean floor, shelves with books and a propane stove.

"Would you all like some herbal tea?" David offered before he went to a trap door outside the cabin and retrieved more letters from Ted that had been stored in the underground location. Lee sat at a small table outside the cabin and inventoried each of the letters as Kathy and David sipped on the hot tea David made for them.

"This has been very difficult for you David. We understand," Kathy comforted him.

The trip paid off, as David was able to account for years of his brother's whereabouts with the additional letters and postmarks on the envelopes that he had maintained at his Texas cabin. Even better, none of the information showed any conflict with the timeline of UNABOM events.

About a week after the trip to Texas, David and Kathy were talking on the telephone.

"Have you been able to eliminate Ted as a suspect?" David asked, hoping for a definitive yes that would never come.

"We're still working on this David. We just don't know yet how this might end," Kathy responded as she would many times during February and March of 1996.

* * *

Terry called Max in Nebraska to make sure he was aware of the latest developments in the case and our shift in strategy. On February 23, Terry's call to Max abruptly ended his vacation. Terry and I had sent Dave Weber, John Gray and Candace De Long, all of whom were San Francisco based FBI agents assigned to the UTF, to Helena, Montana with specific instructions to brief Senior Resident Agent Tom McDaniel on the details of our investigation. We wanted Max to fly directly to Helena from Nebraska and assume supervisory control of our work in Montana. The weather in Nebraska was terrible and a blizzard delayed his departure for two days. By the time Max caught up with his small contingent of agents in Helena, they were checked into the Park Plaza Hotel, on Last Chance Gulch, under aliases to protect the confidentiality of our investigation.

"You need to get some Montana cold weather clothing, Max," Dave Weber cracked when he and John Gray met Max at the airport.

A trip to Capital Sports and Western Wear on Helena Avenue enabled Max to get cold weather clothes that would securely wrap him in his covert role—Wrangler jeans, plaid flannel long-sleeved western shirts, thermal long underwear, a wool stocking hat, a pair of Danner insulated Elk hunting boots, and a baseball hat with the Capital Sports logo. He already had gloves since Nebraska was almost as cold as Montana this time of year.

"That's a good look for you Max. Now people will come up to you on the street and say howdy partner," John Gray quipped.

"At least I can stay warm while I'm skulking around Montana," Max snapped back.

Joel caught up with Max by phone at the FBI Resident Agency in Helena, where Max had stopped in to talk with Tom McDaniel and the other agents in the office.

"Hi Max, and welcome to the Montana outpost of the UTF. We've been lining up some leads to get you guys started on that end. There's no record of Ted owning or registering a vehicle in the state, so check out any sources where he might have rented a car—maybe from a Rent-a-Wreck type place.

"You might find out some background info by reviewing hunting and fishing licenses for Kaczynski and have the local office run an historical DMV records check for any previous registration information.

"Contact the Bureau of Land Management and find out the exact location of Kaczynski's cabin and property, so we can have the correct legal description for the search warrant affidavit that Terry is drafting. Oh, your team has already found out that Kaczynski's cabin is stained red, doesn't have any eaves, is near a creek, and has a root cellar on the property.

Before he ended the phone call with Max, Joel had one more thing to say, "Kaczynski apparently knows the librarian in Lincoln, which could lead to an interesting interview later on— but we'll discuss that angle with you later. The Postal Inspection Service's Assistant Inspector in Charge John Burkhardt assigned here in San Francisco told me he knows the postmaster in Helena and believes him to be trustworthy. We'll work through Burkhardt back here to initiate a mail cover on Ted at the Lincoln Post Office. We'll talk more real soon. Good luck!"

Early the next morning, Max hit the road with agents Dave and John to tackle the hour-long drive through the snow-covered mountains between Helena and the small village of Lincoln, Montana. Lincoln is located on Montana Highway 200, midway between Missoula and Great Falls at an elevation of over 4500 feet. Stemple Pass Road, the old stagecoach route over the Continental Divide from Helena to Lincoln dead-ends into Highway 200 in the center of Lincoln.

Four miles south of Highway 200 on Stemple Pass Road, Max and crew found a cluster of four mailboxes with one bearing the name, "Ted Kaczynski." The mailbox was near an entrance to the property of the Gehring Lumber Mill. Snow-covered trees were everywhere and blocked any view of Kaczynski's cabin, which was located nearby in Coldwater Creek Canyon. Continuing back into Lincoln, they observed a compact town with the essential businesses to support tourism, hunting, camping and fishing, but not much more. Along Highway 200, Lincoln's main street, were a Post Office, a bank, a hardware store, the local high school, a public library and several restaurants and bars.

Garland's Dry Goods was set up to outfit all manner of hunters, fishermen and other outdoor types. Max and Dave went into Garland's, as well as into the Grizzly Hardware store in an effort to determine if either store sold one inch avocado paneling nails, similar to those nails that served as shrapnel in the bomb that killed Thomas Mosser in New Jersey. They quickly determined neither store sold those nails.

While in Garland's store, Max bought a baseball cap with the logo, "Legendary Fly Fishing, Blackfoot River," emblazoned in yellow around a "bunyan bug." As Max later expounded to all that would listen, the "bunyan bug," a mythical insect, is an artificial fly or fishing lure that is a favorite of many fishermen in Montana's fertile trout streams, including the Little Blackfoot River that runs through Lincoln.

After taking numerous photos in and around Lincoln, Max and his group returned to Helena for an afternoon meeting with Helena Senior Resident Agent, Tom McDaniel. Tom had set up a meeting at Max's request with Assistant United States Attorney

Bernie Hubley, who was Steve Freccero's counterpart in Montana. Max, Dave, Tom and Bernie met at the Rialto, a cozy, small bar located on Last Chance Gulch.

As soon as Tom made introductions, Max began, "Bernie, I'll be direct and to the point. We need your help! I know you're going to find this hard to believe, just as I do, but we're here because the UNABOM Task Force thinks that one of your local residents, Theodore Kaczynski of Lincoln, may be the Unabomber."

Hubley's reaction—shock and probably near cardiac arrest— these are all understatements. Bernie was a former FBI agent, now a top-notch federal prosecutor and was about to become a valued UTF team player. As Bernie figuratively picked himself up off the ground, he pledged total confidentiality and joined into a relationship with us that would become deep and profound in its impact on our investigation. As happened so many times during the UNABOM investigation, Bernie was exactly the right person, in the right place, at the right time.

One of the skill sets that Terry, Max and I shared was the ability to develop valuable sources of information. For Terry, it was developing counterintelligence "assets" in New York to target against and disrupt the efforts of Russian intelligence officers. Max recruited criminal informants to help destroy organized crime and labor racketeering on the docks and in the warehouse districts of San Francisco's seaport market place. And, I had done a lot of each during assignments ranging geographically from Los Angeles to Miami and then to Hawaii.

Quality sources of information were the ingredient that "made" or enhanced complex cases, and the trick was in deciding who and when and how to approach people. Having them don and wear the "team jersey," as Terry was fond of saying, was the objective. If an approach was spurned, it carried tremendous risk to the investigation and wasn't for the faint of heart. One wrong move by talking to the wrong person at the wrong time could compromise our carefully crafted and discreet Montana investigation. To be successful, we had to surround Theodore Kaczynski without him ever knowing we were there.

Max and his team were on the ground in Helena, with periodic and discreet forays into and through the tiny community of Lincoln and the surrounding area. But, I was raised in a small town, rural environment—Clayton, located in northeastern New Mexico. The cattle in the county outnumbered the people about 100 to 1, if not more. And, we knew (or thought we did) every time an agent of the FBI or DEA or any other three-letter agency came to our town. It was impossible for an outsider to remain discreet and anonymous, while asking questions and taking pictures without arousing suspicion.

Max's background was similar to mine, having been raised in a small rural community in Nebraska. He shared my concerns, understanding that remaining anonymous and covert in a small community like Lincoln would be nearly impossible.

Selecting key personnel was critical. Max had highly recommended and supported the decision to send Dave Weber to Montana, as part of his small UTF team, for exactly that reason. Dave, a Montana native, knew the local customs, language and behavior. He had traveled through the state during his employment prior to joining the FBI and he blended in nicely.

In Lincoln, however, we urgently needed an insider or two working on behalf of the UTF. We had keyed on the possibility of approaching Butch Gehring, who owned the lumber mill adjacent to Ted's property and whose father had sold Kaczynski his property, and perhaps Sherri Wood, the Lincoln librarian. But, we were unsure of their relationships with Ted and decided that trying a direct approach with either might be a critical mistake.

First, we needed someone to validate our selected targets.

Ordinarily the FBI would reach out to trusted law enforcement contacts that lived and worked in the community. When Max broached the subject with Tom McDaniel at the Helena Resident Agency, our path became clear. Tom told Max that the most knowledgeable, competent, and trusted law enforcement person in or around Lincoln was U.S. Forest Service Police Officer Jerry Burns.

Following Tom's recommendation, Max was introduced to Jerry Burns and they hit it off immediately. Jerry was a life-long resident of Lincoln and his duties included patrolling the Helena National Forrest, which bordered Kaczynski's property. Not only did he know everyone in Lincoln, he even knew Ted by sight, as they had one or two brief encounters over the years. Jerry referred to Kaczynski as the Hermit of Mount Baldy and acknowledged that most residents of Lincoln considered Kaczynski to be "eccentric." Jerry was immediately enthusiastic about working with the UTF. His only request was that we obtain the permission of his supervisor.

On that score, it didn't hurt that Burns' boss was another former FBI agent, Tom King, the U.S. Forest Service Regional Special Agent in Missoula, Montana. Max called and spoke to Tom. He gave Max the go-ahead to use Jerry's assistance, as well as the resources of the Forest Service, without requiring any explanation of why we needed their help. King simply asked in return that we keep him advised of anything that could negatively impact his department. We were happy to oblige and Jerry became the newest member of our "de facto" UTF in Montana.

What an absolute bonanza. From knowing nothing at all about Lincoln and its inhabitants, we had gained a trusted source that became our eyes and ears. Jerry knew everyone in Lincoln and could tell us who could be trusted and who could not.

Less than twenty-four hours later, Burns was leading Dave

Weber and Tom McDaniel on U.S. Forest Service snowmobiles along the Humbug Contour Trail, that meandered through the mountains a couple of miles south and above Kaczynski's cabin. High on top of a ridge, they parked their snowmobiles and began crawling down the snowy mountainside, coming to within 200 yards of the hermit's reddish colored dwelling. Even from this vantage point, they were unable to get a clear photograph of the cabin that was hidden among a thick stand of Lodge Pole pines.

Suddenly, the creaking of a door and its subsequent slamming echoed through the dense forest, prompting them to beat a hasty retreat back up the mountainside. They mounted their snowmobiles and sped back to the trailhead where Max and John Gray awaited their return.

"Too many trees Max. We tried. We just couldn't get any good pictures."

Max was disappointed. But, the little setback of not getting a photo of the cabin was completely overshadowed by the success of gaining a strong foothold in Lincoln. Another advantage of having an inside source was learning about good places to eat. On Jerry's recommendation, Max and the team stopped for dinner near the Great Divide Ski area, at what soon became a 5-star attraction for the UTF in Montana—the Marysville Steakhouse.

CHAPTER FIFTEEN

WE WON'T BE USING THE HOSTAGE RESCUE TEAM

(The Hostage Rescue Team or HRT is the FBI's premier tactical team, earning campaign ribbons in the middle of the 1990's for assaults against armed and barricaded positions in places named Ruby Ridge and Waco. My concern was not the tactical team, but the manner in which it deployed with "go/no go" decisions made from a command center in Washington, D.C. My San Francisco Office had a first class SWAT team, so the decision was a no-brainer for me—but highly unpopular at FBIHQ).

I BECAME SERIOUS AS I SPOKE WITH TERRY DURING A BREAK AT THE annual seminar for San Francisco FBI supervisors in Pacific Grove, CA. "This thing in Montana is the real deal and it's only going to get more intense. It's time. You and I need to escalate our presence there and turn up the heat before something happens to tip off Kaczynski. We can't be left empty-handed without the evidence needed to convict him."

Terry nodded and replied in kind, "You're not kidding. It would be catastrophic for the Unabomber to slip out of our grasp and become a fugitive."

There it was; we had both acknowledged it openly. Ted

Kaczynski is the Unabomber. Ted Kaczynski is the Unabomber!

Although we had been edging ever nearer to that finding of fact, the latest developments had been the final straw for the two of us. A telephone discussion with Max and agent Candice DeLong earlier in the day had cemented the deal in our minds— particularly Kathy's discovery of a "Ted letter" to his brother, posted in Lincoln, MT, that referenced a health article in *Scientific American*, a la the Unabomber's manifesto. We discussed with Max that it was a priority to discreetly determine if Ted received the publication by mail subscription or perhaps he was a regular visitor to the Lincoln Library. But, I was not yet willing to allow Max to contact the librarian directly for concern that it might divulge our presence beyond our tight circle in Montana.

It was a shame that more of our UTF personnel were unable to share in our exhilaration about how the pieces of the puzzle were fitting together. The persistent skepticism about the new direction of the investigation, as voiced by some experienced agents, was understandable and I surmised that it could be traced to one or two causes. First, we had restricted knowledge of the latest developments to a small group of individuals on the UTF in San Francisco and a handful at FBIHQ and Main Justice, where each was identified on a "bigot list" to guard against leakage of the information.

The second limiting factor was simply that many had been down this road before with equally as compelling suspects and knew that word and phrase comparisons to Kaczynski's writings were short of the evidence needed to convict someone of these heinous crimes.

For Max, this was certainly true. My eyes widened as Terry described a recent telephone conversation with him:

"Terry, you know how I feel. I'll be your point man on this if I'm the last person standing; but I just don't see it. This guy lives in the middle of nowhere, doesn't have a job, people we've talked to said he's a hermit who has never left Montana, he has no water, no electricity, no income and lives in a 10 by 12 cabin with hardly any room to turn around. His only known mode of transportation is an old bicycle. Yet, we somehow think he's the Unabomber? It's a hard sell and I'm having trouble buying it."

Max paused to let his words resonate and then continued. "Remember this—right after the killing of Gil Murray in Sacramento, the profilers in Quantico told us that it was a direct response by the Unabomber to the bombing of the Federal Building in Oklahoma City. If true, the timing would require more than bicycle power on the part of Kaczynski. And, the forensic experts at the FBI Lab have told us the Unabomber has used power tools and kilns to build his most recent bombs. That's quite a feat in a snow-bound shack without electricity.

"But, don't worry. You and Jim have given me this assignment and I'll do everything you guys ask of me. I'll gather all the facts that are out there—but at some point, well…" his voice had trailed off.

Before the San Francisco supervisor's seminar wrapped up, I asked Terry to give a high level view of recent UNABOM case developments. It was amazing that even by limiting details to the 50,000 ft. view of the investigation; he literally brought the house to their feet in acknowledgement of the outstanding work that was being achieved in this highly unique case.

Everyone headed to the exits for lunch and then a Friday afternoon drive back home. I motioned for Terry to step out on a balcony.

"That was a great conclusion to the conference. Now, as I was saying—we're going to turn up the heat in Montana and I'm going to be directly involved from here on out. Get ready to travel—we're paying a visit to Max and his team. From this point forward, I'll be spending a lot of time in Montana and I want you back and forth as needed to get the affidavit ready for either an arrest or search warrant. That affidavit is our top priority in the near term."

Terry smiled. "I completely agree. I'll let Max know we're flying out for a strategy sit-down, which will be welcome news to him. I can work on the warrant affidavit as easily from Montana as anywhere. Joel will be our point man for UTF here in San Francisco."

After a weekend of intense planning with the UTF leadership team in San Francisco, Max picked us up at the Helena airport and appeared relieved that he no longer had the weight of the Montana investigation solely on his shoulders.

By now Max had moved his small team of investigators out of the Park Plaza Hotel on busy Last Chance Gulch and into a small Victorian bed and breakfast, the Appleton Inn located away from downtown Helena.

"Max, your team has done a great job here. Everything is coming together nicely," Terry encouraged Max to feel good about what he had accomplished.

When I first arrived in Montana, only a few people knew we were there. Besides Max, his team consisted of SF-FBI agents Dave Weber, John Gray, and Candice DeLong in Helena; Agents Chuck Pardee and Dan Atchison were temporarily assigned to handle UTF leads in Salt Lake City; and Agents Phil Lowell and Jim Huggins were dispatched to Missoula. Max' primary point of contact in Helena was Agent Tom McDaniel of the Helena Resident Agency, which was a satellite office of the Salt Lake City FBI Division. With additional UTF manpower on the horizon, it was imperative to deal immediately and discreetly with the logistics of having our own covert office space, telephones, utilities, and rental cars—all located a discreet distance from the Helena Resident Agency.

The challenge was doing this without attracting unwanted attention indicating that a secret FBI operation was gearing up in the Helena-Lincoln-Missoula triangle. Our saving grace was the existence of a large and overt FBI operation in eastern Montana involving an uprising of the extreme right wing group, the Freemen. Hundreds of FBI agents, support personnel, and other law enforcement officers were making daily headlines and news reports in that part of the state. Although some distance away, the Freemen operation was a convenient diversion for us. When our identities as FBI agents became known, people just assumed we were affiliated with that other investigation. An overt FBI operation became the perfect cover for a new covert operation in an entirely separate region of Montana. Lady Luck was smiling on us.

On Tuesday, March 12, 1996, in Helena, MT, I met with Terry and Max to outline the organizational structure of the new UTF base in Montana. There was no reason to be so formal, but I did not want a failure of communication at this critical stage when frankly—our rear ends were showing.

"First of all, the three of us now constitute the SAC, ASAC, and Supervisory Special Agent of this separate branch of the San Francisco-based UTF. We are located within the field office boundaries of the Salt Lake City FBI Office and I have yet to give formal notice to the head of that office of our expanding presence in Helena—which is highly irregular and generally unacceptable. The Director knows, but that's about it."

At that, Terry jerked his head up in surprise. "Now, I suppose you've replaced Max as Public Enemy #1 over there in Salt Lake."

Max was quick to assert that he had mended his fences in the Salt Lake City office months ago.

I continued, "I doubt that it's quite that dramatic. Besides, that entire office is consumed with the Freemen investigation in eastern Montana and don't need the distraction of UNABOM right now. I'm about to make a phone call to explain to each of the SAC(s) of Newark, Salt Lake City, and Sacramento that a conference call is being scheduled for tomorrow when we will brief them, along with the Assistant U.S. Attorneys assigned to the UTF case in their cities, on the recent developments. There will be representation from FBIHQ and Main Justice attorney Tom Roberts will also be on the call. All of this UTF focus on Montana and a suspect named Ted Kaczynski will be breaking news to all of them. It'll be hard to contain the information after that phone call, but it has to be done."

Terry added, "I'm still coordinating the full UTF, as in the past, but Jim and I have agreed that my main focus will be cataloguing and assembling the supporting facts in the affidavit for the search of Ted's cabin."

Max added, "…and any supporting structures. We have indications that Ted added a root cellar with a roof somewhere outside the cabin structure."

Terry continued, "Max, you will continue to supervise the investigation and evidence collection by all of the Montana UTF investigators and that number is increasing by two on Thursday with the arrival of Postal Inspector Paul Wilhelmus and agent Michael Grady of ATF. In addition, we're sending Lee Hayden over from San Francisco to manage all of the logistical needs, such as contracting for office space, etc."

Next, I dropped a bomb of my own that they had not anticipated. "For my part, I will be in Montana most of the time until that warrant is served—whether it is an arrest warrant for Ted or a search warrant for his cabin or both. I firmly believe that time is short; as we begin to tighten the noose around Lincoln and start interviewing townspeople it will greatly increase the risk of a public disclosure. When that happens, we have to be ready to move very quickly. I have informed the Director and have his concurrence for delegating the SAC responsibility for the San Francisco FBI Division to Associate SAC Charlie Matthews for the duration of my absence."

Their jaws dropped with knowledge that this likely had never happened before in the annals of the FBI—relinquishing a field commission to take charge of a tactical mission of undetermined duration. Then, no SAC previously had this opportunity to solve UNABOM; and to me it was worth it—win or lose.

Wednesday, March 13th was an incredibly busy day that began in the Helena FBI office with coffee and pastry substituting for a healthy breakfast. Then, Max led us through a review of hotel records for the Park Hotel in Helena where Ted had signed the register for 31 stays during 1980—1995. Of obvious interest to us in updating Ted's timeline was whether any of these known dates were in conflict with the Unabomber's timeline of known times that he had mailed packages or placed bombs. As the hotel dates were entered for a side-by-side comparison of the 31 visits, not only were there no direct conflicts but there was a correlation of movement where additional investigation was needed to see if Ted had expanded his travel beyond Helena by bus or rental car or other means to carry out the Unabomber's deadly business.

While stating my concern that these overnights in Helena were perhaps the first or final step of Ted's travel to or from UNABOM events, I was interrupted by Max. "Jim, I have already assigned leads in Helena and Missoula to interview rental car dealers and commercial bus drivers looking for someone of Ted's description transiting the area. There's a lot of work to be done in tracing potential travel routes through Salt Lake City to Sacramento and to San Francisco. It's a big country out here— they didn't name it Big Sky Country for nothing."

Terry and Max advised me that two teams of SF-FBI agents, Jim Higgins and Phil Lowell had been assigned to handle leads in the Missoula area, and Chuck Pardee and Dan Atchison were setting up in Great Falls to handle leads generated in that area. The circle had closed in a rough100 mile circle around Ted's cabin in Lincoln. Max had implemented coverage by agents John Gray and Candice DeLong to the only form of public transportation leaving Lincoln this time of year—one bus traveling west-bound and one bus going east-bound per day. The instruction was to ascertain if Ted or anyone looking like Ted boarded a bus in either direction and then to provide notification to the agents in Missoula or Helena, which would allow at least an hour's advance notification of arrival at either destination. Above all, they were to remain in covert status throughout their time in Lincoln.

According to Max, "The rest are busy checking motel/hotel records, pulling financial records for banks in Helena and Missoula, interviewing bus drivers, and also checking college and university libraries in a reasonable radius to determine if a record existed of Ted having checked out the very books or publications mentioned in the Unabomber's manifesto and other writings."

At noon, Terry and I retreated to a quiet location within our Montana office space to participate in one of the routinely scheduled conference calls we frequently had to brief Federal prosecutors in Newark, Salt Lake City, and Sacramento—sites of the three UNABOM murders—as well as Department of Justice Attorney Tom Roberts and Deputy Assistant Director Bill Perry of FBIHQ's Criminal Division. The prosecutors were "competitors" for Federal jurisdiction in the event of the Unabomber's arrest. For the most part, they were hearing for the first time about our location in Montana, the suspect's name, and information regarding his brother David and my negotiations with the brother's attorney. There were some of the usual questions, but also a stunned silence from others.

As the shock wore off, it became apparent to me that few would be willing to accept the risk to their careers by naming the UTF suspect in a warrant; and then being wrong. It was a hot potato where extraordinary production of evidence was demanded. In my years of experience, I knew that we had already exceeded the threshold for a search warrant in routine criminal cases and were at the point of sufficient probable cause to support an arrest warrant.

But, ironclad evidence was the threshold that we were asked to equal or exceed because no one was yet willing to accept that this hermit in the mountains of Montana was in fact the Unabomber. And, many of my agents were included in that number.

Terry and I were finally able to get outside the confines of the small Helena office in the early afternoon. Max had arranged a tour to Lincoln in a 4x4 SUV via the snowy and non-paved Stemple Pass Road. Our objective was to survey the area of Ted's cabin and to get a feel for the town of Lincoln. Following the requisite viewing of the Kaczynski mailbox, the neighboring Gehring sawmill, and downtown Lincoln, we were on our way to meet Max and crew for dinner at the Marysville Steakhouse. On the way, I was astonished to see a moose and calf in a meadow and a group of mountain goats clinging to a rocky outcropping above the highway. This was Big Sky Country all the way—and the steak was deliciously prepared against the backdrop of an old mining camp.

On Thursday morning, March 14th, I conducted a conference call with the FBI-SAC of Salt Lake City and the regional managers of the ATF and U.S. Postal Inspection Service and gained their agreement to isolate the de facto "UTF—Montana Office" from non-UTF personnel in each of the three agencies despite the presence of overlapping jurisdictions and physical boundaries. It was a critical step in prolonging our ability to remain covert and undetected until we had sufficient evidence to at least get a search warrant for Ted's cabin.

We met with AUSA Bernie Hubley at his office in Helena and discussed the status of the voluminous affidavit for the search warrant that Terry was assembling these days as he traveled between San Francisco and Helena. That document initially would need the endorsement of AUSA Steve Freccero in San Francisco, but the cabin's physical location in Montana meant that ultimately Bernie Hubley would have a lot to say about filing it before a U.S. District Court Judge in Helena.

I wanted Bernie to be aware that this case could implode or explode (no pun intended) without warning if the suspect somehow becomes aware of the investigation. Our discussion explored legal options in the event that an emergency search warrant became necessary to protect against the destruction of evidence. He was far more receptive than the feedback I had been receiving from Freccero.

Before calling it a day and catching a late afternoon return flight to San Francisco for a long weekend, I sat down in the office with Max and Terry to discuss and decide the next critical interview. The three of us recognized that if Max was successful in turning Butch Gehring, the owner of the lumber mill who sold Kaczynski the land to build his cabin on, to our side, then we will have advanced our "eyes and ears" to a position that is directly down a narrow country lane from the cabin of our Unabomber suspect.

Based on Jerry Burns' personal knowledge of personalities in and around Lincoln, we became convinced that Butch would agree to assist us and would hold our confidence. The plan was to have Jerry vouch for and introduce Max to Butch, probably at the lumber mill. I concurred with Terry's recommendation that the time and place should be worked out in close coordination between Jerry and Max to gain the best possible advantage. After gaining assurance that I would be informed immediately of the results, I left for home with an indicated return date—four days later on Tuesday, March 19th.

* * *

It was frigid and snowing lightly when Jerry Burns introduced Max to Butch Gehring, while standing on a log deck next to a small office shack at Gehring Lumber Mill. Gehring was an independent soul, relaxed and comfortable in the wilderness. He listened intently as Max explained he was an FBI agent investigating

Kaczynski for sending threatening letters through the mail. He did not invite Max inside to enjoy the comfort of a small wood-burning stove.

The colder it got outside, the more comfortable Gehring seemed to get, as he followed Max' story about his loner neighbor. Although Max was grateful for his Danner elk hunting books, insulated socks, and clingy long underwear, it was still bone-chilling cold.

"Do you mind if I take a few notes?" he asked Gehring, who nodded assent. But, the ink in his government-issue ballpoint pen had frozen and rendered any writing attempts to be futile. Max held the pen in the front pocket of his jeans for warmth and in a couple of minutes his body heat did the job. As snow began to fall on the pages, Max jotted down some notes from the interview.

Gehring saw all this and finally smiled, "Would you like to step into my office to finish our talk?" he questioned.

"That's a great idea," Max accepted the invitation and returned the smile. Apparently, he had passed a Montana test of endurance and the interview proceeded as planned.

Then, in an unexpected development, Gehring offered to take Max and Jerry on a walk up his skid road to show them Kaczynski's cabin. When they were within about forty yards of the dwelling, Max had his first unimpeded view of the place and was transfixed. Later that day Max described, for both Terry and I, his first encounter with Kaczynski. In fact, he told me the story multiple times before he had the chance to tell it to Terry on the phone, who was back in San Francisco.

"So suddenly, Gehring's dog started barking really loud while it went after a deer and flushed it from a thicket near the cabin. The deer and dog ran past Kaczynski's cabin and Kaczynski obviously heard all the racket. As we watched kind of helplessly, the cabin door swung open and this wild looking man stared at us intently. I was speechless just looking at this guy off in the distance."

Max paused so Terry and I could take it all in. Then he continued. "So Butch didn't miss a beat and just waved and hollered, 'Hi, Teddy,' as if nothing was out of order. Just as quickly, Kaczynski nodded in Butch's direction and disappeared back into the cabin."

"And I couldn't believe what I had just seen," Max went on, "My God—is that what we've been looking for all these years?" It was his first face off with Theodore Kaczynski, but was not to be his last.

* * *

Getting photographs of Kaczynski's cabin for tactical planning was not an easy task in this Continental Divide region of Montana. And, creating a reliable radio communications system to keep us in touch with each other proved to be equally challenging. The FBI's sophisticated surveillance aircraft, dubbed "Night Stalker," had completed a flyover for a photo reconnaissance attempt that provided a beautiful picture of Canyon Creek, but did nothing to penetrate the canopy of snow-clad trees that completely obscured the cabin. The shadowy plane wasn't even that discreet.

"Did you guys get a good picture of me yesterday?" Butch Gehring joked with Max, who obligingly denied knowledge of any such fly-over. After Jerry and Butch observed that the State Fish and Game Department frequently used a small plane to monitor a herd of elk living at nearby Mt. Baldy, Max decided that Ted wouldn't be suspicious of a small plane flying near his cabin because he was familiar with their monitoring of the elk herd. Our local Helena FBI agent J.R. McDonald, who was also a pilot, rented a small plane. Dave Weber hung out of the plane's window with a Nikon 35mm camera and a 200mm zoom lens getting great and clear shots of the cabin and surrounding area. The problem was solved.

Had *Life* magazine still been in business, Weber's resulting photographs would have won the photo/journalist prize for 1996. Rich in detail, they would have captured the secluded lifestyle of America's Most Wanted Terrorist—living in a small, isolated cabin in the middle of a snow-covered wilderness, visible only from the air and separated from the view of neighboring cabins by mountainous terrain and acres more of thick Montana forest. Years before the advent of Google maps, they gave the UTF an accurate overview of the trails, vantage points, and vulnerabilities of Kaczynski's woodsy house that could be used to plan our tactical approach without his knowledge when it was time to affect an arrest.

The radio communication solution was not as simple. The FBI's technicians in Salt Lake City had never been able to build a workable radio repeater system in the mountains that surrounded Lincoln and get that signal all the way back to Salt Lake City. Jerry Burns pointed out that his employer, the U.S. Forest Service (USFS), had effective communications through its solar powered repeaters in fire lookout towers on Stonewall and Granite Butte Mountain. Their equipment was not designed to beam a signal back to Salt Lake City, but we had no need for that either. Reliable radio communication along the western slope of the Continental Divide around Lincoln and Missoula was a critical need, with an extended range to Helena being a stretch goal. Max had contacted our San Francisco technical agent Larry Long and asked him to complete a communications survey for us.

Ultimately, it was concluded that we could adapt the Forest Service radio communications system to ours and we dispatched technicians Bill Hagle and Rick Etheridge to Montana to install FBI equipment on the USFS transmitters. Once again, Max looked at Dave Weber to lead an expedition into the wilderness terrain.

Weber and Burns decided they would need four snowmobiles to get everyone and their equipment to the surrounding mountaintops. The USFS had two snowmobiles and Weber rented two more. He and Burns gave Hagle and Etheridge a quick course on operating snowmobiles before the four launched into the rugged mountains.

The installations were successful, but as they were returning down the steep and snow-covered slopes, Hagle lost control of his snowmobile and it veered out of control directly toward a cliff. Before taking the steep plunge, it hit a tree and Hagle was thrown into a snow bank—sparing his life. Even so, Hagle was rushed to a nearby hospital with a head injury and possible concussion.

Early the next day, Weber and Burns used rappelling gear to rescue the snowmobile that miraculously suffered only minor damage. After some repairs and tender care, they restored its luster and returned it to the rental agency. And, for the first time, the mountains that protected Kaczynski's secluded cabin from every form of outside intrusion were alive with the chatter of FBI communications from Helena and Missoula to Lincoln's most private and guarded spots.

* * *

I was back in San Francisco on Monday morning for a full day of briefings with the UTF leadership team regarding the progress being made by our Montana contingent. It was also an opportunity to touch base with Associate SAC Charlie Matthews regarding the myriad of other investigations and operations that were ongoing in the San Francisco FBI Office. On Tuesday morning, March 19th, I was back in the air on my way to Helena, MT.

Upon meeting with Max, we toured the rented office space that would be occupied on Wednesday morning by the UTF staff. We dubbed it the High Country Offsite Office of the UTF. For the rest of that day, we occupied ourselves with the constant task of reviewing the results of incoming interview reports and tagging the pertinent times and dates to Ted's timeline while comparing it to the Unabomber's timeline.

UTF agents had confirmed multiple hotel/motel stays by Kaczynski in Helena and in Missoula; two bus drivers on routes beyond Missoula had identified photographs of Ted as a passenger and established the dates of travel; and Ted's bank records in Missoula had been accessed by subpoena with additional findings of dates and locations where he had stayed and made payments. There were no discrepancies between the parallel timelines and by Thursday afternoon we had amassed a preponderance of damaging evidence that pointed directly to Ted Kaczynski as the Unabomber.

On Thursday, March 21st, at the High Country Office, I relished the moment and made a notation in my day planner at precisely 3:30 pm to mark the occasion when Max Noel finally declared, "Jim, I know it's been a long time coming. But, I now believe based on all of these facts that Ted Kaczynski is the Unabomber. It's amazing, but true."

"Alright, Max. That's an occasion worthy of tearing Turchie away from his search warrant work back in San Francisco. Why don't we give him a call and tell him that you have joined the fold of believers." The few moments of laughter that followed provided relief from the tension that we'd been feeling.

The next priority was for Max and I to reach agreement on a search/arrest plan. My primary objective was to serve an arrest warrant, but in either event we needed to follow up with a search warrant for the cabin. At minimum, Max and I were anticipating the need for a temporary detention of the subject while the cabin was assessed and deemed to be a safe and secure environment for the UTF search team. Despite the diminutive size, Ted's cabin was potentially a veritable bomb factory that would require a slow and deliberate examination of its contents.

Our initial plan was to wait until Kaczynski came out of his cabin for a ride into Lincoln on his bicycle, as we had determined he did periodically. The weather was improving and the roads becoming more passable for bicycle travel each day, which made it a viable option. We'd stop him on Stemple Pass Road where he'd be easily placed into "investigative detention" while the UTF search team completed their work at the cabin. The likelihood of Ted having a concealed and easily accessible weapon or bomb on his person, as he went into Lincoln to purchase supplies and/or pickup mail, was remote.

In the process of reviewing photos of the cabin and terrain maps for the mountainside, we sketched out the various locations of private cabins that could be used as staging and observation areas in addition to the nearby Gehring lumber mill. A call was also made to our SWAT Team Coordinator in San Francisco to get him out to Lincoln for a survey of the immediate area.

On Friday, March 22, we called all nearby Montana UTF personnel into the High Country Office for a full discussion of the preliminary search/arrest plan. Terry was on the conference phone and both he and Max emphasized the need to complete all interview report forms and evidence logs for purposes of finalizing the search warrant affidavit. Terry reported that the document's thickness was now approaching 30 inches or more, but there was a process underway for constantly culling and prioritizing the material that would make it into the final affidavit. As he pointed out, the highest priority evidence was what was now being developed on a daily basis and it was imperative to get that material to him in a timely manner.

Terry was joining our phone call from Schenectady, New York, where he had flown that day from San Francisco, along with Kathy Puckett and Lee Stark. The trip to New York was prompted by an animated debate that took place earlier in the week on the timing of our interview with Ted's mother, Wanda, who was in the process of moving from Lombard, Illinois to an apartment in Scotia, New York, the week of March 18. David had taken time off his job to help Wanda with the relocation. Max and I were pushing to use the opportunity to gain access to Wanda and find out what she knew about her son Ted. Terry had been working with Kathy, Lee, Max and I to identify questions we should ask of Wanda and David based on recent developments in the investigation.

In a subsequent private conversation with Terry, Max and I shared our view that Kathy was moving slower than we wanted or needed and we couldn't afford more of the same at this critical juncture in the case. The mother was a key interview target and we expressed a need for Kathy to press hard for information, if necessary. We already knew that Ted was isolated from telephones and outside contacts while holed up in his cabin for the winter, so Max and I were willing to take a slight chance on premature exposure in exchange for gaining a potential knock-out blow in evidence from the mother. Terry and Kathy disagreed.

"It's time for Kathy to interview Kaczynski's mother," I argued, wanting David to pave the way for the UTF interview team to meet with her immediately.

"Kathy believes strongly that David simply isn't ready to introduce us to his mother or even discuss with her that her older son might be the notorious Unabomber. David can't guarantee Kathy yet that Wanda might not write a letter and tip off her son that we're asking about him. Kathy thinks David himself needs more time to digest all that has happened because he still routinely calls to ask whether we've eliminated his brother as the Unabomber. She thinks that David expects that one day she will tell him what he really wants to hear- yes, we've eliminated Ted as the bomber. But we all know that isn't going to happen. David is a chronic worrier and Kathy wants more time to bring him around to what is likely to happen here," Terry wrapped up his defense of Kathy and his position.

"Terry, stop, we're done discussing this. Get Kathy on the phone, get some advice and help from Bisceglie, whatever, but I want that interview this weekend and she and Lee are going to go to New York to do it—and you're going with them!" Our discussion complete, Terry got Kathy back on the phone. She wasn't happy with my decision, but she had no choice but to follow through.

Just as I hoped, Terry guided Kathy through a plan to get Wanda's cooperation. After he got her moved into her Scotia apartment, David sat down with Wanda and broke the news that he had called the FBI about Ted. Wanda took it amazingly well, consoling her younger son, while expressing every confidence that he was wrong and that his brother Ted wasn't the Unabomber.

Per the plan they had developed, after he talked with Wanda, David contacted attorney, Tony Bisceglie, who relayed the message by mobile phone to Kathy and Terry that she was amenable to talking.

"She's ready to talk to the FBI. She even asked David when he thought you might show up." Bisceglie added laughingly. It was Saturday, March 23, and it would prove to be a significant day in the history of the UNABOM investigation.

Within minutes of the green light from Bisceglie, Kathy, Lee and Molly Flynn walked up the stairs to knock on Wanda's door. Molly had shown up at the last minute, so Terry opted out of the meeting and made plans to debrief the team later that evening to discuss their findings. The little apartment was already going to be overflowing with three FBI agents, and Terry didn't like the visual picture of several hunkering FBI agents confronting the small grandmotherly figure. David had tears in his eyes as the introductions ended, and Wanda moved quickly to comfort him. She reassured him that she wasn't mad at him for not telling her he had been talking to the FBI about his brother Ted. She gave no indication that she was surprised or upset by the day's developments and listened intently as Kathy explained to her why the FBI was at her door.

"We'll want to ask you some questions about Ted, how he currently lives and how he manages to get by when he doesn't appear to work," Kathy slowly and sympathetically laid out for Wanda. "We'll want to know about his upbringing, hobbies, what he reads and how he gets along with other people. We'd like to know about any of his friends and perhaps see any letters he has written to you." Kathy stopped for Wanda to take in what was happening in the living room of her tiny apartment.

"I understand," Wanda began, with her own sympathetic demeanor setting an example of courage for everyone else in the room. "Ted has always been different and alone. He lives in the wilderness because he likes it there. I think it suits his personality and lifestyle. He's never needed much in the way of money because he grows all his own vegetables and hunts animals for meat. I have an old footlocker that belongs to Ted here in the house. I brought it with me during the move this week. Ted hasn't seemed interested in it for many years. It has letters and other writings and things that I've kept over the years."

"Could you please show us the footlocker when we're finished talking with you?" Kathy probed, as Lee Stark could hardly conceal his appetite to look inside it.

"Yes, when you tell me you're ready, I will show you where it is," Wanda was becoming at ease with Kathy while her younger son David, sat quietly and followed the interview of his mother.

As Wanda Kaczynski patiently described Ted's wilderness lifestyle, hobbies and her memories of his upbringing, she located and readily handed over copies of letters Ted had written to newspaper editors and magazines during 1969 and 1970 that talked about technology and freedom. One letter referred to the U.S. Commission on Violence, which suggested to Kathy and Terry that Ted had certainly read, *The History of Violence in America*, one of four books cited by the Unabomber in his Manifesto.

Wanda gave the agents another rough draft letter in her son Theodore's handwriting, which stated that:

"...*modern technology has led to the concentration of economic*

and political power...by Big Business and Big Government..."

Theodore Kaczynski's words echoed those written by the Unabomber in the UNABOM Manifesto:

"...The conservatives are...exploiting his resentment of Big Government to promote the power of Big Business."

One by one, Kathy led Wanda through each of the UNABOM events to determine whether she knew Ted's whereabouts during the bombings.

"I remember walking Ted to the local commuter train in the fall of 1979," Wanda told Kathy, as Kathy's brain voiced to her that this recollection of Wanda might effectively place Ted in Chicago during the time of the bombing of American Airlines flight 444 in November of 1979.

"These are some cancelled checks dating back to 1985 for money I've sent to Ted over the years, Kathy gently received the checks from Wanda as Lee counted over her shoulder that they added up to almost $14,000.

"My husband and I visited with Ted in Montana during the mid-1980's. He had built a root cellar into the side of a hill about 150 feet across from his cabin. When we went to see Ted I had taken him a portable, manual typewriter, or I might have shipped it ahead at his request, one or the other," Wanda volunteered to Kathy, as Lee took copious notes.

"I believe Ted also had another manual typewriter that he took with him from the family home when he left Illinois in the late 1970's," Wanda finished, casting a look at Kathy that seemed to ask for approval of the job she was doing.

"Wanda, this is very helpful and we are so appreciative," Kathy reinforced, "Could you take us to the footlocker now?"

"It's about time," Lee silently thought as he jumped from his chair, following Kathy, Molly and Wanda to the trunk.

Wanda led the way into her bedroom, while David moved the trunk out of the closet. She sat down on the floor next to the trunk and opened it, pulling out documents, papers, and other items and placed them on the floor.

"All of these are things that Ted just didn't want anymore, but I kept them anyway," she told Kathy, as they all relived the lifetime of Theodore Kaczynski through his written hand.

From items found in the footlocker, the agents made one fascinating discovery after another. The old footlocker Ted Kaczynski had left at his parent's home yielded the carbon copies of his 1971 essay and other letters and notes. Of great interest to Kathy and Terry was a letter signed by Ted that he had written to his mother Wanda. The letter read, in part:

"...We will be sacrificing some of the materialistic benefits of technology, but there just can't be any other way. We can't eat our cake and have it too."

The discovery represented a direct link to paragraph number 185 in the Unabomber's Manifesto, which included the identical phrase:

"As for the negative consequences of eliminating industrial society-well, you can't eat your cake and have it too. To gain one thing you have to sacrifice another."

All of us realized that the common usage for the phrase was "you can't have your cake and eat it too" and for those of us assigning great weight to the word and phrase comparisons, it was a smoking gun. This phrase was destined to receive top billing in the probable cause section of Terry's search warrant affidavit—along with Wanda's knowledge of manual typewriters at the cabin and now an indication of Ted's habit of retaining carbon copies of his writings. Damning evidence was quickly piling atop more and more of the same.

Wanda gave the agents an article Ted had written titled, "How I Blew Up Harold Snilly." Ted had used the pseudonym, Apias Tuberosa, when he wrote the article while living in Lombard, Illinois. In his story, he recounted how a high school classmate blew up a mixture of chemicals that Ted had provided him:

"When I was in high school, I took a course in chemistry. There was only one aspect of the subject which interested me, as any chemist could have seen from a brief inspection of my rather specialized collection of home reagents; powdered aluminum, powdered magnesium, powdered zinc, sulfur, potassium, nitrate...in suitable combinations these things are capable of exploding."

Not surprisingly, the chemicals that Ted listed were among those used in the early UNABOM events. And, the use of the pseudonym evoked the "Enoch Fischer" letter sent to Percy Wood by the Unabomber in 1980 and "Ralph Kloppenburg," who sent the "thesis" paper to Professor James McConnell at the University of Michigan in 1985.

The "Harold Snilly" story was consistent with a letter Wanda had written to Harvard University in 1958 on her son's behalf:

"Much of his time is spent at home reading and contriving numerous gadgets made up of wood, string, wire, tape, lenses, gears, wheels, etc.; that test out various principals in physics. His table and desk are always a mess of test tubes, chemicals, batteries, ground coal, etc. He will miss greatly, I think, this browsing and puttering in his messy makeshift lab."

In parting, Wanda again emphasized to the interview team that Ted liked his privacy and enjoyed living alone in the wilderness.

"It's upsetting that you would suspect Ted because of his lifestyle. I don't believe he is the Unabomber, but if it is him, he must be stopped," she told Kathy.

* * *

Terry returned to San Francisco the next day and spent hours updating Max and I on the phone as to the full details of the interview of Ted's mother; as well as time spent with AUSA Steve Freccero and FBI Legal Officer Gordon McDonald, updating them on our investigation and adding pertinent paragraphs to the search warrant affidavit.

In Montana, I sat down with Max and Tom McDaniel. Max wanted to be heard on his proposal to lure Ted outside the cabin so that he could be detained without incident, should we need to do so. This was Plan B, where we might not have the luxury of waiting for him to leave his cabin for a bicycle trip into Lincoln. And, it was far more dangerous to implement.

"Okay, Max. We talked about this moment many months ago and here we are. I don't want the HRT out here in Montana. I don't want another Ruby Ridge or Waco. And I don't want any screw-ups. What have you come up with?"

To my satisfaction, Max and Tom had spent considerable time putting together a plan for the approach to Kaczynski's cabin. Their plan was based on information from Butch about how protective Kaczynski was of his property. The previous summer, Butch had leased to Kennecott Mining Company the exploratory mining rights on his own property, which actually surrounded Kaczynski's 1.7 acres. Ted had been very upset when he found out and the two had several discussions about it. Last December, Butch talked with Ted again and told him of a new lease with a different mining company and their people, who would be coming around the property this next summer. Ted was furious and Butch told him to "just deal with it," but he assured Ted that he wouldn't let the mining company employees encroach on his property. Max and Tom saw an opportunity here that could be exploited.

The plan Max proposed would have him and Tom McDaniel openly approaching Kaczynski's cabin from the direction of the Gehrig sawmill and being in the company of fully uniformed, USFS Police Officer Jerry Burns, who would do all the talking. At the appropriate time, Burns would announce that Max and Tom were the representatives of a Golden Colorado mining company. Jerry would ask Kaczynski to come out of his cabin to show them the corner posts marking his property. Once Kaczynski took the bait and stepped from the protection of his cabin, they would grab him and handcuff him. Max would display FBI credentials and advise Kaczynski of his detention during the service of a federal search warrant for his cabin and surrounding property.

"I like it Max." I moved our discussion ahead. "Now let's discuss how we're going to work our San Francisco SWAT team members in close to provide support to the operation in the event of trouble or in case Ted tries to rabbit over the hilltop."

That afternoon, Max and I traveled to a location that was under consideration to serve as our forward command post once the search/arrest plan was set in motion. It was the Seven-Up Ranch Resort and Supper Club, located just off highway 200 about five miles east of Lincoln. It was owned by Wayne Cashman and his family, who were deemed by Tom McDaniel to be capable of holding our confidence. Aside from serving good food, the property was big enough to assemble all the UTF agents for briefings and serve as a staging area for vehicles and SWAT personnel. It was close enough for us to shuttle back and forth from Kaczynski's cabin and far enough away to afford operational separation and security from the media and curious townspeople. We booked the entire facility from that day forward for the duration of our investigation in and around Lincoln.

We had also identified two cabins in the canyon near Kaczynski's to be used as observation platforms. The cabin nearest to Ted's was a small elk-hunting cabin, owned by Glen Williams. It was never used in the winter because it wasn't winterized. The second cabin was owned by the Miller family and was a few hundred yards further down toward the mouth of the canyon; and importantly it was winterized. UTF agents located and spoke with both absentee owners and secured their cabins for our use.

When the property arrangements were in place, we deployed agents Jerry Webb and Chuck Durr to the Miller cabin, so they would be close enough to Kaczynski to move in on a moment's notice if it became apparent that he was taking evasive action or destroying evidence.

Our plan was structured for an orderly process to unfold, if only Main Justice would name a lead prosecutor to the case— preferably someone that would make a decision. My telephone requests for a lead prosecutor had not received attention.

Soon, I learned that the timing, and potentially the element of surprise had been taken from our hands—by a leak to the media.

CHAPTER SIXTEEN

END OF THE TRAIL

"I hate the technological society because it deprives me of personal autonomy."

(Everything we'd done and all the decisions we'd made in our two years working on the UNABOM investigation came together on April 3, 1996.)

MONDAY DAWNED IN MONTANA ON MARCH 25TH, LIKE MOST other days—weekends and weekdays had merged into a continuum. Our constantly growing numbers of UTF members engaged non-stop in old fashioned, shoe-leather police work involving interviews of motel clerks, shopkeepers, bank tellers, and bus drivers. This flurry of activity added to the stockpile of typed reports, messages, faxes, draft copies of affidavits and statements of probable cause that were exchanged hourly with Terry and the FBI's legal team in the San Francisco FBI Office.

Napoleon said that an army marches on its stomach, but during these days the UTF lived and died by its ability to digest its own paperwork. And, prosecuting attorneys have an insatiable desire for facts and never admit they have enough; whereas investigators like me aim for "just enough." Terry reported that the draft affidavit for our warrant had grown from a foot-high stack of papers two weeks earlier to something of mountainous proportions.

The public's attention was stirred up to such an extent about the search for the Unabomber that getting any kind of a warrant regarding a suspect looked like it would require virtual assurance of a conviction before an AUSA would put their personal reputation on the line. Terry and I faced a hard sell in any case, but marketing a snow-bound hillbilly of a hermit as the notorious and stealthy Unabomber became one of our most formidable challenges.

After my conference call to the Assistant United States Attorneys (AUSA) with jurisdiction and venue in the Federal Judicial Districts covering the three UNABOM murders, I had been pushing hard with Deputy Director Bill Esposito to get a lead prosecutor named for the case. Then I followed up with Howard Shapiro, the FBI's Chief Counsel, and learned that my request was meeting a lot of resistance. It turns out there were multiple interests at Main Justice and among the U.S. Attorneys that were vying behind the scenes to control the ultimate prosecution—but only after the Unabomber was identified and arrested. None seemed to see the contradiction in that arrangement.

I was disappointed and angry, but also unaware that forces beyond our control were about to turn our strategy and timetable upside down.

Lowell Bergman, Executive Producer for the CBS News show, *60 Minutes*, telephoned my SF-based media representative, George Grotz, on Tuesday, March 26th, and requested a meeting with me to discuss confidential information in his possession that the FBI was working a viable UNABOM suspect in a nearby western state. Wham! There it was—the unwelcome news of a media leak.

I was in Montana at the time, but Janet and George were dutifully representing to all callers that I was in my usual business mode in San Francisco to avoid adding to any suspicion. I told George to stall Bergman while I reached out to FBI Headquarters. Esposito told me that Bergman had called there first and he had passed him my name.

George feigned casual interest and set the meeting with Bergman for Friday, which bought us valuable time. I alerted Max and Terry to the seriousness of the situation and we immediately began emergency planning. There was now a very real probability of a media story naming Kaczynski as our suspect. We agreed that AUSA Steve Freccero in San Francisco and Bernie Hubley in Helena should be alerted and be prepared to act accordingly, if an expedited warrant was needed. Then, I booked a flight back to San Francisco for my "routine" meeting with Lowell Bergman.

At the appointed time, Bergman was escorted into my office. George handled the introductions and I rose from my desk, shook hands, and motioned to the side chairs and couch for our discussions. From its start, this meeting was unlike any that I had experienced with a representative of the media at any level. My expectation was a request that I confirm his information, along with veiled or even open threats for additional information. But, that's not the way he handled it—he didn't ask for or appear to want confirmation. Instead, Bergman represented that he was simply doing the courtesy of putting the FBI on notice.

Trying not to appear overly interested, George and I strained to listen and retain the gist of what he was saying until we could write it all down after the meeting. In a nutshell, Bergman said that he had multiple sources on our UNABOM investigation; he repeatedly made the points that he was a player, he had sources, and that he did not want to jeopardize the integrity of an FBI investigation. He claimed not to be in a hurry to release his story, but then stated his concern that media competitors might obtain the information and beat CBS News in breaking the story.

The odd meeting concluded the same way it started—with

Bergman summarizing his intention to put the FBI on notice. We were careful not to say anything to cause the information to be confirmed, nor did we ask him about the identity of his sources. We stood, shook hands, and he left.

George had a quizzical look on his face and I just shrugged my shoulders, as we sat down in my office to review what had been revealed. I asked Janet to track Terry down to join us.

Terry arrived and I brought him up to speed. "Bergman does have it right that we have a primary suspect and there was something he said about a brother of the suspect, but it was all wrong. Still, he has a source of information that's telling him about a suspect in Montana and somehow it involves the suspect's brother. This is not good. Not good, at all."

It wasn't as damaging as it might have been. Terry quickly ran down a list of his next steps; giving even more urgency to the affidavit preparation, updating Joel and Max and the other UTF leaders, notifying FBI Headquarters, and kicking off a new phase of emergency planning.

I returned to Helena that weekend. As before, I registered at the motel under another name to avoid detection by reporters that might be making pretext phone calls to the front desks in an effort to confirm the existence of UTF activity in the area.

Max and I called an immediate meeting with the UTF staff at the offsite office to advise them of the immediate threat of media exposure that could jeopardize the investigation at any time. There were anxious looks and expressions of concern about the integrity of the investigation, but they took the news in stride without any concept of just how fast that locomotive was coming down the track.

On Monday, April 1st, I received news from George Grotz of more calls he had received from Lowell Bergman over the weekend. I also had a message from Bob Bucknam, a Special Assistant to Louie Freeh, stating that the Director had received an inquiry from CBS News in New York City about a UNABOM suspect.

It was Bergman who seemed to be driving the story with his information sources and while he didn't have the exact name of the suspect, it now was phonetically close to Kaczynski. In a matter of hours, CBS News confidentially told Bucknam that the state of Montana was the location of the UNABOM suspect investigation. Next, Bergman told Grotz that he knew FBI agents had been flying into Helena and Missoula, MT, to work on this case. A quagmire of leaked information was forming around us—probably a result of the steadily expanding universe of insiders with knowledge of our covert operation in Montana.

The ball was solidly in CBS' court, but no story had yet appeared. Max assured me that our UTF agents had not seen or heard any unusual movements around the Kaczynski cabin. The news from Terry was that the legal work on the search warrant affidavit was moving at a feverish pace to organize and highlight the most relevant items of evidence.

Terry had commented dryly on a phone call, "The affidavit is now measured in feet, not inches." He added that Steve Freccero was working alongside our legal agents and attempting to stay current on the intake of new data.

I had to ask, "Terry, have you told Steve about the media leak?"

"Only in very general terms of a potential leak," was the response. "I'm waiting for the other shoe to drop before lighting him up."

Be careful what you ask for, was my first thought. Within the hour, Grotz called to relay the message that CBS News was virtually certain that other news organizations, the *New York Times* and *Washington Post* in particular, had similar information that the FBI had a UNABOM suspect. It was unnecessary, but he said it anyway: "CBS News is not about to be scooped by the competition."

The bombshell revelation was their stated intention to break the story during the Tuesday evening news—the next day!

I motioned across the room to where Max had a phone

propped on his shoulder and I mouthed the words, "Let's talk—now!" Next, I telephoned the San Francisco office for Terry to join in our huddle.

"OK, the down and dirty of it is this. CBS News is going live on the Montana suspect story in the next 12 to 24 hours and it looks like the major newspapers also have the story and are set to publish. Max, I want you to pull the trigger on final preparations to execute the plan at Kaczynski's cabin door. We'll need to move quickly after the story breaks. Ted is isolated from a TV news report without electricity and he has no telephone, but there's no guarantee he doesn't have a battery-operated radio or that someone in Lincoln might hear the news and drop-by for a visit."

Max was on it before I finished speaking. "Terry, that affidavit is more critical than ever. I need you to get it pared down to the most critical and essential elements that even an attorney can understand. When you have the first cut, send it to me to look at. Get the full UTF team involved in coordinating the logistics of moving essential people and equipment to Helena on the first available flights. Talk with Charlie about adding some administrative help for alerting and moving the SWAT team and the Evidence Response Team as we planned. And, Terry, don't forget to book flights for you and Grotz. You guys figure out who is needed beyond that; and put your support resources in San Francisco in touch with Lee Hayden at the Helena Offsite—have them book flights, tickets, rental cars, motel rooms, etc."

Max had rejoined the conversation after giving out some urgent instructions to whoever was in the next room, but he heard my last comment and offered a comment, "Jim, let's not wait on that, I'll have Lee rent every available rental car today; whether they're in Helena or Missoula, or within a hundred miles. They're going to be one precious commodity when this gets cranked up."

Following my burst of instruction, I was breathless. "I agree—and you guys know what has to be done."

Max was the first to take advantage of my pause. "That's one hell of a scheduling nightmare. It's a physical impossibility to get everyone here from San Francisco and to execute everything you've just said by late tomorrow afternoon. If it comes to that, I have enough people here in Montana to fill in and pull off the arrest scenario at the cabin."

"The problem with that," Terry offered, "is that I have to get the search warrant affidavit authorized by Freccero and then get it in front of a Federal Judge here in San Francisco. You can serve the search warrant in Montana as soon as it's official—it doesn't have to be in your physical possession. And, I can fax a copy of the warrant itself to Bernie Hubley in Helena. But, everything has to work like a Swiss watch in order to get all that done by tomorrow afternoon."

"We may be forced to act without everything being in place and perfect. My next call is to Esposito and Bucknam at HQ, and to Louie if necessary, to tell them all that we've put in motion and the challenges that are cropping up."

Max had one more thing to say before I did that. "Jim, we've been holding back on doing some key interviews in Helena and Lincoln out of concern that our covert investigation might leak out. Can I assume that we now have the go-ahead to conduct those interviews?"

Terry quickly agreed with Max it was time to do the interviews and I nodded my consent. This was understood to include the librarian in Lincoln, to learn the degree of frequency that Ted came to the library and to determine if some or all of the books and publications quoted in the Unabomber's manifesto were available there; and also the manager of the Sylvan Learning Center in Helena because investigation had established that Ted had a brief affiliation there and the Sylvan Learning Center was one of the few businesses mentioned in the manifesto.

After a lengthy call to Headquarters, I drove to my motel room without a thought of dinner and slept fitfully through the night.

Arising early on Tuesday morning, April 2nd, I felt my back being pressed against the wall. Due to the time difference with California, I had to wait an hour before connecting on a call to AUSA Steve Freccero. After a short greeting, I proceeded to present my own summary of the facts as justification of an arrest warrant for Theodore J. Kaczynski, or at minimum a search warrant for Kaczynski's cabin. At this stage in the investigation and with Steve's involvement with Terry in the preparation of the draft affidavit, my assumption was that my recommendation would be well received. I was astonished by his answer and the intensity of the response.

"No, I don't think you have enough probable cause to obtain a search warrant; and even if you did I wouldn't authorize it!" Freccero stated.

My response was ineloquent and to the point. "Bullshit! I've got enough probable cause for an arrest warrant and a search warrant! And, I need it now. There's been a leak to the media that will alert the suspect to destroy evidence in that cabin...." My voice trailed off and I realized this was going nowhere.

Within the hour I was speaking by telephone with Director Louie Freeh, Deputy Director Bill Esposito, and FBI Legal Counsel Howard Shapiro, who collectively recognized the serious consequences that could result from an airing of this story on the news. I reprised my earlier presentation to AUSA Freccero and began a detailed description of probable cause that was based in part on Kaczynski's personal writings being virtually identical in a side-by-side comparison to certain unique phrases in the Unabomber's manifesto; and with identical linguistic patterns in more than 100 of Ted's personal letters to his brother. I gave particular attention to the inverted phrase "they can eat their cake and have it too" that was written by Ted and appeared in that identical way in the manifesto. Next, I shifted to a description of Ted's bill payments by check, dozens of postmarks on Ted's letters showing dates and locations of postings, as well as motel receipts and bus tickets that provided trace evidence of Ted's travel patterns–and none being in conflict with the dates and places of known Unabomber activities.

The Director provided an immediate response. "You have ample probable cause here for a search warrant. And, in view of the media threat to go public, I want it served today!" I was elated to receive the Director's personal support, but I still needed an AUSA that would file it; and that wasn't happening—not today in any case.

When I called Terry to brief him on my conversation with Louie and my dismay at Steve Freccero's assessment of our probable cause, he told me to relax.

"Jim, I know Steve can get really anal. But he has been working his butt off and is clearly on our side here. The search warrant is solid and gets better with every hour. Steve is our greatest supporter from my view and we'll have the warrant ready for a Judge to sign, whether that Judge is here in San Francisco or in Montana."

Relief that afternoon was spelled B-U-C-K-N-A-M. He came through with news of a phone call from Director Freeh to CBS News President Andrew Heyward that resulted in a stand-down from their threat to go public that next evening on Tuesday, April 2nd, and instead there was a commitment to hold the story for 24-hours. On Wednesday, CBS would be announcing a statement that "the FBI has identified a primary UNABOM suspect and have him under surveillance in Montana, near Helena and Missoula."

Without being explicit either way, CBS had received confirmation of their source information and we got the time we needed—time to get our assets in place and to file for the search warrant.

Terry coordinated the move of close to one hundred UTF agents, analysts and professional support personnel from San Francisco to Montana between noon and midnight on April 2. He was one of the last FBI agents getting off the final Delta Airlines flight into Helena at midnight. As he rode the escalator down to the main airport lobby, he saw Max waiting for him, tired but excited by all the action.

"Jim's waiting for you Terry to go over the warrant. I'm going to drop you off, get a little rest and then head for Lincoln early. Good luck with the warrant today."

Terry arrived at the airport in Helena with the affidavit in hand, as our revised plan was to file it before a Federal Judge there. He had worked on it up until it was time to leave San Francisco. Just before boarding the flight, Steve Freccero gave him the leftover half of a turkey sandwich he had bought for lunch, but never had time to finish.

That evening, Terry and I drafted and re-drafted the affidavit in the High Country Offsite until 2:00 a.m. the next morning. Terry worked with Bernie Hubley another two and half hours, faxing parts of the affidavit between San Francisco and Washington, D.C., until almost 4:30 am. Steve Freccero was at the other end of the fax machine in San Francisco and between the three of them, the final copy of the warrant was finished and ready to present to U.S. District Court Judge William Lovell at 8 am the morning of April 3rd.

Max was moving in multiple directions at once—meeting with the arriving SWAT team and others from San Francisco to brief them until the wee hours in preparation for an early morning deployment to the Seven-Up Ranch near Lincoln.

While attempting to grab two hours of sleep, I lingered in thought to wonder just how long it might have taken to get a decision on a search warrant without having the extraordinary pressure of an external deadline. I fell asleep without the answer, and then the alarm was ringing loudly. It was an hour's drive to establish our forward command post at the Seven-Up Ranch, five miles east of Lincoln, MT. I felt anticipation at the prospect of meeting up with the Unabomber.

* * *

It was before dawn on the morning of April 3, 1996 when I gave the word for the SWAT snipers to move into place so we could keep an eye on Kaczynski's cabin door. The UTF investigative teams, Evidence Response teams, analysts, and all of the other personnel who had arrived in Montana overnight assembled at the Seven-Up Ranch and Supper Club. The hot coffee, flowing pitchers of orange juice, and pastries supplied to the assembled teams was the only food many had known for well over sixteen hours. We'd moved so many people to Montana so quickly that most had little opportunity for lunch or dinner the day before. The SWAT members were suited up in winter white, military-style "Ghillie" suits to camouflage their appearance in the snowy terrain, which inspired some good-natured ribbing from their peers.

Along with SWAT Commander Tom LaFreniere and Max, I briefed the group on our operational plan to remove Kaczynski from the cabin and render it safe while the search commenced. Now all we had to do was to wait for Terry's call on his meeting with Federal Judge William Lovell in Helena.

Judge Lovell had arranged juice, coffee and donuts for his staff, Bernie and Terry while he reviewed the search warrant and supporting affidavit. After spending considerable time pouring over every paragraph and asking detailed questions of Terry, Judge Lovell put his signature on the search warrant and told him to get it served. Upon receipt of the news from Terry that our search warrant had been filed and that he was on his way to Lincoln with the signed warrant and affidavit in his briefcase, it was time to implement the next phase of our plan.

Max, Tom McDaniel and Jerry Burns led the SWAT personnel to the Gehring saw mill property and provided directions so that they could begin their careful and quiet ascent up the mountains behind Gehring's house. Their objective was to gain a vantage point to view Kaczynski's cabin from the other side of the skid road. Their job was two-fold: containment of the subject from escaping and emergency response in the event that Max and his team received a dangerous response from the subject.

The timely deployment of SWAT was rendered all the more difficult by a decision to follow the book on procedure and tote their heavy body armor and loads of other equipment along with them. I already knew it would take the teams about 45 minutes to hike into location. Dave Weber and Max had paced off the precise number of steps required to reach the location at which they would leave the upper skid road and camouflage themselves in the forest surrounding Kaczynski's cabin. There they would wait, and if everything went as planned, there would be no need for their services.

I moved forward as far as possible by accompanying John Steiner, the senior SWAT team leader, to the Miller cabin under the escort of Jerry Webb. This served to physically establish a forward command post for my decision-making that was away from the proximity of an attorney from Main Justice who had taken over one of the few telephones at the Seven-Up Ranch. Steiner had radio contact with SWAT members as they were slowly easing into place, which also allowed us to remain in close contact with Max and his team at the sawmill location. Candice De Long, John Gray, Paul Wilhelmus and Mike Grady were positioned at the elk-hunting cabin of Glenn Williams as a precaution to confront Kaczynski if he somehow eluded detention and escaped down the canyon toward the road leading to Lincoln.

As the sun raised high in the sky and our SWAT elements were still shuffling into place, I gave Tom McDaniel the green light to provide details of our covert operation to the Sheriff of Lewis and Clark County, fully realizing that he was a close associate of the FBI and the rest of the law enforcement community in Montana. I knew that he would be very unhappy about my decision not to include him or members of his department until the last moment of making our play at the Unabomber's cabin. But, it was a sound decision that we had applied uniformly to our other non-UTF personnel and FBI offices alike to forestall leaks of information that could destroy the fruits of over 17 years of investigation. Tom didn't eagerly anticipate having to break this news to the Sheriff, but he carried it off like a true professional. I'm sure that he stood up and received the anticipated anger that was aimed my way, but Tom didn't mention it.

Still, the SWAT members moved agonizingly slow and everyone else waited. Max, Jerry Burns, and Tom McDaniel relaxed on Butch Gehring's log deck, confidently reviewing their plan for approaching and detaining Kaczynski. Butch supplied them with a pot of coffee and continued laughing at the sight of the SWAT team scaling the mountainside in their "chicken suits."

An hour, then ninety minutes, and Steiner stated that the team wasn't fully in place. My impatience and apprehension was boiling, as all it would take was for Ted to come out of his cabin and see a fresh footprint in the snow or hear rustling in the brush and we would have a barricaded subject on our hands. An armed and dangerous subject in a cabin having only one door and a single window—and presumably with enough provisions to last out the winter. This was not going to happen!

Finally, Steiner reported to me that all were in place except for one member that was still moving into his place of hiding. On that note and noting it was now past noon, I told Steiner to order that agent to hunker down in his Ghillie suit in the best cover available as "phase two" of the operation was about to begin. Steiner sighed in frustration and explained the reason for their long delay. After hiking only a short distance in the high altitude with all of their equipment, the team had decided they needed to cache their unnecessary "stuff" before proceeding with their deployment. So, they made a decision to hike far up the skid road to a location where they could safely stash their gear. They had finally made it back to the designated area—concealed in the forest around Kaczynski's cabin. At last, we were ready and I gave the go-ahead to Max and his team to proceed.

The interesting thing about Max's plan for approaching the cabin was that it was completely open and loud. In fact, the success of their ruse to entice Ted out of his cabin hinged on Kaczynski hearing them coming and looking out to recognize the U.S. Forest Officer Jerry Burns, who would do all the talking. Max, Jerry Burns, and Tom McDaniel set off on their short hike up the canyon and talked among themselves in somewhat normal tones. We could hear their voices at the Miller cabin, but not enough to make out their words.

As they stepped off the skid road and onto Ted's property, Jerry Burns began calling out the hermit's name to make sure he was aware of their presence. Repeated calls failed to elicit any response.

Worry lines began to crease across Max' forehead, as he considered their options if Kaczynski didn't buy their charade. Finally, sounds of someone moving about inside. Whether the movement was hostile or one of curiosity was unknown.

Reaching the structure's only door, Tom McDaniel and Jerry Burns positioned themselves directly in front. Max stood at the cabin's front corner. The door abruptly cracked open and someone leaned outside with a look of anger—or maybe annoyance.

Jerry Burns was dressed for full visual effect in his USFS uniform. He directed his remarks to an unbelievably dirty and disheveled individual that he recognized as Theodore Kaczynski. "Ted, I'm escorting these two men from the gold mining company that has leased the mineral rights on Butch Gehring's property. They want to locate your boundary stakes, so they don't get on your property when they come back up here in a few weeks."

A high-pitched voice answered from the shadows within.

"The corners of my property are clearly marked with corner stakes."

Jerry didn't hesitate, as the occupant opened his door a little wider. "They're covered with snow. Can you come out and point out the location of the stakes for us?"

"I need my coat," Kaczynski said while turning back inside. In one motion, Burns grabbed Ted and yanked him backwards to prevent his disappearance into the cabin. The packed snow and ice was slippery and they almost tumbled backward. Like a towering grizzly, Tom McDaniel wrapped them both in a huge bear hug that held all of them upright.

Kaczynski struggled desperately until Max strode up to them, drew his Sig Sauer Model 226, and pointed it directly into Kaczynski's face. "We're with the FBI and have a Federal warrant to search your cabin." Max sternly delivered that message and Kaczynski stopped trying to get away.

With the suspect handcuffed behind his back, the foursome walked the 200 yards to the Glenn Williams' elk hunting cabin that had been designated as the point of detention while the cabin was being searched pursuant to the court order.

"The handcuffs are too tight," Kaczynski complained to Burns. "Can you loosen them?"

"That won't be possible until we get to the Williams' cabin," Jerry told him.

"Am I under arrest?" he asked Max.

"No," was the curt answer.

"Can you remove the handcuffs?"

"No," was the short response.

"Am I free to leave?" his eyes searching Max for a longer discussion.

"No," Max repeated again.

"It kind of sounds like I'm under arrest," Kaczynski continued.

* * *

I looked at my watch and it was 12:38 pm when word was passed that the suspect and cabin were secure.

When they arrived at the Williams cabin, Max seated Kaczynski at a table in the center of the room. Candace De Long placed a jacket over his shoulders and blanket around his legs. ATF agent Mike Grady tried to start a fire in the wood-burning cook stove, only to have the cabin fill quickly with smoke. Kaczynski looked at Grady with a kind of contempt before offering advice and instruction on how to properly light a fire and get the chimney to draw. Grady followed the directions and the ensuing fire warmed the cabin. Everyone but Paul Wilhelmus, Max and Kaczynski left the scene.

Max placed the UNABOM Wanted Poster, a "data sheet" for Major Case 75, the composite drawing of the Unabomber, and three photographs of Kaczynski on the table in front of him. The cabin wall had already been covered with a UNABOM timeline and overlapping Kaczynski chronology. All of the charts, data and photos were placed in the cabin on the advice of the Behavioral Science Unit at Quantico. Kaczynski seemed to ignore it all, never once asking any questions about the museum like displays.

Max and Paul formally identified themselves again. Max gave Kaczynski his Miranda rights and began trying to interview him.

"Am I free to stand up and leave the Williams cabin?" Kaczynski drilled Max.

"You're not free to leave. No," Max emphasized. "Is there anything in or around your cabin that could endanger the lives of the agents doing the search?"

Kaczynski ignored the question, instead responding, "Obviously I have been suspected of something and they always say don't talk."

Kaczynski studied a copy of the search warrant Max gave him.

Max assisted him while he read it by turning the pages since Kaczynski was seated at the table with his hands cuffed behind his back.

Finally, Kaczynski agreed to talk with Max and Paul Wilhelmus about general subjects as long as they didn't ask him about the search or as Kaczynski put it, "the case." For the next five hours they sat inside the Williams cabin, with Kaczynski asking questions and getting acquainted with his new found but unwelcome, wilderness mates. He asked about the well being of Glenn Williams and noted that his cabin was at an elevation of 4,800 feet. He spoke about his cabin, hunting rabbits, deer and elk, but said he avoided fishing because it took so much time and wasn't a reliable food source.

"Were you the one in the blue coat making noise at the Miller cabin yesterday?" he suddenly asked Max

"No," Max answered. Max was fully aware that he had been wearing a blue parka, as was Jerry Webb, while he was staying at the Miller cabin.

"Were you or some of the others you're with trying to take motorized vehicles up the Hum Bug Contour Road several weeks ago?" Kaczynski pressed on.

"No, what makes you think that?" Max shot back.

"I saw evidence that such vehicles had been on the road and found footprints in the snow coming down the mountainside towards my cabin." After making his point, Kaczynski returned to conversation about hiking trips in the mountains, his garden and growing vegetables.

He complimented Max on the ruse the team had used to lure him from his cabin. He explained to them that pretending to conduct a mining survey was the only way he could have been successfully induced to leave his cabin, especially since he had been holed up in it all winter long, not even making any trips to Lincoln.

Their conversation returned to Kaczynski's wilderness lifestyle—how he gathered wild mushrooms and herbs, and how he routinely melted snow for drinking water. As Kaczynski spoke, Max recalled the words the Unabomber wrote in his Manifesto, which became a part of the FBI search warrant affidavit:

"...When primitive man needed food he knew how to find and prepare edible roots...hunting not for sport...but to get meat that is necessary for food."

It was close to 4:00 pm when Terry and I arrived at the Williams cabin. By that time it was apparent Kaczynski wasn't going to discuss anything about his "case," negating any further need for us to stay clear. Max introduced Kaczynski to us by name and I explained the warrant process to him, letting him know the search of his cabin and property would continue through the remainder of the day and likely continue into the next. He didn't seem interested and kept staring at Terry while I spoke. When I finished, he looked immediately in Terry's direction.

"Are you the Terry Turchie who is the affiant in the search warrant?" he asked.

"Yes, I am," Terry confirmed.

"Can I read your affidavit?" Kaczynski tried another avenue to see the evidence against him.

"The affidavit is filed with the Federal District Court in Helena and is sealed. You'll be able to see it at the appropriate time and that isn't now."

"I'll take up the issue with the Assistant U.S. Attorney," I added.

Terry and I then walked up the skid road to check on the status of our search at Kaczynski's cabin. We stood at the doorway as bomb experts Pat Webb and Donald Sachtleben explained the array of items strewn about inside. Pat and Don had already determined the cabin was a literal bomb factory and presented a dangerous situation for our agents involved in the search. They cautioned that it would take a significant time to proceed safely. The forested pathway leading to the cabin door was dangerous, slippery and wet from a combination of dirt and snow sitting atop sheets of ice. The afternoon was quickly passing us by and the sun's faint heat was no longer with us as the cold tugged at layers of clothes we were wearing.

"How in the world did he get by out here when the winter weather hit?" I kept thinking to myself, answered by the sights of wilderness survival strewn around us. Across the creek adjacent to the cabin there was a lean-to where a dead snow-shoe rabbit was hanging in a dry spot, likely aging so it could become one of Kaczynski's dinners.

Garden areas were located near the cabin, obviously irrigated by water from the creek. A screen hung from the ceiling in his cabin. (Meanwhile back in the Glen Williams' cabin, Kaczynski was busy explaining to Max and Paul that he used the screen to dry the vegetables he took from his gardens, the carrots, broccoli, onions, radishes, and spinach).

First to catch my eye was the small, dirty window on the left wall, with only a bit of a table and bench, attached to the wooden planking of the wall. It had to serve as the focal point for food preparation, reading, writing, and perhaps typewriting, as it was the only table. Two vintage hunting rifles hung on the wall over what appeared to be a bed or cot. The most prominent feature was a pot-bellied stove of cast iron that stood opposite of the door. It didn't appear to be vented to the outside.

There were nondescript, wooden shelves nailed to the walls with large and small alcoves holding bottles and jars, cans of nails and screws, hand tools, books, newspapers, and food cartons. A low, wooden cot was along the right side and I could make out a prominent smear of black dirt on the wall apparently caused by Ted's bare shoulders and hair rubbing against the wall. It was impossible to get out of my head the picture of Kaczynski's filthy body covered in black soot from the poorly vented stove. Just seeing and smelling the carcinogenic ash led me to the conclusion that Kaczynski was a walking cause of cancer from second hand smoke if my agents were exposed to him for too long. In the corner, there was a pattern of wooden planks on the wall that served as a ladder to reach a storage area in the cabin's loft.

Don called out chemicals and other materials he saw in front of us that could be used to make a pipe bomb. Various types of containers filled with powders were labeled "KCIO3," which is potassium chlorate; NaCIO3, sodium chlorate; sugar, zinc; aluminum powder and silver oxide. Making explosive materials requires an oxidizer and a fuel. Combining the sugar, zinc, aluminum powder, lead and silver oxide, which can all serve as fuels, with potassium or sodium chlorate that are oxidizers, easily resulting in the creation of an explosive material.

Three-ring binders stacked neatly on homemade shelves above the cabin floor were filled with pages of handwriting, some of it diagrams and notes detailing the manufacture of destructive devices. Some of the diagrams showed cross sections of pipes and electrical circuitry commonly associated with building bombs. There were sketches of boxes which could have been used to contain and transport explosive devices. The handwritten notes were in both English and Spanish and described chemical compounds that could be mixed together to create explosive charges.

Metal, plastic and copper pipes; C cell batteries; electrical wire; and a collection of tools such as mechanical drills, drill bits, wire cutters, and a roll of solder, were all indicators to Don Sachtleben that components inside the hermit's cabin were ready to be assembled into a functioning explosive device. The extensive notes in Spanish and English handwriting and several books on electrical circuitry and chemistry simply validated the extent to which Kaczynski's cabin was the Unabomber's factory.

It required discipline not to launch into the room and begin rummaging through everything like on a kid's treasure hunt. We reminded ourselves this was the lair of the Unabomber. The search had to proceed sensibly and systematically to avoid destruction or contamination of evidence, and in a manner providing the maximum safety for the examiners who might be working among detonators, explosive chemicals and materials, or even package bombs rigged to explode upon opening or movement.

Each of us took a final look around the 10 by 12 feet square shaped room, breathed in the stench of human waste—obviously, Ted's waste—that was buried in a shallow hole carved out in the dirt, beneath the cabin's thin wooden floor and felt the chill of the Montana mountain air seeping in through the open cabin door. We couldn't do anything at that moment to improve our creature comfort. There was no electricity, plumbing, running water, phone lines, television, or coffee pot inside the dirty, smelly cabin. I was fairly certain that Kaczynski didn't entertain other people too often. It was time to close down the search scene for the day.

Without adequate lighting, I quickly decided that it would be a tedious and dangerous proposition to begin the work of examining and removing the dozens of books, stacks of papers, boxes, cartons, jars, sacks, buckets, clothing items, bedding, and cooking utensils that were strewn about in multiple tiers. Instead, we concentrated the immediate efforts of the Evidence Response Teams on sealing off the site and towards acquiring and bringing forward the tools of their trade, with gasoline-powered electrical generators being the immediate need. The search would begin in earnest the next day.

Our observations inside the cabin, with the explanations from our bomb experts Don and Pat, were enough for me to return to the Williams cabin, where Terry and I pulled Max aside and told him to arrest Kaczynski and inform him he was being charged with possession of explosive materials. Max was eager to oblige. Rejoined by Tom McDaniel, they walked Kaczynski to Tom's white Ford Bronco, parked a short distance down the skid road, and placed him in the back seat. Paul Wilhelmus sat on one side of Kaczynski, Max on the other, and Terry in the passenger side front seat, as Tom pulled away in the direction of Stemple Pass Road, while I followed them.

As we turned right off the skid road and onto Stemple Pass, our two-car convoy passed by dozens of media representatives who had assembled during the day and were being kept off of Gehring's property by teams of FBI and ATF agents. Stopping briefly at the Seven-Up Ranch to tell the Forward Command Post we were taking Kaczynski to Helena, Terry jumped into the car with me and followed McDaniel's Bronco up the mountain to begin our one hour journey to Helena. It wasn't long before the radio crackled with noise and a feint voice in the background, advising Terry and I to stand by for the Director.

"That doesn't sound good to me," I looked at Terry, whose eyes stayed focused on McDaniel's car, but who nodded in agreement.

What transpired that evening was an unbelievable comedy of bureaucrats gone wild. Tom Roberts, the attorney from Main Justice that we had left at the Seven-Up Ranch and who I had later prevailed upon to authorize the arrest of Kaczynski had used the time of our travel to Helena for second-guessing and sowing the seeds of doubt at his home base in Washington.

Even before we arrived at Helena, the Director was calling. We were receiving a constant message on our portable radio, "SF #1, you are being called by WDC #1. He needs a call ASAP." We could receive, but were out of range for transmitting an answer. Terry and I had no choice but to keep on driving. I didn't have a good feeling about any of it.

When we arrived at the FBI's Helena RA, I realized that Max, Tom and Paul were exhausted from the long day they had spent with Kaczynski. Unfortunately, our job wasn't finished and their day would get a lot longer.

"Just take him into a room and keep getting to know each other while Terry and I find out what's going on back east," my frustrated tone collided with their bewilderment at having to spend even more hours with Kaczynski.

Paul, Tom and Max accepted our situation as it was. The easy part was over. Now we had the second guessing bureaucracy to deal with. Realizing that Kaczynski must be hungry since he had turned down their offer of fried chicken earlier in the afternoon, only eating a Snickers bar, Max asked Ted what he wanted to eat for dinner.

"A peanut butter sandwich on whole wheat bread and a quart of milk," Kaczynski answered.

When Paul visited a nearby restaurant to fill the order, he returned with a menu so Kaczynski could make another choice. "You're out of luck on the peanut butter sandwich. They don't have them so you can choose something else from this," he said handing the menu over.

Kaczynski made another selection and Paul returned from the restaurant a second time with grilled cheese, potato chips, several slices of dill pickles, and two large Coke bottles filled with milk. They all settled in for a long evening, giving Kaczynski a newspaper to read, while Terry and I contacted the Bureau to determine our fate.

A lot can happen when high-powered people without the facts begin to formulate contingency plans for the most outrageous imagined circumstances. It didn't take long for my instincts to be proven right. Upon arrival at the Helena RA, a phone was shoved into my hands and on the other end of a conference call was Louie, Howard, and Bill—along with more strident voices that I assumed were from across Pennsylvania Avenue at Main Justice. Without pausing to ask me for the facts, a myriad of erroneous legal assumptions were being put forward—the most outrageous was their consideration of charging the suspect as a material witness. That one floored me and I probably said something inappropriate for the distinguished audience, but my comments had no effect.

It was as if I had not been at the scene, had not looked into the cabin, and had not heard Kaczynski being questioned. Before the Director came to the phone, another Bureau official told us that the Department of Justice was raising serious concerns about our arrest of Kaczynski. The Director was going to authorize us to arrest and detain him on a material witness warrant so we would be covered while the debate swirled back east. Tom Roberts, the Department of Justice attorney assigned to the case had gone so far as to tell the Director we needed to let Kaczynski go until we could secure an indictment.

Arghh! I was no longer in charge. The party was over. The inmates were back in charge of the asylum and the asylum was Main Justice!

While I argued the point, Tom McDaniel knocked on the door and summoned Terry from the room. He gladly left.

"Bernie wants you to call him right now!" Tom emphasized. "He's at his office."

Terry called Bernie Hubley at the U. S. Attorney's Office and the conversation was short and sweet.

"Terry, I know what's going on with you, Freeman and Main Justice. Get Freeman off the phone now and the two of you get to my office."

"He's on with the Director…" Terry started to explain.

"Get him off the phone now and get him over here!" Bernie hung up the phone.

It was close to 10:00 pm when I read the scribbled note Terry stuck in front of my face. But it got me off the phone and we told Tom, Max and Paul to hang in there, while Terry and I went off to meet Bernie.

During the next two hours, Bernie, Terry and I were joined by Don Sachtleben and eventually Tom Mohnal, who was on one of the first flights out of Washington D.C. to Salt Lake City and then Helena that morning. Our conversations weren't civil, as Mohnal insisted we couldn't charge Kaczynski with possessing explosives materials if Mohnal hadn't been at the cabin. But San Francisco's own bomb expert, Sachtleben, had seen the cabin up close!

We'd stood there with Don as he crouched in the doorway, captivated by the myriad of small jars and bottles on the shelves that he couldn't wait to get his hands on and examine more closely. And, where the rest of us saw generic powders of various colors and granularity, he had observed and noted the characteristics of certain chemicals that would always be found in a bomber's cookbook. He provided exactly the detail that Bernie needed to get this arrest and prosecution back on-track, firmly within the jurisdiction of the U.S. District Court in Helena, Montana, and beyond the grasp of Washington bureaucrats—at least temporarily.

As it all played out, Bernie studiously took notes and every once and a while turned to Terry for a clarification on something I was saying. Then, as if matters couldn't have gotten worse, the Bureau called for Terry and me on one phone, while the Department of Justice attorneys were calling for Bernie on another.

As Tom Mohnal and I exchanged insults, Terry left the room to field the calls. While he was outside in the hallway of the US Attorney's Office, he had an idea and got on the phone with John Behnke. In the meantime, Bernie and I were formalizing our approach to use Don Sachtleben to file explosive possession charges against Kaczynski based on what he saw in the cabin.

"John, I know all Hell is breaking lose back there," Terry explained to Behnke over the phone. "But if I can just talk to Howard Shapiro (the FBI Chief Legal Counsel and a close confidant of Director Freeh who, along with John Behnke, had become close with Terry during the past year) for a minute I think we can get all of this handled."

John immediately got it and summoned the Director's Legal Counsel to take Terry's call in a room away from the commotion.

"Terry," Shapiro started in, his tone reflecting the storm swirling on Pennsylvania Avenue.

"Just give me ten minutes Howard. I promise you will be glad you did," Terry appealed and Howard listened. Terry explained what had happened throughout the day, our session with Bernie, and Don Sachtleben's observations, closing with telling Shapiro that Kaczynski was the Unabomber and there was no mistaking it.

"We've been misinformed back here Terry. All of this makes perfect sense. We have great trust in you and Jim Freeman, so go on and implement your plan."

Bernie wasted little time when he heard the results of the conversation. He and Sachtleben decided to meet early the next day and discuss an affidavit and criminal complaint. Terry and I went back to the Helena RA to tell Max, Paul and Tom they were authorized to book Kaczynski into the Lewis and Clark County Jail.

Max and Tom McDaniel escorted a handcuffed Kaczynski on what was an unintended "perp-walk" from the office back to the car and on to the county jail, as Terry and I walked behind. A camera crew and a photographer closed in around them and the spectacle of a tattered Unabomber and his UTF captors appeared on the next cover of Newsweek. America wasn't ready for what it saw. Kaczynski had a wild-eyed look that seemed more an embellished Hollywood creation of a mad man than reality. His thick dark hair and beard, showing the last few days of dirt he had picked up both inside his cabin and outside in the harsh weather, his wrapped face concealing everything but his hollow, expressionless eyes.

His dark-colored, hand-me-down clothes were ragged from wear. He had every appearance of a homeless man in the middle of a big city that had been brought in from the cold. But it was those eyes that gave him away. He wasn't the homeless stereotype of first glance. He was America's longest running serial bomber— eighteen years and sixteen bombs and never a clue to his identity— Until now.

That was the beginning of a media circus that lasted for days and engulfed the hamlet of Lincoln and the road near the cabin. I posted teams of agents on 24-hour perimeter duty to protect the integrity of the search site. It struck us as ironic that the Unabomber's warped view of technology had now engulfed his home site in a forest of TV vans sprouting satellite dishes and antennae.

Two days into our search of the cabin, everything came to a screeching halt. We found what appeared to be a live bomb underneath the cot Kaczynski used as a bed. It took three more days to carefully remove the carefully planted bomb by a remotely controlled robot. It was disabled by our first-ever use of the PAN bomb disrupter that the UTF had commissioned to be built by Sandia Corporation.

PAN stands for Percussion-Actuated Nonelectric and was developed by Chris Cherry and his team of researchers at Sandia Lab. In the year prior to Kaczynski's identification, the UTF sought help from Tom Mohnal at the FBI's Lab in Washington, D.C. in the development of a disrupter that could disable a UNABOM device. The Unabomber's bombs had so many redundant systems that trying to disable one with the technology available at the time would likely have failed.

The UTF's proactive approach to UNABOM increased the possibility that a bomb might be found in the mail stream, so it was important to have the capability to disarm it. Mohnal had a solid relationship with Chris Cherry and Sandia, turning to them with the challenge of designing and building just such a device.

We sent an airplane to bring Cherry and his team to Lincoln. Rod Owenby, also from Sandia, and Vic Poisson, who worked for the Riverside, California Police Department, as well as Special Agent Patricia Clothier of the Los Angeles Division, who was a also a Bomb Expert and member of the team arrived in Montana a day after our call for help went out. They worked non-stop with Mohnal, Pat Webb and Don Sachtleben to make preparations to remove the live bomb from Kaczynski's cabin. They built a wooden ramp up the trail to Kaczynski's cabin so the bomb could be safely carried out. In one of the open fields near the cabin, they constructed a sheltered area where the bomb could be placed for the controlled detonation.

When everything was finally built out and in place and they had time to discuss the possibilities surrounding the removal and detonation, Don Sachtleben drove the robot up the trail. He carefully maneuvered the explosive package out of the cabin, delivering it safely to its resting spot in the field.

It was placed between mountains of sawdust and next to an aiming device that combined x-ray and laser for precise targeting. There weren't any wires to cut to stop this bomb from exploding. This wasn't the movies. Terry, Max and I stood at a safe distance with just a little apprehension about the success of the technology. There was much riding on preserving a live bomb from Kaczynski's cabin. If everything worked perfectly, the FBI Lab would be able to compare its components with those from UNABOM crime scenes. The noose around Kaczynski's neck would quickly tighten if all the forensics added up.

"Jim, we're ready, why don't you step up and fire this off," Cherry grinned at me and I was eager to play a role in detonating the bomb.

After all the preparation and anxiety, there was hardly any noise as the bomb responded to the PAN disrupter and detonated harmlessly in the man-made cradle in the middle of the Montana outdoors. Two shotgun projectiles simultaneously severed the electrical wiring between the battery source and the detonator. It worked! The bomb was recovered intact and ready for a courtroom appearance as key evidence. It would be the last such detonation of a UNABOM device in this wilderness, experimental or otherwise.

We had shown up at Kaczynski's cabin just in time. It appeared that he was already planning to break his pledge of ceasing his delivery of terrorist bombs. The batteries of the package bomb found under the cot were charged and ready to go. It was wrapped for mailing, lacking only the mailing label. There was a return address—the street address of the Seattle FBI Office. This time the joke was on the Unabomber.

We even found evidence suggesting the bomb's next target. Kathy Puckett's assessment had proven right-on. Kaczynski couldn't stop mailing bombs even if he wanted to. And this bomb, which we called UNABOM Device #17, wasn't intended to "commit sabotage." It's deadly design could have taken the life of more innocent victims.

For several more days, portable x-ray equipment was used to examine every package and box remaining in the attic of the cabin. There, at the bottom of the very last box (an old ammunition container) was where the old manual typewriter was found. It checked out to be the one he used for composing his manifesto, his letters to the New York Times, and his deadly mailing labels. And, what appeared to be the original of the Unabomber's manifesto was found among papers on the first floor.

The search and arrest of the Unabomber was complete vindication for all of the years of work, frustration, and disappointment. The UNABOM Task Force had prevailed. The guy with aviator sunglasses and a gray sweatshirt was clever, perhaps brilliant. But, in the end, justice was served.

The thousands of pages of handwritten notes found during our subsequent search of Kaczynski's one room with a loft cabin left no doubt we had the right man. Living in seclusion in the mountains, he recorded his every thought:

"To make an impression on society with words is...almost impossible for most individuals and small groups...if we had never done anything violent and had submitted the present writings to a publisher, they probably would not have been accepted..."

"In order to get our message before the public with some

chance of making a lasting impression, we've had to kill people."

"I intend to start killing people..."

"...I want to release all my hatred and just go out and kill."

"My motive for doing what I am going to do is simply personal revenge. I do not expect to accomplish anything by it...I am motivated by a hatred for what is happening to freedom."

His mother's wish turned out to be prophetic. She didn't think her son Ted was the Unabomber, but, "if he did it, he must be stopped."

CONCLUSION

ONLY A FEW WEEKS AFTER RETURNING TO SAN FRANCISCO FROM Montana, I walked down the hallway from my office to break the news to Terry. He was immersed in the next phase of UNABOM—coordinating the prosecution stage and preparing to testify before Federal Grand Juries in Sacramento and Newark, New Jersey, to seek the indictment of Theodore Kaczynski for the UNABOM crimes. Aside from Director Freeh, Terry would be the first FBI colleague to learn of my closely held secret.

"Terry, I came down here to let you know of a personal decision and I need you to keep this to yourself until I announce it to the office later this morning. I've decided to retire from the Bureau and accept an outstanding offer to work in the private sector."

At first, the news didn't seem to register, and then he sat back in a chair he had pulled up to a table while reviewing photographs of the search site in Montana. After drawing a deep breath, he said "You're serious, aren't you?" "I'm not kidding around. This is a monumental decision for me. On the one hand, I am at the pinnacle of my FBI career; but there is the nagging question of what more do I want or need to accomplish. I now have an enormous opportunity in private industry to build an organization from the ground up; to make it mine. It's an opportunity not to be missed; it's time to pick up and leave the only career that I have known since college."

"Jim, we've been through so much together—I don't know what to say."

For a few moments, we were drawn together into a vortex of shared memories. We had been through hell and high water together and spoken platitudes between us were unnecessary. I didn't need to affirm my continuing confidence in him to lead the UTF through the same careful process in getting the case ready for trial that we put into identifying Kaczynski—that was a given. Terry was prepared and ready.

In fact, the Director had heard us loud and clear when we recommended the selection of a prosecutorial "dream team" to take the case forward. While we were still tediously sorting through every inch of the bomber's 10 by 12 cabin in Montana, looking for every shred of evidence that would bind him to his crimes in a court of law, their names were announced to the media.

Named to the role of lead prosecutor was Robert Cleary, Assistant United States Attorney in Newark. Assisting Cleary would be the primary UTF counsel in San Francisco—AUSA Steve Freccero, as well as AUSA Steve Lapham from Sacramento, and AUSA Bernie Hubley from Helena, Montana. Doug Wilson from Washington, D.C., completed the roster. We had laughed when I noted for Terry's sake that they were all wearing the team jersey "now."

Eighteen years—that's how long it took to identify and arrest the Unabomber. It represents the longest, unsolved serial bombing case in the nation's history. Even against the backdrop of the 9/11 terrorist attacks on America, the massive scope of the UNABOM investigation remains the most complex who-dun-it in the history of the FBI.

In early, 1998, FBI Director Louie Freeh described its scope and impact:

"In an effort unprecedented in FBI history, thousands of FBI Special Agents and support personnel worked diligently for 17 years to solve the Unabomber case. Once the Unabomber was apprehended, teams of Special Agents were meticulous in the fact-finding and evidence searches that withstood all court challenges." Most of the FBI's 56 Field Offices and Legal Attaches around the world played supporting roles in UNABOM, but the focal points were ultimately in Chicago, Sacramento, Salt Lake City, New Haven, Newark, and San Francisco. Numerous individuals from multiple law enforcement agencies and forensic laboratories played key roles in this investigation over the years; some being identified herein with their contributions or distractions put on display as we experienced them and others were simply too numerous to call outright. All were professional and well-intentioned in wanting to do their best to take this madman off the street.

By the time we identified Kaczynski, the core of the UTF in San Francisco was comprised of fifty full time FBI agents, twenty-five analysts, another fifteen support personnel, and several agents and postal inspectors from the ATF and United States Postal Inspection Service.

During its lifetime, the UTF investigated over 2,400 suspects, assembled 3,600 volumes of case files representing almost 18 years of investigation, compiled 82 million data records, gathered 8,182 items of physical evidence, and over 22,000 pages of evidentiary documents. Terry and Max had obviously found grist for their mill —the Massively Parallel Processor.

As proud as I was of the team that I assembled to approach the UNABOM case in a different way, I realized that the end of the trail for the Unabomber was the right time and place for my new beginning—and the end of my career in the FBI.

* * *

"It'll be different around here without you," Terry finally said as we shared UNABOM trivia and stories in his office, adding with a mischievous grin, "Just when I was getting used to all your meddling."

As I left his office, I reflected on the mentoring process that began just two years earlier when I made the decision to put him in charge of the UTF. That first move, so unpopular in some circles in the Bureau, was a harbinger of the decisions and changes that we would make together along the way. Those decisions broke traditions and rules that were hard-wired into the institution and had guided FBI approaches to major investigations for decades.

Changes that we made in the name of UNABOM challenged time-honored assumptions about the FBI's administrative structure—specifically the perceived mandate and role of various Headquarters components to directly supervise individual field investigations; the gross inefficiencies of elite fiefdoms with artificial boundaries throughout the field office structure; and hopefully exploded the myth that only "sworn agents" are suitably qualified and in sole possession of investigative skills. We offer no excuses for our departure from tradition and for breaking these unwritten rules—it was an expedient means for solving UNABOM, but also a necessity for influencing change and evolution in today's FBI.

I mentally ticked off several areas of change:

First and foremost was the challenge to the culture, structure and strategy in managing and investigating major cases. Strangely enough, this was made possible and accomplished with an undeclared co-conspirator—Director Louie Freeh.

Terry was steadfast in making analysis the lynchpin of our reinvestigation of UNABOM crimes, including suspect and event (bombing) investigations through years of investigation; finding little consistency or comparison of the data between agencies, laboratories, or lead investigators.

Among the UTF members, we encouraged partnering between separate agencies and information sharing equally among support analysts and agent investigators. There were no walls and no topics were off-limits for discussion.

Profiling was driven from the field and not from the FBI Behavioral Science Unit at Quantico. The profile was not the profile forever; it was dynamic and subject to change with the collection of each new confirmed fact.

UTF management prioritized the investigative structure and strategy throughout the FBI's Field Office system—discretion on when and how extensively to support UNABOM was removed by the Director from other Special Agents in Charge.

To insure consistency and quality, UTF investigators were dispatched to other FBI Divisions to conduct and/or coordinate critical interviews and suspect investigations.

I assumed the role of coordinating all UNABOM media contacts by default when it was a career threatening role. This was distinctly an FBIHQ prerogative, but later my unprecedented role with the media was expressly approved by Director Freeh when we demonstrated a viable media strategy that complemented and enhanced our UTF objectives.

The UTF managed and directed the UNABOM investigation—not the FBI Laboratory.

We did not allow layers of supervisors at FBIHQ to derail the implementation of our strategy. As the Special Agent in Charge of UNABOM and the San Francisco FBI Division, I insisted on the final authority in UTF decision making—it was commensurate with my mandate from the Director in taking on the management of UNABOM in the first place.

We never allowed the FBI budget process or program management from FBIHQ to drive the UNABOM investigation. If we had an idea with merit, we lobbied overtly and covertly to fund its implementation. UNABOM was afforded Major Case status and ultimately we were provided a special budget protocol.

As the Special Agent in Charge of San Francisco and jointly the Director-appointed SAC of the UTF, I was prominently and directly involved in the implementation of our UNABOM strategy.

Field-wide and at FBIHQ, there were many agents, supervisors, and SACs that found this highly unusual approach not to their liking because it flew in the face of tradition. For others, it was change and no one likes change. But, I was trying to solve the ultimate unsolvable case—not win a beauty pageant. It worked.

We moved contrary to tradition and the counsel of peers by proposing the publication of the Unabomber's Manifesto, not because we believed the bomber would stop bombing—because of the likelihood someone would recognize the lifelong work and philosophy of the Unabomber and turn him in. The FBI Director and Attorney General agreed with our proposal as part of a larger investigative strategy.

The FBI traditionally maintained a very cautious and arms-length relationship with the news media. Inherent in the publication of the Manifesto was a historic and significant change in the nature of that relationship.

Retaining control of all aspects of the UNABOM strategy required that we "control" various aspects of FBI Headquarters and the Department of Justice if we were to make it to the end of the road with our approach and strategy intact. This road was fraught with the danger of finished careers and potential investigative disasters, but we stayed in the driver's seat by restricting the flow of information about the case to a "need to know" standard. We stayed the course—right up to the day we arrested Theodore Kaczynski.

I decided not to use the FBI's highly competent Hostage Rescue Team (HRT) when it came time to move on Kaczynski's mountain hide-away. It wasn't a lack of faith in the HRT—but their decision-making processes on site at that time were controlled out of Washington. I simply refused to accept that risk and retained the authority.

As the work to identify the Unabomber and safely arrest him was winding down, the FBI came under attack from several directions for decisions and outcomes in other major investigations. Among the criticisms: the FBI failed to identify CIA traitor Aldrich Ames, who passed secrets to the Russians during visits to the Soviet Embassy in Washington, D.C. His visits were caught on FBI surveillance cameras trained on the building.

In standoffs with domestic militants at Waco, Texas, and Ruby Ridge, Idaho, subsequent deployment of the FBI's Hostage Rescue Team (HRT) and resulting firefights, led to years of controversy, talk of government conspiracies and wrongful death lawsuits. The outcomes cut short the tenure of Deputy FBI Director Larry Potts, highly respected over his decades-long Bureau career.

The FBI Laboratory was severely criticized in a 500-page report completed by the Department of Justice. The report called into question laboratory examinations in dozens of past cases, faulting ten lab experts by name.

While the media focused the public's attention on these issues, the UNABOM Task Force was preparing to bring Theodore Kaczynski to trial in Sacramento, California. Despite these distractions, the credibility of the UTF and its work in UNABOM remained intact with Director Freeh and Attorney General Janet Reno fully supportive of the task force and its efforts.

When Kaczynski's defense team offered an unconditional guilty plea, meaning he would plead guilty to all the UNABOM crimes and waive his right to appeals, lead prosecutor Robert Cleary told Terry he would call the AG and asked Terry to determine the FBI's position on such a plea from Director Freeh. Terry contacted the Director and summarized the breaking development of the possible plea deal.

"Bob Cleary wants to know the position of the FBI on accepting the plea or moving forward with the trial." Terry concluded his conversation.

"The position of the FBI is whatever you decide it should be," was Director Freeh's immediate response.

Six months earlier, the *TIME* magazine cover story of April 28, 1997 "What's Wrong at the FBI," described Director Freeh's struggle, as he was attempting to bring "change" to the FBI:

"...Freeh demonstrated a willingness to turn the agency inside out. He set out to cut red tape, transfer 600 desk warmers back onto the streets, embrace new technology, diversify the ranks...insisted on cooperation and shared resources...Freeh's critics resent him not so much for what he did, but for the way he did it."

When I was eventually told the story of the plea deal and read the *TIME* article, I thought—There it was! We had gotten along so well with Director Freeh and his team for a reason. While we were working to re-invigorate UNABOM, the Director was trying to rebuild and retool the FBI itself. The same issues that we and others faced in solving UNABOM throughout the years also stood in the way of the changes Director Freeh wanted to bring to the Bureau. It was an epiphany. The Director had his own UNABOM strategy that ran deeper than ours—it was proof that change was truly needed. UNABOM was a laboratory to experiment with the effects of change.

Louie Freeh left the FBI in the spring of 2001. Terry retired as the Deputy Assistant Director for Counterterrorism on May 1, 2001. And, Max had retired from the Bureau a couple of years after I did. Less than a week before the 9/11 terrorist attacks on the World Trade Center, Robert Mueller, former United States Attorney for Northern California, stepped into the job of FBI Director.

Mueller never had time to sit back and review the FBI's strengths and weaknesses before making the decisions that would leave his imprint on the Bureau. The events of 9/11 put everything the FBI did under the microscope. Some politicians were so confident the FBI was to blame for the success of the terrorists because it failed to prevent the deadly attacks that they wanted to strip national security responsibilities from the Bureau.

Mueller's long and credible career, inside and outside the government, helped him lead the organization through its latest crisis. Almost on the back of his personal honor and the trust he had developed during his years of government service, Mueller convinced Congress and various committees investigating 9/11 that he was capable of changing the FBI.

The "9/11 Report of The National Commission on Terrorist Attacks upon the United States," released in 2004, identified for Mueller some of the obstacles he faced. They sounded all too familiar to me.

The FBI needed to institute an integrated national security workforce of agents, analysts, linguists and surveillance specialists.

Recognizing that cross-fertilization between criminal justice and national security disciplines was vital to the success of both missions, all new agents were recommended to receive training and experience in both areas.

The FBI's budget structure needed to be aligned according to its four main programs—intelligence, counterterrorism and counterintelligence, criminal and criminal justice services to better manage resources and protect the intelligence program.

Information procedures had to provide incentives for sharing and restoring a better balance between security and shared knowledge.

Despite the above recommendations and a few others from the Commission's report, Mueller's work to transform the FBI wasn't easy. *U.S. News and World Report* featured an article, "Remaking the FBI, Why It's So Hard to Get G Men to Think like Spies," in its March 28, 2005 edition.

"That's an organization where the culture is very, very fixed; more so than a place like the Marine Corps," says Deputy Attorney General James Comey in the article. "Unlike the Marine Corps, most people spend 30 years at the Bureau. The culture sets like concrete over 30 years, and to change that is very, very hard.

"Hard, even for a decorated ex-marine like Mueller. 'I've come to find that one of the most difficult things one has to do...is to bring an entity through the development of a change of business practices.'

"Changing any large bureaucracy is difficult, but at the FBI it is especially so. Mueller's challenge is both simple and enormous...spotting terrorists and stopping them before they attack. That's not just a whole new mind-set. It means creating a new infrastructure to assess threats, communicating that information rapidly (to)... agents, offices and executives, and sharing it with analysts and operatives outside the FBI."

By the time the article was written, some in Washington were already criticizing Mueller for his style and impatience with some veteran agents. Senator Patrick Leahy of Vermont, a veteran FBI critic, went so far as to say Mueller "came in with so much goodwill on the part of both Republicans and Democrats, and that goodwill is just being thrown away."

But the proof is in the pudding, as the saying goes. Director Mueller didn't leave the FBI for another eight years—two years beyond the term limit of ten years for his position. Between Mueller and Director Freeh before him, the FBI transformed itself to address the most significant national security and crime challenges America faces today, just as it had, by necessity, transformed itself at other important times throughout its one hundred year existence.

UNABOM was, and will remain an example, of how one investigation can impact changes in an organization overall by influencing the thinking of its leaders. We understood early on that UNABOM would never be solved if we didn't break time honored rules and traditions that literally changed the FBI institutional approach to such cases. In the wake of further domestic terrorist attacks and the subsequent attack on the World Trade Center Towers and the Pentagon, many of the very rules and traditions we challenged became the flashpoints for change in the FBI itself.

We also found that the effective delivery of change depended on the personalities and in depth involvement and understanding by an organization's leaders. Positive changes need time and consistency to settle in. It's a good sign that former Deputy Attorney General James Comey understood this in 2005 when he explained to *US News and World Report* that a "culture sets like concrete over 30 years and to change it is very, very hard."

As Director Mueller was moving out of his office on the 7th Floor of the J. Edgar Hoover FBI Building in September of 2013, James Comey was moving in.

EPILOGUE

LOOKING OVER MY SHOULDER

THE SOMETIMES BRILLIANT RECLUSE WAS REMOVED FROM SOCIETY, convicted, and placed in life-long solitary confinement in a Maximum Security Federal Penitentiary in Florence, Colorado. It is designed to hold the most dangerous of inmates and is often called "The Alcatraz of the Rockies."

In a wooded mountainside near Lincoln, Montana, his tiny cabin was unceremoniously ripped from its foundation and transported as evidence to the criminal proceedings in Sacramento near the grisly scene of one of his three murders.

A faint scar remains on the earth where the cabin had stood. The Kaczynski mailbox no longer stands on Stemple Pass Road. Trees and underbrush have quietly reclaimed the land, while rabbits, squirrels and porcupines have returned in abundance after being hunted and killed for food by the hermit that had called this home for some twenty years.

His journals described the widening circle around the cabin that became devoid of small game because of his hunting and trapping for food. As his personal story unfolded, it was eventually necessary for him to trek across the rugged mountain trails in search of larger game and to kill and eat from a more diverse menu.

On the day of his arrest, there were remnants of an elk's carcass tossed aside in the snow. The antlers, bones, and hides of various animals were strewn about the property. Despite the passing of years, I am amused by a remembrance of Ted's recipes for wild game that we retrieved from the cabin. At one point, his diary described a particularly satisfying concoction of coyote stew and root vegetables.

His vegetable garden was in a nearby plot of ground that was partially sunny outside of the winter months, but was not sufficiently fertile; so his writings detailed how his green thumb was augmented by fertilizing with his own feces. Given that the cabin offered no running water for basic sanitation—or a toilet of any type; we found an iota of "gallows humor" at the thought of coyote steak simmered among rutabaga slices with a lingering aroma of home fertilizer around the fire pit.

Ted's emaciated frame at the time of his arrest will be long remembered, and not the least by Max who emerged from the brief struggle with grimy, soot stained hands.

When I came upon the scene, Max was trying to wipe his hands clean by rubbing them in the snow and pulling pine boughs across his palms. It helped a little, but the stench remained oppressive for hours. In witnessing the place and the condition of its lone occupant, it was a wonder to me that anyone had survived the repetitive rigors of winter and the pervasive threat of serious illness or disease.

When it was no longer needed due to the Unabomber's guilty plea, Kacynzki's cabin was released from the court's jurisdiction and eventually found its way to the Newseum in Washington, D.C., for all to see.

It is now one of several exhibits in the Newseum highlighting the historical relationship between the FBI and the media. His manifesto is largely forgotten or ignored.

Theodore Kaczynski, aka the "Unabomber," is now confined for life in a one-room maximum security cell. It is equipped with a desk, a stool, and a bed made mostly of poured concrete—not the natural wood materials that he favored when fashioning his home-made killing devices.

The cell is fitted with a few conveniences of modern technology—a toilet and a shower and a sink. His view of the expansive Montana sky has been replaced by an elevated slit in the wall that is four inches wide by four feet tall.

Kaczynski's fate is a fitting and satisfying culmination of the extraordinary hard-work and dedication of the men and women of the UNABOM Task Force. More importantly, the UNABOM investigation is a validation of the vital role played by an alert public and engaged media in bringing dangerous criminals to justice. If we learned anything from UNABOM we learned that it is only through the public's trust in law enforcement that we can remain a nation guided by the rule of law. Striking that balance in this age of terrorism will determine our fate as a nation of laws.

INDEX